A Primer For
WRITING TEACHERS

Theories, Theorists, Issues, Problems

A Primer For

WRITING TEACHERS

Theories, Theorists, Issues, Problems

DAVID FOSTER

BOYNTON/COOK PUBLISHERS, INC.

Library of Congress Cataloging in Publication Data

Foster, David, 1938-
 A primer for writing teachers.

 Bibliography: p.
 1. English language—Rhetoric—Study and teaching.
I. Title.
PE1404.F67   1983   808'.042'071   83-3791
ISBN 0-86709-053-7

For information address Boynton/Cook Publishers, Inc.,
52 Upper Montclair Plaza, P.O. 860, Upper Montclair, NJ 07043

ISBN: 0-86709-053-7

Printed in the United States of America
 84 85 86 10 9 8 7 6 5 4

Preface

This is not a book about what to do on Monday in the classroom. There are books to be had for this purpose: the best are in the "List of Further Readings" for Chapter IV. Of course, readers will find many suggestions here about methods they might like to try in Monday's class. But that's not the main purpose of this book, and if it is merely quarried for classroom strategies—important as those are to all writing teachers—it will not have served its intended purpose.

The purpose of this book is to clarify and evaluate the concepts and methods available to teachers of writing today. Though many of the ideas and strategies described here have college-level contexts, most are quite appropriate to high school situations also. And because recent claims about better ways to teach writing can't be adequately evaluated without knowing something about their theoretical backgrounds, the psychological, rhetorical, and linguistic elements of composition are also discussed in these chapters. Though some of these elements appear remote to teachers facing full classes and reams of student writing, they are important to understand, not because the methodologies they generate are all for the best, but precisely because they aren't. One of the biggest mistakes teachers can make is to accept some "new and improved" technique or textbook without looking closely at its origins and its probable effects upon students.

This book, then, seeks to help teachers formulate the questions that need to be asked about current ideas and practices in writing pedagogy. For example, high school and college teachers are often urged to teach students more "grammar," more "basics," so that they will write more "correctly." The usual result of these urgings is to drive teachers to grammar drills and error hunts, on the principle that what Ann Berthoff calls "drill-for-skill" will result in more literate competency tests and application letters. Yet it's more than sufficiently clear that all the grammar instruction in the world neither increases fluency nor decreases error in student writing. Warriner's texts and their clones in high school and the publisher-of-your-choice handbooks in college abound, but they don't do much to help people learn to write.

Many years ago when I began teaching writing at a large university (in the megaton range), I was handed a syllabus in which error-correction figured prominently. I had had no training in teaching writing; I was innocent of any grasp of the psychological and linguistic dimensions of writing; and I had no familiarity with any classroom strategies. Moreover, we TA's who actually met the students had no hand in planning the syllabus or making any of the pedagogical choices that might have taught us something about the craft of writing. If it was Tuesday, we had to talk about comma splices (whether our students indulged in them or not); on Thursday it was "A Modest Proposal," nominated because irony was the element of the day (whether irony meant anything to the students, or they to irony).

Most of us were indifferent to the process of composing; it was something one did in order to get a grade, a chore that we had learned to handle because we were English majors. Possessing some modest language ability ourselves, most of us failed to grasp how difficult and complex writing is or how to help other students a few years younger learn to compose in a course directed mostly at grammar and editing skills. We failed to teach, and the students mostly failed to learn, or learned despite us. Behind us loomed the larger failure of the institution (and "higher education" itself in those boom days) to create genuine learning opportunities for undergraduates by helping its graduates—their frontline teachers—learn about their discipline. Things have changed to some extent since then: many graduate programs today do have courses in writing pedagogy, and graduate students and new teachers are increasingly encouraged to take writing seriously as a teaching emphasis. For those present and future teachers particularly, this book is intended.

Many people helped this book along. Al Kitzhaber gave some early chapters a bracing commentary that cleared the writing of some of its murkiness. Bill Pixton, a friend from the swarming hallways of CCCC meetings, read much of the manuscript as it developed and provided suggestions and encouragement throughout. Ann Berthoff, though she doesn't know it, had a large influence on this book through her writings, which everywhere reflect the same anti-drill-for-skill bias as this book, but with far more learning and wit. Both Frank D'Angelo and Linda Flower generously provided unpublished work of theirs which helped me better understand the nature of their respective research undertakings. To my colleagues Bruce Campbell and Thomas Swiss of Drake I owe special thanks both for reading portions of the manuscript and for the countless friendly discussions that helped me formulate my own ideas more sharply. It is no exaggeration, however, to say that Bob Boynton, publisher, adviser, and critic, is primarily responsible for making this book possible, though not for the shortcomings it contains. His help at all stages has been crucial and appreciated. So, finally, has the labor of Fran Marks, who typed and retyped the manuscript while forbearing to ask why it took me so long to get it right.

Contents

Chapter I
TEACHING WRITING
Tradition and Change

In the last decade teaching writing has not been an honored task. In the 1970s it was discovered that a student named Johnny couldn't read or write, and that this was mainly the fault of the schools. We were also told that English teachers were living "one of the most personally and socially destructive forms of life known to middle-class man"; "what students are learning from these teachers," it was discovered, "is that learning to write is simply not very important."[1] Teachers of English have felt doubly wounded by such charges. They are hurt by their own knowledge that, after all their labor, they have not found the magic key to unlock Johnny's powers of language. And they feel unjustly singled out for infamy when, they like to think, the causes of Johnny's failures lie deep in the culture that nourishes him.

The difficulty with "English"—particularly that branch of it labeled "composition"—is that it has traditionally been given a perverse educational mission. English teachers are asked to teach writing while they instill in students the humane values of literature—under the traditional assumption that true literacy includes both the ability to use language and the capacity to appreciate it. But the public tends to see only speaking and writing skills as functional in the marketplace. When language aptitude scores decline, no defense of the liberalizing force of literature offsets a public outcry against "illiteracy." Public wrath over students' reading and writing failures particularly annoys English teachers because they know how difficult it is to prove that writing instruction works at all. Some studies, they know, have demonstrated little or no improvement in student writing after a course in composition. They know that it's far easier to discover whether students have learned the muscles of a cat or the causes of the Civil War than to determine whether students' writing has really improved. Indeed, the often ambiguous results of writing measurement indicate how difficult, on the face of it, the task of "teaching" writing is. Thus, English teachers often console themselves that writing cannot actually be taught at all, only watched and nurtured, as a potted plant is tended.

If we cannot adequately measure the results of writing instruction, how can we talk sensibly about teaching methods? In the following chapters we'll take a leap of faith: we will analyze various approaches to teaching writing, distinguishing the more effective from the less, though we will remain aware that measurement studies may not furnish us empirical proof of our preferred methods. Our justifications will rest primarily on reason, common sense, and the support of contemporary philosophical, psychological, and linguistic insights. In the chapters that follow, we will examine why some traditional aspects of writing instruction are ineffective and counterproductive, which of the many recently proposed teaching strategies and theories are most useful, and how to plan and run an effective writing course.

We'll start by considering what, after all, we're doing when we teach writing.

Teaching writing isn't so very different from teaching a science, mathematics, music, or any other discipline that requires some factual knowledge and some mastery of a process or set of skills. Yet writing teachers are tempted to envy math, history, or physical education teachers, who can at least measure their teaching success by the number of equations solved, dates remembered, or chin-ups counted. Despairing at the lack of measurable results often appearing at post-test time, writing teachers may resort to the psychotherapist's excuse: the patient didn't want to change after all. And the writing problems students still have after finishing composition courses make writing teachers vulnerable to criticism from colleagues in other disciplines. An inability to focus and organize a paper, a difficulty in constructing coherent paragraphs and sentences, or, particularly, editing and proofreading failures mark students as victims of English department malpractice.

Teaching writing is a uniquely thankless job. Indeed, writing teachers may be excused for thinking their job today is even harder than it used to be because they are assailed by so many competing ideas and goals. The theories of linguistics, psychology, and epistemology mingle with the practicalities of technical writing, business writing, and myriad academic writing purposes. Writing teachers are prone to feel nostalgic over the popular image of the nineteenth-century English teacher single-mindedly shaking out of her pupils all the rude differences of language inevitable in an immigrant society, in favor of the formal idioms of McGuffey's reader. Yet the history of English education in America reveals educators at different periods defining the purposes of writing instruction in oddly familiar terms. At least three major concerns recur in English educational policy: the value of writing as a form of power, the interdependency of language and thinking, and the primary importance of literacy instruction in the English teacher's job.

Writing has often been justified as an instrument of power. One nineteenth-century headmaster, using the code words of the Protestant work ethic, associated language learning with character-forming labor: "the earnest, laborious student of language develops a power which no other training could possibly give him, and in comparison with which all his acquisitions of mere knowledge sink into utter insignificance."[2] The kind of power conferred by language mastery was spelled out nearly a hundred years later by the Commission on the English Curriculum, which asserted that the "power to use words orally and in writing" allows the student to "achieve adequate adjustment for himself and his teen-age friends." [3]   The emphasis on language's life-adjustment power reflects the impact of progressive education upon language goals, and foreshadows the Dartmouth conference's advocacy of language play as a means of personal growth.

But interest in the kind of power language confers upon students is not the only link between traditional and contemporary writing pedagogy. The current fascination with process in writing expresses the same faith in the connection between reasoning and language shown almost a century ago in the *Report* of the Committee of Ten, which argued that "if the pupil is to secure control over the language as an instrument for the expression of his thoughts, it is necessary . . . that every thought which he expresses, whether orally or on paper, should be regarded as a proper subject for criticism as to the language." [4] This conviction that thought and language are instrumentally related has traditionally stood behind assertions that language mastery is a form of mental discipline. The various psycholinguistic models available today do not agree on the exact relationship language may have to thinking. But recent studies of language and discourse have a distinctly mentalistic emphasis, with various models of mind as their bases (see Chapter II). Such an emphasis appears, for example, in the concept of persona, the embodiment in language of the specific attitudes and sensibility of the discourser, for whom style is a presentation of self in language. Sentence combining is another example of stylistic strategy—pedagogical in its use—that has emerged from the emphasis upon mental process in linguistic theory. Ironically, because it is a-rhetorical in its primary focus on syntax, sentence combining can become merely a five-finger exercise for students unless it is given a larger rhetorical framework for its sentence manipulations.

The place of writing instruction in the English department is another subject of longstanding debate in American education. Debates over the relative importance of literacy instruction, as opposed to literary training, have heated teachers' lounges for at least a hundred years. In the later nineteenth and early twentieth centuries "composition" was a general term for instruction in rhetoric, usage, and correctness, with particular attention in schools to correcting the nonstandardisms of immigrant and minority children. Under pressure from the Committee of Ten *Report* and other efforts to standardize college and preparatory studies, literature gained stature in English instruction until, by the early twentieth century, school and college writing was taught as an element of, and a tool for, the study of literary culture. [5] Later, composition in the schools began to receive a different emphasis with the coming of progressivism: "Our major task in the ordinary school is to teach all our pupils to read ordinary matters with ordinary intelligence and to express ordinary thoughts with reasonable clarity," remarked an NCTE president in the mid-1930s. [6] Following Dewey's insistence that the business of education was designing proper experiences for students, English curriculum planners emphasized the role of writing in students' self-development. Advocacy by participants in the 1965 Dartmouth conference of developmental goals for the English curriculum—e.g., the self-awareness gained from increased mastery of language skills—has reinforced the progressive tradition in English curriculum planning. Unfortunately, within English departments today tension between the commitment to literature and the obligation to provide composition instruction persists. Thus teachers who love literature *and* who find value and pleasure in teaching writing are vital to the psychic health of English departments.

Ambivalence and shifting emphasis characterize writing pedagogy because writing is a complex blend of innate abilities and learned skills. Writing is—to borrow from the vocabulary of education philosophy—both an "open" and a "closed" capacity. As John Passmore points out, a closed capacity is one that eventually "allows of total mastery," while an open capacity is "never fully mastered to perfection." "Somebody else—or ourselves at some other time— could do it better." [7]   Examples of closed capacities, he suggests, are adding and subtracting, playing tic-tac-toe, performing an assembly-line operation, solving equations, or operating a complex machine. All these tasks may in time be mastered completely and accomplished at a speed only surpassed by machines or computers programmed for the same tasks. Open capacities, on the other hand, are never completely mastered; there is always more to be learned about improving chess skills, suggests Passmore, in contrast to tic-tac-toe (41). Any task that requires imagination, judgment, or creativity involves open capacities, whether manual or mental, in trades, management, or the professions. An open capacity may depend upon a closed capacity. Determining the effectiveness of a drug or a teaching method may depend upon skill in applying measurement statistics and drawing the proper inferences from them. Such a determination requires the closed capacity to work statistical procedures in order to produce data; drawing conclusions from the project requires the open capacity (a combination of imagination and judgment) to interpret the data and make decisions from such interpretations.

Writing, and teaching writing, are open capacities. Yet many of the actions and skills contributing to their success are closed, needing only to be mastered to fill their place in the larger effort. Successful writing instruction depends upon the instructor's understanding which elements of writing depend upon closed capacities, at what point writing must be treated as an open capacity, and what attitudes and methods are appropriate to each kind of capacity. Teaching an open capacity as though it were a closed capacity may be profoundly counterproductive, yet perhaps no more so than to attempt to treat some of the closed capacities in writing as though they were actually open.

The process of writing depends upon many closed capacities. Most obvious is the skill in editing mechanics: spelling, punctuation, error-avoidance, and the correcting of typographical errors. The application of such skills is often what people—even some writing teachers—mean by writing "correctly," and writing handbooks enforce the view that teaching such skills is a primary mission of composition instruction. The detailed elaboration of grammar rules and the etiquette of documentation, for example, imply that these elements of the written product ought to be supremely important to student writers. But documentation, for example, is a closed capacity governed by formulas. A perfect footnote is possible for careful students to achieve. Insisting on accurate spelling often draws a large amount of the writing teacher's energy, because it's the most visible evidence of "illiteracy" to many readers. Yet spelling correctly is a closed capacity that can be trained into students. Finally the error-orientation that underlies many handbooks' emphasis upon rules suggests that error-free writing should be the writing teacher's main goal. But error-free writing can easily enough be achieved and is not necessarily effective writing. The pedagogical emphasis upon "correct" writing may inculcate in students a narrow adherence to rules as the governing intention in writing. Learning most surface conventions requires detailed, painstaking labor; it does not require imagination, inventiveness, or reasoning power.

Even activities requiring these abilities may involve closed capacities. The specific heuristic strategies described later in this chapter are systems whose elements, once learned, are intended to be used in the same fashion for each inventive task. There's a danger that such strategies could become sterile exercises for students who, having learned the basic heuristic steps, satisfy themselves with applying them routinely without real insight or discovery. Some traditional ways of imposing structure upon paragraphs may also inculcate closed capacities in students. For example, the notion of a topic sentence in paragraphs has been maligned frequently in recent years, on the grounds that pedagogical insistence upon a topic sentence ignores the many possible paragraph arrangements that do not have one. Yet methods of structuring paragraphs without obvious emphasis on topic sentences—Becker's Topic-Restriction-Illustration (TRI), for example—may develop equally readily into a closed, limiting procedure. This can happen if writing teachers forget that most paragraph models are extractions from the modelmaker's survey of x number of paragraphs, representing the form taken by sentence groups on the page, not the processes by which they are generated. Of necessity, paragraph models emerge from the empirical forms of the written product, not the generative process behind the product. Teaching students to generate paragraphs according to given models risks teaching them that following a format is the same as making a good paragraph. It may encourage them to practice what must be an open ended capacity as a closed, form-bound skill. The same danger lurks in other strategies as well: teaching expository discourse by the five-paragraph model, teaching inventiveness by means of outlining, or teaching sentence-making as an exercise in combining coordinate clauses into more "efficient" syntactical structures.

Producing effective writing requires the mastery of various closed capacities. But these developed skills, to be meaningful, must be used in the service of the infinitely *open* capacity which is the writing process. Passmore suggests that an open capacity makes it possible for the student

> to take steps which he has not been taught to take, which in some measure surprise the instructor, not necessarily in the sense that no other pupil has ever done such a thing . . . but in the sense that the teacher has not taught his pupil to take precisely that step and his taking it does not necessarily follow as an application of a principle in which the teacher has instructed him (42).

Certain aspects of writing, of course, cannot be taught as open capacities: putting commas and periods in the right place, spelling correctly, and using quotation marks appropriately require precise applications of principles. Diverging from mechanical conventions is dysfunctional, not creative. Adhering to them requires students to learn precise, rule-governed behavior which, though contributing to good writing, does not constitute it.

The fundamentals of good writing behavior must *always* be taught as open capacities. Following the composing models discussed later in this chapter, we can divide these fundamentals into three groups: inventing and developing a discourse, arranging and structuring it, and revising and reordering it at all levels. We must also keep in mind that most composing models present these elements as recursive, continually interacting in a circular fashion. Inventing and developing may both precede and accompany the actual writing of an essay. Some students may discover their argument more effectively, as many writers do, simply by writing a first sentence and building on it, without any elaborate prewriting activity. Making outlines before writing may encourage students to think they have the entire discourse under control; practiced writers know how often a pre-established intention vanishes under the pressure of a clearer, firmer direction emerging during writing itself. Only when students understand that inventing and developing occur at any point in writing will they be able to exploit these capacities in a truly open way. And only if they see every draft as an incomplete intention, open to further development, will they be able to exploit the revising process as an open capacity.

This flexibility, an intuitive awareness of the incompleteness of any text, is at the heart of all good writing behavior. It is this uncomfortable tension between what is done and what is still unrealized intention, so familiar to practiced writers, that makes the act of writing and its teaching so difficult. And it is just this relativity of "completed" intention that dismays students. For they can finish the math problem and find that they have the right answer, or absorb the sociology text and score well on a multiple-choice test, or perform the lab experiment and fill in the worksheet correctly. But never, it seems, can they fully please their writing teacher, who always manages to find some way in which they might have written a piece more effectively. When students find it more expedient to blame the writing teacher's intransigence than their own efforts for the evaluation they receive, then they have not grasped (perhaps because they have not been sufficiently taught) the probationary condition of even the best of writing intentions. Only rigorous instruction in this principle will bring home the complex, humane effort that is writing. Unfortunately, schools and colleges are generally not adapted to such teaching. Instead, they feel pressured to seek the obvious remedy for what they take to be writing's obvious ill: its failure to obey rules. For such a problem, the manifest solution is to teach students rules so that they can write more correctly.

The Handbook Tradition

The best way to understand popular opinion about teaching writing in today's schools is to consider a major tool of that teaching—the composition handbook. Nearly every trade publisher of college texts offers one or more versions of the writing handbook, often competing directly with one another. And just because it's so difficult to prove the effectiveness of a particular teaching method, most writing handbooks are written without regard to any coherent teaching plan. Printed on heavy-grade, glossy paper and securely bound to withstand a life of eternal recycling between bookstore and student, these texts urge the making of outlines, the writing of thesis sentences, and careful editing. The uninitiated writing teacher, charged with selecting a text and correlating a course syllabus with its contents, might conclude that in its few hundred pages live all that a student needs to know about writing. Their content and organization are formulaic. Early chapters focus on how students should begin their writing assignments: they are usually urged to formulate thesis statements, build clear beginnings, middles and endings, and develop support for generalizations. This standard advice only takes a few chapters to impart, however; much of the rest of the typical handbook is given over to mechanics, usage, spelling, diction, and common errors in syntax and idiom. Handbooks, that is, tend to focus on the form of the written product. The bulkiest texts are the ones with the most thorough collation of rules. They signal the unmistakable message that format and editing codes are the student writer's most important goals.

In writing handbooks, the written product itself is made the focal point of the writing course. The presentation of sentence patterns and errors, for example, is based on traditional word-grammar analysis in most texts, in which parts of speech and their structures are the basis of stylistic discussions and error analysis. In the handling of stylistic questions, emphasis is on what has been called "the rhetoric of the finished word."[8] Sentence-manipulation and word choice are presented as part of the editing process, surface manipulations of syntax and vocabulary in pursuit of clarity and variety. The bulky sections of the texts devoted to grammar and usage rules reflect clearly the major goal of language instruction from the handbook writers' point of view: bringing students' writing into conformity with the decorums of standard usage. Such a goal is not without advocates. Handbook authors defend their approach to teaching writing as essential to preserve the normative function of written language. Indeed, the written form of a language changes much more slowly than its oral form, as E. D. Hirsch points out: "the conservatism of written speech has. . . been the foundation of a genuine *lingua franca* within every large literate community in the world."[9] This linguistic fact lies behind the tacit agreement among handbook writers and publishers that writing teachers' main task is to teach students the editing codes of standard written English.

Debate over written language's normative function is widespread today. Opponents of the normative position say that it's both invalid and culturally insensitive. It's invalid, critics say, because modern language theory deems any standard dialect a function of what the majority actually speak and write, not the result of grammatical "laws" formulated by the harmless drudges who make dictionaries and textbooks. The "prescriptiveness" of modern handbooks, argue critics, is a vestige of earlier days when the established rules of Latin grammar were taught to youthful and recalcitrant speakers of a living language like English. Moreover, an insistence on the necessity for a standard form of the language is intolerably authoritarian, critics persist, because dialectal variation represents cultural variety. To insist on an "official" dialect is to encourage social and cultural leveling. The educational establishment ought not to deny a particular dialect the right to flourish in a society historically tolerant of diversity.

The text-makers counter that such an argument overlooks the basic function of language in a diverse society: to make communication possible amid cultural and ethnic variety. There are many countries of the world claiming to be nations which are, in fact, separate regions kept separate by different languages or dialects too dissimilar to allow communication. If any language is to permit fluid interaction among all elements of that language community, then one of two conditions must exist. All dialectal variations of the language must be readily understood among the dialect groups; or one common dialect must be spoken and understood by all groups, in addition to their own. It has been the standard written English taught in schools and colleges, argue the text-makers, which has been a major contributor to the geographical and political unity of the United States. And to maintain the normative power of standard English, they persist, educators must insist on its primacy in schools and colleges. The key element in teaching standard English is the codification of its visible codes —its idioms, usages, mechanics and spellings—in universally available sources: handbooks. Without firmly established codes there can be no standard dialect, and without handbooks to purvey them, codes cannot remain firmly established.

This dialectic offers theoretical justification for either position. For teachers in practical situations, however, the normative, handbook-aided approach often confuses technique with technicality. As we have already seen, writing is a complex, amorphous activity whose openness can never be comprehended by rules or conditions. Handbooks that emphasize editing codes misrepresent writing just as do teachers who emphasize spelling and punctuation over other elements of the process, by forcing a false equation between the open-ended process called "writing" and the rule-bound activity called "editing." Writing is more than editing; editing is an important, last stage in writing. Editing requires students to learn exactness and attention to detail, referenced by established etiquette. Inventing and developing require infinite choices, with the writer's shaping purpose the only reference. Inventing, organizing, developing— these processes are difficult to teach precisely because they have no norms of right or wrong, but only the value of effectiveness with respect to the governing purpose. Editing is much easier to teach just because it is controlled by rules. Thus, writing handbooks seize on the pedagogically easier aspects of writing, giving them disproportionate attention at the expense of the crucial, subjective phases of writing that precede editing. In thinking out their courses, teachers of writing must begin by realizing just how limitedly useful handbooks are, nearly in inverse proportion to their availability.

The Rhetorical Tradition

Handbooks' disproportionate attention to editing rules suggests, in the terms of classical rhetoric, the sway of style over invention and arrangement in the classroom. We need now to consider briefly the importance of the rhetorical tradition for teaching writing today. The story of rhetoric from its classical origins to its modern forms has been well and frequently told, and requires no recounting here.[10] The elements of classical rhetoric are deeply embedded in all types of discourse and its study; until modern times rhetoric formed a major part of school and university curricula in Europe and America. Derived from the Greek word *rhetor*, which means "orator," rhetoric in the classical period centered on spoken discourse, and had five aspects: invention (the discovery and development of content), arrangement (the organization of the discourse), style (e.g., figurative language, sentence patterns), memory and delivery. The first three of these aspects—invention, arrangement, and style—continued to be emphasized during the Renaissance and Enlightenment periods of western culture, particularly in philosophical and religious discourse. Schools and universities through the nineteenth century emphasized training in rhetoric for speaking and writing. In America, however, the early twentieth-century split between the disciplines of English and speech allowed rhetoric thereafter to be identified primarily with speaking. While speech departments carried rhetoric into their camp, viewing it as their birthright, English departments claimed only that part of rhetoric applicable to the study of prose composition. As a result, English department "rhetoric" tended to be reduced to matters of style and form, the study of discourse forms, sentences, diction and usage. The handbook tradition discussed above is a continuing manifestation of the rigidified notion of rhetoric typical, until recently, of English department attitudes.

In the last decade or so, a rhetoric "revival" of sorts has brought the true range of rhetoric renewed attention from teachers of writing.[11] The major parts of rhetoric—invention and its concern with topic development, arrangement with its formal concerns, style, and the rhetorical situation involving speaker-audience, writer-reader relationships—have been rediscovered in their relevance to the writer's task. All inexperienced writers must learn them if they are to be capable of effective writing. When English professor Richard Ohmann calls for students to be familiar with the "concept of liguistic structure" and the "intricate regularity of patterns of English," he is confirming the importance of style.[12] When rhetorician Dudley Bailey asserts that rhetorical training should include analysis of "the logical and psychological patterns which listeners and readers . . . anticipate in our discourse," he is calling for a contemporary version of the classical "topics" to help writers shape their work for their intended audience.[13] In this and later chapters, we will explore further the role of rhetoric in contemporary understandings of how and why we write. First, however, we must consider how a much younger discipline has combined with rhetoric to give new insights into writing.

The Influence of Psychology

Teaching writing today is not only a continuation of traditional rhetorical training. Two other major disciplines—psychology and linguistics—have strongly influenced what writing teachers do to help students understand and master the writing process. We'll consider certain specific aspects of recent linguistic theory in Chapters II and III, which deal with such issues as the role of grammar and sentence combining in teaching writing, and the relevance of dialect differences to writing instruction. The rest of this chapter examines the contributions of modern psychology to our understanding of how and why we write. Cognitive psychology has provided crucial insights into writing and its teaching by offering some persuasive interpretations of language as a function of thinking.

Piaget, Vygotsky, and Bruner

Jean Piaget has presented a seminal interpretation of language as an activity of mind. As the originator of what he termed "genetic epistemology," the study of how the developing mind structures knowledge in systematic ways, he studied the stages of learning through which children pass from birth to late adolescence. His method was both speculative and empirical. He observed individual children or small samples of a particular age group, wrote descriptions of their learning behavior, and built theoretical constructs of the learning process. Because in his early years as a researcher this methodology differed radically from the controlled experiments of the behaviorist school, his influence did not begin to spread until after World War II, two decades after he began publishing his work. In the composition field his influence has appeared only recently, long after it had risen to dominance in psychology and educational theory. His description of the cognitive stages of childhood, the core of Piaget's theories, is a useful starting point for a consideration of his influence upon the teaching of writing.

The periods of cognitive growth, each consisting of certain "operations" which the child becomes capable of, are in Piaget's view successive but not strictly linear. They are overlaid upon one another, the capabilities typical of each period synthesized in the development of the succeeding period, and integrated in the mature individual. The first period Piaget terms "sensory-motor," the phase of growth before language when the infant learns to respond to its environment in non-linguistic ways. Language has a central place in Piaget's theory of learning, but this first period reveals "that the rudiments of intelligent behavior evolve *before* language develops."[14] Infant behavior demonstrates that human learning depends not on the ability to generate language, but upon a more basic ability of which language is a manifestation. This capacity Piaget terms "semiotic ability"—the human capacity to communicate with symbols. During the "sensory-motor" period the child gradually learns to represent experience internally—to think, in other words. "From an organism whose most intelligent functions are sensory-motor, overt acts," the child alters after the second year into one "whose upper-limit cognitions are inner, symbolic manipulations of reality."[15]

This transition marks the child's entry into the second learning stage, the "period of preoperational thought," during which the child extends the ability to symbolize experience in various ways. "Individual semiosis," says Piaget, includes "imitation, symbolic play, and the [mental] image"; language is the most articulate form of "semiotic thought."[16] By the third year, the child is making sentences, revealing an innate capacity to articulate thoughts according to syntactical rules that cannot be attributed merely to imitation of other speakers. Once the child begins to use language, the rate of learning increases because the child can assimilate experience in an "increasingly complex and efficient fashion. The progress from the "preoperational" to the period of "concrete operations" (which begins about the eighth year) is made possible largely by an increasing ability to represent reality abstractly. The "concrete logical operations," which involve such things as the ability to perceive quantities and relationships, are products of the growing capacity for symbolic manipulation of reality.

The last stage of cognitive growth, the period of "formal operations," reveals the child's enhanced ability to deal not just with concrete elements of reality, but with abstract verbal issues and complex logical problems. The child begins to deal with the possible as well as the real, with the past and future as well as the present. "Language is indispensable to the elaboration of thought" in this period.[17] The process of abstraction, says Piaget, "detaches thought from action and is the source of representation. Language plays a particularly important role in the formative process," for it is "elaborated socially and contains a notation for the entire system" of cognitive functions.[18]

For Piaget, then, language has two major functions in the child's intellectual growth: it permits the development of increasingly complex cognitions, and through a process Piaget calls "decentering" it enhances the child's ability to understand other perspectives on reality and distinguish them from his own. Decentering is the process by which he escapes from the "cognitive egocentricism" characterizing the early years of growth. In these years his awareness "is marked by unconscious preferential focusing," a "lack of differentiation between one's own point of view and the other possible ones."[19] That is, he begins by perceiving the world as continuous with his own understanding. He is unable to grasp people or events as "outside" his own world and different from the way he sees them or thinks them to be. He attempts to communicate by means of "egocentric speech," whereby he "talks for himself," although he "thinks he is talking for others and is making himself understood" (*Comments,* 8). Decentering is the child's gradual liberation from egocentricism through the ability to understand experience from more than a single perspective. "The progress of knowledge," says Piaget, is "a perpetual reformulation of previous points of view by a process which moves backwards as well as forward . . . this corrective process . . [obeys] the law of decentering" (*Comments,* 3). Decentering is essential to the maturing process, and language is essential to decentering, by permitting the child to interact with others. As language enhances the ability to "see" various perspectives on experience, it also greatly increases the capacity to develop concepts about the relationship between self and world.

Piaget's theories about language's communicative and conceptualizing functions were extended and altered in the work of L. S. Vygotsky, a psychologist and contemporary of Piaget. Vygotsky's provocative study of the relationship between thought and language is another major contribution to our understanding of language processes.[20] Vygotsky emphasizes that language is not merely the expression of thought, but provides "reality and form" (126) for thought. His interpretation of the term "egocentric speech" insists on an integral relation between language process and thought process. Piaget, says Vygotsky, defines egocentric speech as an expression of the child's egocentric understanding, so that when decentering occurs egocentric speech vanishes. Vygotsky argues otherwise: the decrease in egocentric speech, he says, "denotes a developing abstraction from sound, the child's new faculty to 'think words' instead of pronouncing them" (135). What emerges as the child matures is an "entirely separate speech function" characterized by the dominance of predication, simplified sentence structures, and shifting, flexible word meanings. This internalized language use Vygotsky calls "inner speech," a concept which Piaget himself eventually came to accept. Inner speech is a mature process of thought, "a dynamic, shifting . . . thing, fluttering between word and thought," a "thinking in pure meanings" (249). Meanwhile the capacity for external speech, obedient to the conventions of socialized language, also evolves. The mind of the mature individual thus depends upon language in two ways: language as inner speech is part of the thinking process, while language as external speech is necessary for communication. "Speech structures mastered by the child become the basic structures of his thinking," while "intellectual growth" in turn depends upon the child's "mastering the social means of thought, that is, language" (52). Inner and outer speech are reciprocal processes, both essential to the maturity of the individual. Written language is perceived by Vygotsky as the fully developed offspring of inner speech, whose predication and condensation give way in writing to fully developed syntax and word specificity. Vygotsky also suggests that the composing process itself—the movement from "mental draft" to written draft to final draft—reflects the process by which inner speech becomes external speech. In the process of composition, reflection in language (inner speech) becomes communication through language (external speech).

Vygotsky and Piaget, however, carefully avoid saying that language-making and thinking are identical, despite their relatedness. Rather, thought and language are seen as two intersecting circles, with verbal thought the crucial ability emerging from the interaction of both. For Vygotsky "there is no rigid correspondence between the units of thought and speech"; "just as one sentence may express different thoughts, one thought may be expressed in different sentences" (149). Language is essential to the development of intelligence because grammatical structures express logical relationships similar to those expressed in nonverbal forms of thought. Piaget also sees language as a crucial form of cognition, but not its only form: "the roots of logical operations lie deeper than the linguistic connections," he suggests; "language is thus a necessary but not sufficient condition for the construction of logical operations" (*SPS*, 98). The development of intelligence in the child is catalyzed by the growth of language, but language is not "the source of all logic for the whole of humanity" (*PC*, 87). For logic is not, in Piaget's views, simply "generalized syntax." Mathematical logic is an important mode of thought, as are image-making and other nonverbal processes. Language is a crucial but not an exclusive form of intelligence.

Another noted spokesman for the discipline of cognitive psychology, Jerome Bruner, follows Piaget and Vygotsky in arguing that language is "at the center of the stage" in intellectual development. He maintains that language is an "instrument of thought" because the syntax of language organizes human experience into "hierarchical categories" which underlie all human experience. [21] These categories, which he terms "causation, predication and modification," make possible the child's ordering of his world. [22] "The medium of language . . . [is] the instrument that the learner can use himself in bringing order into the environment" (*TTI*, 6), says Bruner. But he's not suggesting that language constitutes reality, or that thought is made up of language. In saying that language is "a tool for organizing thoughts about things" (*TTI*, 105), Bruner means that language expresses the mind's drive to categorize experience, and provides a method by which thought can deal with experience. Bruner reaffirms Piaget's principle that language enables the developing mind to objectify experience by abstracting from it and communicating about it. Ultimately language expresses the quality of the intelligence which uses it: "the shape and style of a mind is, in some measure, the outcome of internalizing the functions inherent in the language we use" (*TTI*, 107). Like Piaget and Vygotsky, Bruner insists on language's crucial ability to make learning possible.

New Modal Systems

The changing concept of mode in discourse is one important sign of psychology's current influence on composition. The idea of modes, or "forms of discourse" has traditionally drawn meaning from some kind of psychological framework. Associationist psychology is the basis for the most influential nineteenth century modal system, that of Alexander Bain. There are "three ultimate modes of mind—Feeling, Volition, and Intellect," he suggested, and the "forms of Discourse" correspond to each faculty:

> Those that have for their object to inform the Understanding [Intellect], fall under three heads—Description, Narration, and Exposition. The means of influencing the Will [Volition] are given under one head, Persuasion. The employing of language to excite pleasurable Feelings, is one of the chief characteristics of Poetry:[23]

Furthermore, "the Will can be moved only through the Understanding or through the Feelings." Thus three of Bain's five "kinds of composition" embody an association between actions of the intelligence and the moving of the will—i.e., between what the writer wants the reader to understand and what he wants the reader to believe or do, Bain might say. This linkage among psychic components reflects the mechanistic tendencies of associationist psychology, and to the modern eye appears reductive and outmoded. The very same terms are used, with very different premises, by another nineteenth century rhetorician, A. D. Hepburn, who classes the "forms of Discourse" according to the "objects of thought" each one addresses:

> 1. Description [is] the exhibition in language of the parts of a simultaneous whole. 2. Narration [is] the exhibition of the parts of a successive whole. 3. Exposition [consists] in the explication of general notions and propositions formed from them. 4. Argumentation [treats] the truth or falsehood of a proposition.[24]

Hepburn bases his definitions on the subject matter of the discourse types, rather than upon their psychological function. While Bain's categories are based on the writer's subjective intentions, Hepburn's "Forms" are defined by their objective, referential content. John Franklin Genung, an American rhetorician of the nineteenth century, echoes Hepburn by asserting that description, narration, exposition and persuasion are "the particular forms that invention adopts, as it has to deal with material of various kinds."[25] Bain, Hepburn and Genung use nearly identical terms to define categories of prose composition yet define those categories in radically different ways. No contemporary rhetorician has sought to clarify or to reconcile the conflicts within these traditional modal categories. Yet these categories still appear today in many rhetorics and readers, often without any definition of their conceptual basis.

What has long been needed is a reformulation of the concept of mode on clear and unambiguous psychological premises. With the help of contemporary psychological and linguistic understandings, James Britton has developed the most persuasive and useful current theory of discourse forms. Britton has suggested three "function categories" of writing in schools, described in terms of the audience for the writing ("who is it for?") and the purpose the writing serves ("what is it for?").[26] Britton acknowledges the convergent influences of cognitive psychology, linguistics and epistemology, with Piaget and Vygotsky as generative sources. Britton's interest in audience and purpose would appear to derive from classical rhetoric's interest in the speaker-audience relationship. However, his definition of the writer's audience-sense utilizes a contemporary frame of reference. Britton does not analyze the writer-audience relationship as always purposeful, i.e. involving a writer seeking to inform, persuade or move an audience. Instead, drawing on recent analyses of "language roles" in human interaction, Britton suggests that the writer, purpose and audience of a piece of writing are all related in one or two basic ways. If writing reveals an intention to "get things done," whether by instructing, persuading, "speculating," or "theorizing," then it serves "some end outside itself" (18). This is "writing in the role of participant" (18), and Britton suggests the term *transactional* to describe it. If writing renders "experiences real or imagined" in order that the audience (which may be only the writer) may "contemplate narrated experiences" (19) as a means of understanding them more clearly or judging their value, then that writing becomes an end in itself, and its form and style important in themselves. This use of language Britton calls "writing in the role of spectator" (19), and he suggests the term *poetic* to describe it.

Britton's scheme may be represented in the following diagram:

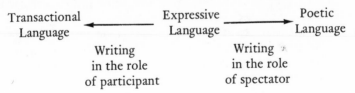

At the center of the spectrum is *expressive* language, which may include both spectator and participant role, but which assumes shared interests and "close relations" between writer and audience. This is the most common use of language in speech or writing, especially in children, because it does not require adaptation to an outside audience, but permits the writer or speaker to explore the world within the security of "shared contexts" (32). As the child matures, or as the adult defines his writing or speaking purpose, expressive language differentiates "into specific forms to meet specific demands over a wide range of transactional and poetic tasks."[27] Britton argues that "expressive language signals the self, reflects not only the ebb and flow of a speaker's thought and feeling, but also his assumptions of shared contexts of meaning, and of a relationship of trust with his listener"; "[expressive language is] the mode in which young children chiefly write." [28] Thus when schoolchildren are asked to write communicatively (i.e. , aim at an audience beyond their immediate world) rather than expressively, they will succeed to the extent they can visualize and address an audience outside their familiar experience.

What Britton perceives as the ubiquity of expressive speech and writing in schoolchildren leads him to propose a "major hypothesis" for school writing: "what children write in the early stages should be a form of written-down expressive speech. . . . As their writing and reading progress side by side, they will move from this starting point into . . . broadly differentiated kinds of writing." [29] This progression has begun to inform writing texts for the college market as well. A number of recent rhetoric texts explicitly follow this pattern in their major sections, moving from "personal" writing (diaries, journals) through "descriptive" and "informative" to "persuasive" writing. Though there are differing forms and changing intentions involved in this sequence, there are also different audiences implied for the various types. Personal writing suggests a "relationship of trust" between writer and reader, while persuasive writing, at the other end of the spectrum, suggests abstract topics and a more distanced, generalized audience. Such a polarity may be seen, for example, in the assignments of the writing-test portion of the National Assessment of Educational Progress (NAEP), a nationwide program for measuring the educational gains of schoolchildren at different grade levels in the United States. The second round of this testing seeks, according to the program's official bulletin, to measure skills in "personal writing" as well as in the functional writing tasks measured by the first round.[30] The test program has been broadened in order to discover whether children are learning the flexibility needed to perform a variety of writing tasks for a variety of audiences.

One important example of Britton's influence on current thinking about modes appears in a well-known empirical study of students' composing processes. In *The Composing Processes of Twelfth Graders,* Janet Emig scrutinizes the physical and psychological minutiae of some high school seniors' writing habits, and induces composing patterns associated with the writing types she finds. In devising her categories, Emig notes the diagram of writing types constructed by Britton and his colleagues, which posits "expressive" writing as the primary mode of writing, especially for students. Agreeing with Britton's insight, she suggests that "all student writings emanate from an expressive impulse" (37). But then she argues that the other two terms in Britton's tripartite scheme "are at once too familiar and too ultimate" (37). Instead, she suggests two terms which describe the "relations between the writing self and the field of discourse": *reflexive* and *extensive* (37). Her diagram closely resembles Britton's:

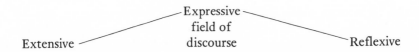

Extensive — Expressive
field of
discourse — Reflexive

By "field of discourse" Emig says she means "areas of experience" (33). But her definitions make it clear that "field of discourse" is more than the relation of the "writing self" to the experience being handled in the writing. "Field of discourse" in Emig's system also includes the audience for the writing, and actually—like Britton's "function categories"—defines the complex interaction of the writer's intent, the nature of the subject matter, and the audience to which that matter is addressed.

For example, although Emig rejects Britton's term *poetic* in favor of her term *reflexive,* both terms delineate a writer-subject-audience relationship. Writing reflexively, the "writing self" ponders and evaluates experience, attempts to answer the question "what does this experience mean?" (37), and is aimed at the self as the "chief audience" (91). Emig's term *extensive* identifies writing in "a basically active role"; such writing answers the question "how, because of this experience, do I interact with my environment?" (37), and is aimed at "adult others, notably teachers," as the "chief audience" (91). In other words, the *extensive* mode parallels Britton's *transactional* category, in which the writing self is in a "participant" role and intends to "get something done" with the writing. Emig's categories are limited to the school writing her students were engaged in, and lack the larger range of examples upon which Britton builds his categories.

Another instance of Britton's influence—and a certain belated counter-reaction to it—can be found in John Dixon's retrospective essay in the third edition of *Growth Through English,* his interpretation of the gist of the 1965 Anglo-American "Dartmouth Conference" on writing.[32] Dixon suggests that the conference emphasized the importance of language in the role of *spectator*—the imaginative and reflective uses of language. But, continues Dixon, "what was left unexplored was the contrary role that [Harding] and Britton drew our attention to (yes, even in the seminar)—the role of participant. This is their generic term for the roles we take on when we use language to inform, advise, convince, persuade, report, invite, order, request, instruct . . . ." (123). Admitting that this is "a very large body of language to neglect" (123), Dixon suggests that nevertheless the Conference participants were so fascinated by language as meditation and play that they ignored language in "the role of informing and explaining." This function—Britton's "transactional" category—requires the student to "imagine an audience other than himself and his classmates," and to organize language "on behalf of, in the interests of, and for [its] effect on, another person or other people" (124). The Conference's omission of transactional writing from its program encourages a distorted view of what writing in schools ought to include, says Dixon. The need for students to "master language in the participant role," he concludes, requires that students should be asked to do more than just use language to "represent" the world to themselves. They should also be asked to use language to "communicate"; that is, they should be required to display a "social competence" in language, embodied in such intentions as "explanations, requests, directions, invitations, reports, instructions" and the like (125).

What Dixon is arguing is what most writing teachers already know: that writing done by young writers must appeal to their own experience even as it relates that experience to others. It's false to talk about student writing as though it could be either entirely self-oriented or wholly social and other-directed. Any writing task that is to mean something to younger writers must fall within their experience and be directed at an audience meaningful to them (see Britton's audience categories in Chapter II for a clear formulation of this point). A journal, for example, can reflect the writer's own feelings about events and people while being formulated as a private-letter-to-the-teacher. Behind Dixon's advocacy of other-directed writing for students lies the idea of decentering. Audience awareness is precisely the writer's recognition of other points of view than his own, and his recognition of the ways in which his words strike others. Linda Flower has formulated the term "writer-based" prose to describe writing which fails to communicate with an audience because such writing exhibits the qualities of the "inner and egocentric speech" described by Vygotsky and Piaget.[33] Such prose must be transformed into "reader-based" writing through the writer's imposition of reader-oriented structures upon his writing. In Piagetian terms the growth of audience awareness is a function of decentering, during which the writer gains the ability to perceive his work objectively.

Despite Dixon's second thoughts, however, the Dartmouth Conference has been influential in encouraging the use of students' personal experience in writing assignments and their participation in a wide range of language-using activity. Since the conference, some composition texts have urged group activities such as panel discussions, role-playing, and simulation games, in addition to small-group work that encourages independent, self-motivated activity. One popular text advocates writing as a way of learning "self-management" for those "trying to claim more control over their own lives."[34] An NCTE Commission on Composition has urged language as a mode of self creation: "through language we understand, interpret, enjoy, and in part create our worlds. . . . [language] can help students . . . live more fully."[35] It argues that "the teacher should encourage writing from personal experience" ("Teaching Composition," 219), and discourage the use of literature in writing courses. Such pronouncements notwithstanding, writing teachers need not consign their outside readings to the shelves and restrict themselves to assignments about summer vacations. The insights of Piaget and psychologists influenced by him make it clear that writing growth will occur most readily when what students write about relates directly to their own experience. Topics need not always come *from* their experience, merely be available *to* their experience, confirming, expanding, or challenging it. Students' attitudes and expectations must be brought into play; nearly any topic can fit this purpose. Setting the context for a writing topic is the teacher's responsibility; it can be done by establishing the rhetorical situation, to include the writing purpose and the audience. Contextualizing writing gives it the psychological fullness which alone invests writing with meaning for students (see Chapter IV for a discussion of the importance of context in making writing assignments).

Invention Strategies

Psychology's most spectacular impact on composition has come in the area of invention, that element of rhetoric concerned with the development of the topic. In classical rhetoric invention means developing proofs for an argument, using "topics" which help the speaker think up and marshal the elements of proof. Topics are themes or "places" of thought to which the speaker can turn for help in developing his own proofs. Aristotle lists four "universal" or "common" topics which are to apply to any matter: the possible and the impossible, past fact, future possibilities, and degree, or relative magnitude. He also develops a number of special topics (division, classification, analysis of consequences, etc.) which have application to a narrower range of subjects than the common topics. Later classical and Renaissance rhetoricians expanded the study of topics to include a very wide range of named exigencies in argumentation, so that the orator could find something to say about nearly any subject that might confront him. "Invention" within the rhetorical tradition thus does not mean finding new and unique truth about a given subject; it means producing fresh, persuasive arguments from time-tested sources already mastered in outline by the arguer. Also following Aristotle, classical rhetoricians generally identified oratory appropriate to three situations: deliberative oratory, concerned with persuading hearers to believe or act in a certain way; forensic, concerned with judicial questions of right and wrong; and epideictic, concerned with celebrating an event, person or public institution. Thus the purpose and main focus of the discourse is fixed by circumstance and context; invention is "discovering" the proofs which might put across the purpose most effectively.

The concept of invention has undergone something of a sea change in recent years. Shaped by modern psychology, invention—finding something to say—has recently been adjudged as much a psychological activity as a rhetorical method. The models of the composing process discussed below show the extent to which invention has recently been defined as a self-fulfilling activity of mind. Implicit in them is Piaget's definition of learning as a constant search for the resolution of "disequilibrium," a condition "in which our ways of thinking and acting become inadequate to deal with a change that has taken place within or outside ourselves."[36] Psychological "disequilibrium" occurs when the mind confronts an experience it cannot categorize or put adequately into perspective. Because, in Jerome Bruner's words, language is "a powerful instrument for combining experiences" (*TTI,* 105), it is the primary means by which the individual reconciles the unfamiliar with the understood. Bruner argues that "the combinatorial or productive property of language" is an invitation "to take experience apart and put it together again in new ways" (*TTI,* 105). "This is what the teacher of composition has in his charge," concludes Bruner (*TTI,* 105).

Thus, the basis for defining invention has shifted to some extent from rhetoric to psychology. In the perspective of the new psychology, all acts of composing begin as explorations of new ways to understand experience: the urge to write begins in the hope of discovery. This definition of writing's beginning point has helped to create interest in several contemporary systems of invention. We will examine four of them: problem-solving, tagmemics, dramatism, and prewriting.

The problem-solving approach to discovery derives from the positivist terminology of behaviorism. Its source is the theory of "cognitive dissonance," derived from Piaget's "disequilibrium." Dissonance stimulates "activity oriented toward dissonance reduction just as hunger leads to activity oriented toward hunger reduction." [37] Dissonance spurs the mind into action aimed toward eliminating the dissonance, in a psychological parallel to the body's drive toward physiological balance. This reductive analogy between mind and body is a major point of objection to problem-solving as a composing strategy, as we will see. All problem-solving procedures rely on some kind of "heuristic," a term deriving from a Greek root meaning "to discover." Webster's *New Collegiate Dictionary* defines it as "providing aid or direction in the solution of a problem but otherwise unjustified or incapable of justification." A heuristic may be a set of questions or analytic categories which help define the issues involved in a problem or "dissonance." The fact that such heuristics are often posed as algorithms in the sciences—closed systems of answer-finding —suggests the rule-bound nature of the problem-solving concept.

The problem-solving approach to discovering what to write is pedagogically appealing in the same way that rules of grammar and usage make handbooks attractive. "Psychologists," remarks one advocate, "have been trying to identify the general features" of heuristic procedures which "should be invaluable for the teacher who is dealing with the creative process of composition." [38] Another enthusiast, citing Piaget and Bruner, asserts that "the ability to read and write sensitively, thoughtfully, and independently presupposes the ability to formulate and solve problems." [39] How may the usefulness of a heuristic be judged? One researcher has offered the criteria of "transcendance" and "flexibility" as essentials. [40] If a problem-solver (i.e. writer) is to take the trouble to master a heuristic procedure, it must be applicable to all writing situations by being larger than any one of them; it must be comprehensive ("transcendent") rather than conditional upon specific data or settings. It must also be flexible so that the writer can utilize any part of it that seems useful to the situation, without having to work from the starting point. If it is limited in its appropriateness, the user is forced to improvise when confronted with a problem beyond its range. The heuristic itself becomes a "problem" requiring a solution, rather than a way of providing one.

Desirable as these features seem, even the first of them—comprehensiveness—suggests difficulties with problem-solving as a general approach to inventing subject-matter. If we begin to write in order to explore our experience, to say what we cannot yet conceive because we have not yet composed it, then we are saying that writing is an infinitely variable process. We have no goal other than to find out what we want to say and how best to say it; we have not targeted a "solution" because there is no specific "problem," only the continuous act of discovery as we make sentences and paragraphs. Writing is too complex, recursive, and unpredictable to be aided by something as narrow as a methodology that can only end in a "solution." The "communications specialists" and scientific problem-solvers who must resolve management or public relations crises or enhance technological systems use the term "discovery" in a narrow, practical sense that does not apply to the composing process. It is the "creative imagination," says Ann Berthoff, the core of the natural resources of mind, which writing teachers must nurture in their students. "For creativity is not an *area*" or a tool for doing a job, she points out, but "the heart of the matter," and writing "conceived as the expression of thinking about experience" is the proper way to describe what the process of discovery serves.[41] Seductively neat and simple as a formulation, problem-solving is ill-suited to describe the generative play of mind that is composing.

Another discovery method with the same limitations is tagmemics. Tagmemics began as a system of language analysis developed by Kenneth Pike, whose purpose was to formulate a heuristic which could aid in the discovery of the grammatical structure of a language. The tagmemic system's universal applicability, Pike argues, derived from its codification of the hierarchical structures of thought inherent in all language. His view is that the structure of syntax is echoed at other levels of discourse, including the paragraph and even larger units. He calls his heuristic "epistemological" because he believes it to be based on the principles by which the mind orders experience of any kind. The text that attempts to put Pike's theory into pedagogical practice is *Rhetoric: Discovery and Change*, by Richard Young, A. L. Becker and Pike. Its makers, influenced by Pike and by the problem-solving approach to invention, intend their heuristic to aid in the "retrieval of relevant information already known, analysis of problematic data, and discovery of ordering principles."[42] Terms like "retrieval" and "data," of course, betray the technological bias of its emphasis upon empirical content.

The tagmemic heuristic rests on two "maxims" that form the basis of a "nine-cell" grid of perspectives. The first is that any experience "can be adequately understood only if three aspects of the unit are known: (1) its contrastive features, (2) its range of variation, and (3) its distribution in larger contexts."[43] The second is that "a unit of experience can be viewed as a particle, or as a wave, or as a field" (122). The resulting grid requires the problem-solving writer to analyze an object, event or experience by asking nine questions about it that emerge from the conjunction of these perspectives:

	Contrast	Variation	Distribution
Particle	1. View unit as isolated, static entity. What are its contrastive features?	4. View unit as an instance of a concept. What is range of physical variation of concept?	7. View unit as part of larger context. What is unit's position in a class? temporal sequence? space?
Wave	2. View unit as dynamic object or event. What physical features distinguish it?	5. View unit as dynamic process. How is it changing?	8. View unit as part of larger dynamic context. How does it interact with environment?
Field	3. View unit as abstract, multidimensional system. How are components interrelated?	6. View unit as physical system. How do instances of the system vary?	9. View unit as abstract system within larger system. What is its position in the system?

A topic "processed" through this system will presumably be developed in a variety of perspectives available to the writer. If it works as its originators intend, it may discover remembered and new information and organize that information for discourse.

The same distortions of the composing process created by problem-solving may be found in tagmemics. English teachers, Ann Berthoff points out, are not "amateurs in the field of understanding the activity of the mind."[44] They recognize the reductiveness of any discovery method that narrows or isolates one part of the writing process at the expense of another. One critic of recent discovery strategies argues that emphasizing heuristics over other aspects of composing may encourage students to make the heuristic process an end in itself, a game which when ostensibly completed may leave the student still needing to compose words into sentences and paragraphs.[45] An over-emphasis on the discovery process may draw time and energy away from simply getting things written down. Perhaps the strongest objection to the tagmemic system is that, in the words of another critic, tagmemics is built upon "a consistently empirical framework" which limits the student writer to the discovery of ideas "through physical features" alone, discouraging exploration of ideas and relationships not open to empirical verification.[46] A close look at the tagmemic grid does indeed reveal a preponderance of empirical terms like "physical features," "physical variation," and "interaction with environment," along with technological terms like "component" and "entity." The tagmemic system seems ill-suited under these circumstances for the exploration of such things as value questions and human relationships.

Another more genuinely open and creative discovery strategy is "dramatism," originally developed by Kenneth Burke as a method of analyzing "forms of thought," e.g., "poetry and fiction," "legal judgments," or "metaphysical structures."[47] His system is based on a "pentad" of queries directed at "what people are doing and why they are doing it" (*xv*). The five components of the pentad are "Act, Scene, Agent, Agency, Purpose." Any "complete statement about motives," says Burke, "will offer *some kind* of answers to these five questions: what was done (act), when or where it was done (scene), who did it (agent), how he did it (agency), and why (purpose)" (*xv*). Noting the parallels between the pentad of queries and the journalists' traditional who? what? where? how? and why?, students of the pentad urge its relevance to the inventing of subject matter. For Burke, notes one pentad advocate, "writing is a transcription of the process of composing ideas; it is *not* the product of thought but its actualization."[48] This commentator suggests that writers use the pentad queries as a self-pacing guide, with the "agent" category addressed to the *persona* the writer is creating, for example, and the "agency" question directed to the kind of process the writer is using to produce the writing.

Recently, however, Burke himself—ever the flexible and wary interpreter of his own theories—has suggested that although his dramatistic terms may be put "to good use" in the classroom, still he did not mean these terms in the sense in which they have usually been applied. While their textbook use relies on their power to "generate a topic," they were really intended, says Burke, "to ask of the work the explicit questions to which its structure had already implicitly supplied the answers."[49] In other words, he intended them for use in analyzing a product, not a process; their application to the composing process itself clearly takes them far beyond their orignal purpose. Burke allows that this is not necessarily bad, for it may have practical usefulness, yet his warning illustrates the distortion liable to occur when theory is too hastily turned to pedagogical purposes. The composition discipline has been prone to haste in its urgency to make classroom use of theory, as our discussion of discovery strategies has suggested.

One other discovery system that has received attention, and has generated indirect classroom influence, is "prewriting." The term itself is often used simply to indicate the early part of the composing process, before the writing or revising phases. But "prewriting" has also become the distinctive label of a discovery method developed by D. Gordon Rohman and others at Michigan State University. Arguing that most students are taught to deal with the abstract "rhetoric of the finished word," Rohman suggests that students need to learn "the structure of thinking that leads to writing."[50] "Prewriting" is a series of activities which "imitate the principles" by which writing is generated: those activities are keeping a journal, practicing meditation, and making analogies. Keeping a journal is intended as a Thoreau-like exercise in the "discovery of myself *for myself*" (109), a way of articulating experience for oneself. Meditating is suggested as a way of imagining abstract ideas into concrete experience; analogy is urged as a method for seeing an experience in a variety of "as if" perspectives. One report on "prewriting" strategies praises it as an effective way to emphasize "sensation, perception, and concept formation" instead of "technical proficiency and rhetorical skill." [51] Insofar as these activities require students to think through an idea, to give it body by developing it through analogies or other mind-play without the false comfort that a "solution" has been reached, they may aid student writers in developing what they want to say beyond the traditional orthodoxies of outlining and thesis-sentencing. A helpful survey of invention systems is "A Critical Survey of Resources of Teaching Rhetorical Invention," by David Harrington, et al. This essay and Richard Young's "Invention: A Topographical Survey" discuss a wide range of texts from which teachers wanting to use such a system might choose.[52]

New techniques of invention clearly must be regarded warily by teachers; *caveat emptor* must rule their enthusiasm. In particular, empirical and behaviorist strategies must be studied cautiously, for they can represent the complexity of composing in a disquietingly reductive way. But the potential limitations of heuristic methodologies are not their only drawbacks. Another difficulty involves the time and energy needed to master a heuristic system. Particularly for a complex set of terms like those in the tagmemic system, learning them well enough for practical use will draw energy away from actual composing for many students. Advocates of heuristics often emphasize the commitment in study and practice needed to make a heuristic system a functional part of a student's composing process. Instructors may well find that this commitment absorbs energy that ought to be spent in other ways: in attending to other phases of the writing process, or in discussion or in giving feedback in the classroom. Taught inflexibly or thrust into a course schedule limited in the necessary time, a heuristic procedure may baffle students and confuse rather than clarify the writing process.

The Composing Process

Still another example of psychology's influence on composition can be found in some recent models of the writing process. In these models writing is presented as an activity of mind. Such a view constitutes a "mentalistic" interpretation of the act of writing, depending as it does on the assumption that writing is a special kind of mental function, not necessarily connected with speech. Invention, the discovery of subject matter, has always been important in rhetoric; but "discovery" in this context lacks the connotation of creative mind-play characteristic of recent composing models.

Analyses of the composing process generally divide it into three parts: the preparatory or conceptual stage, the developmental or incubation stage, and the production stage. This third stage is seen to include the actual writing, revising, and editing upon which most textbooks focus. The middle phase and to some extent the first phase, treated lightly in most texts, are crucial to writing process. The first two stages are generally divided into a variety of sub-stages by researchers, who point out that the apparent linearity in the diagrams they use is an illusion. They are careful to say that the writing process is still largely a mystery; thus their descriptions are inductively devised, or perhaps analogical when applied to the mind's presumed operations.

One thing all theorists agree upon: the stages interact continuously throughout the composing process. The sub-stage labels vary with the biases of those describing them. One systematizer terms "stimulation" the first phase of the writing process (see Figure A), implying a behaviorist orientation in which a "stimulus-response" pattern operates.[53] Another (see Figure B) identifies "conception" as the beginning point of writing, saying that "writing is a deliberate act; one has to make up one's mind to do it."[54] In this model writing is identified with intention and choice, with the understanding that an act of will is involved in writing, rather than simply a responsiveness to a triggering stimulus. A third model (see Figure C) suggests a "cognitive dissonance" as the beginning of writing, and the ensuing stages as attempts to reduce this "dissonance" by means of the writing process.[55] This interpretation derives from a theory about opinion-change which suggests that writing results from the writer's urge to reconcile a clash between conflicting ideas or emotions. Despite the differences in terminology and derivation, however, these analyses share the premise that writing does not just happen. Though it is variously described, some event or state of mind or feeling is seen as precipitating the writing process.

The middle phases of the composing process are variously classified according to the assumptions of the system-maker. The analysis placing "stimulation" at the onset of the process (Figure A) posits such mental activities as "ideation" and "bundling" leading to "verbalizing," the stage in which "ideated material" starts to become writing. This analysis continues to rely on a mechanistic terminology which implies an associationist linkage between phases of the process. In turn, the system placing "conception" at the beginning of the process (Figure B) suggests "incubation" as the middle phase, implying that writing is an organic process whose dissection may threaten to murder it. During the incubation period, according to this model, the writer moves from knowing *that* he is going to write to knowing *what* he will write. Finally, the model that posits "dissonance" at the onset of writing (Figure C) suggests activity leading to "in-

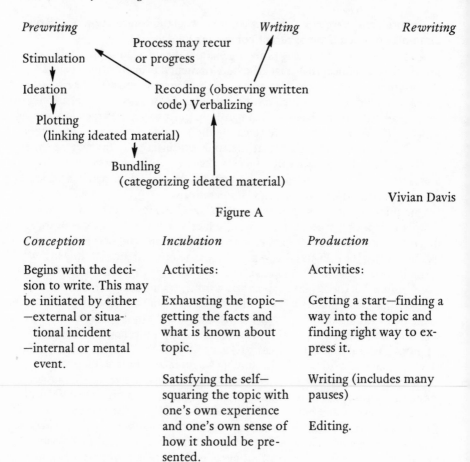

Prewriting   *Writing*   *Rewriting*

                    Process may recur
Stimulation   or progress

Ideation   Recoding (observing written
                        code) Verbalizing
    Plotting
(linking ideated material)

        Bundling
    (categorizing ideated material)
                                                          Vivian Davis
            Figure A

Conception   *Incubation*   *Production*

Begins with the deci-   Activities: Activities:
sion to write. This may
be initiated by either   Exhausting the topic—   Getting a start—finding a
—external or situa-   getting the facts and   way into the topic and
    tional incident   what is known about   finding right way to ex-
—internal or mental   topic.   press it.
    event.
                          Satisfying the self—   Writing (includes many
                          squaring the topic with   pauses)
                          one's own experience
                          and one's own sense of   Editing.
                          how it should be pre-
                          sented.

                                                          James Britton
            Figure B

Starting   *Exploration* *Incubation* *Insight*   *Developing*   *Writing*
Point   *the*   *Rewriting*
              Heuristic Activty   Formula-   *Rhetorical*   *Editing*
A "Cognitive   tion of   *Situation*
Dissonance"   core sentence,
                                           thesis   Envisioning
                                           controlling audience,
                                           viewpoint. discourse
                                                       form.
                                                          Janice Lauer
            Figure C

sight" as a further stage; this transition is seen to be helped by heuristic methods which, like the "topics" of classical rhetoric, aid the mind's exploration of the dissonant elements. This model also suggests that following the "insight" phase, "audience" and "purpose" enter the prewriting phase, just before writing begins.

Whereas the first of these models describes a mental process in loosely empirical terms, the last derives from a blend of psychological theory and traditional rhetorical principles. It needs to be emphasized that in all these models what actually happens as the mind generates written language is not at issue. Despite the authoritative ring of the taxonomy, none of the models makes a claim for psychological reality. These schemes do not attempt to name the mysterious processes of the brain. Instead, they aim at analogical truth; each model represents a metaphor with its own distinct bias of origin. It is not that empirical evidence is lacking about how writers go about their work. It is only that the observable behavior of writers cannot convincingly be reduced to an authoritative theoretical model explaining how language is generated in the mind, and writing in turn derived from this. For example, writing may be related to oral speech, but it is also independent of it; people without speech can learn to write. Even Vygotsky, arguing that the relationship between inner and outer speech may be reflected in the composing of writing, makes it clear that he regards the psychological processes of writing as still largely mysterious. Despite the speculative nature of the composing models, however, educators in recent years have urged the importance of writing in the processes of self-discovery and social maturation.

Attitudes Toward the Student Writer

Noting the persistent afterglow of the Dartmouth Conference, two participants in the event have remarked that since then, "intense interest in self-discovery through language and in self-expression, with writing to realize oneself, has occupied the attention of teachers."[56] In the literature of the composition discipline after 1966, the lore of "Dartmouth" appears frequently. Yet in affirming the power of language to nurture self-discovery and interaction, the Darmouth conferees were, like a presidium, ratifying doctrines about language use already codified in the work of psychologists and the writings of "progressive" educators like John Dewey.

Here again, Piaget's concept of decentering is a major source of interest in the developmental power of language. "One can learn the meaning of perspective," says one interpreter of Piaget, "only by pitting one's thoughts against those of others and noting similarities and differences."[57] "Interaction" is the key: "group activities in the classroom," "discussion sessions, and the like" are the pedagogical methods which reflect the Piagetian faith in cognitive development through communication.[58] Another source of contemporary faith in communicative interaction is John Dewey's insistence that "interaction" is a "chief principle for interpreting an experience in its educational function and force."[59] Dewey argues that any truly educative experience must derive from "both factors in experience—objective and internal conditions" (39). The latter, "personal needs, desires, purposes, and capacities" (42), are too often ignored by teachers, says Dewey, because public education tends to emphasize the control of "external conditions" in the educational process, at the expense of "internal factors which also decide what kind of experience is had" (39). The proclamation of a mid-1970s official of the Conference on College Composition and Communication expresses the same confidence in language's self-developmental force: "good teachers of writing," she asserts, must recognize that "all writers . . . are trying to define their experiences, and, through those experiences, define themselves." Furthermore, she cautions, the writing teacher cannot merely demand writing as other teachers impose essay tests or lab reports, impersonally and objectively: students will "put their selves and their lives into words ... only for teachers who read with sympathy." [60]

The concept of stages in language growth has led to a major change in the way writing teachers view basic or remedial writers. The field of error-analysis has helped writing teachers view writing errors as signs of inexperienced writers' attempts to cope with unfamiliar standard usages. The roots of this view of error lie in Piaget's assertion that as she learns, the child will commit "systematic errors" in the labor of accommodating new cognitive structures to existing ones. In this view errors are seen not as deviations but as signals of the learner's strategies of coping with learning challenges. "Such systematic errors," says Piaget, "are found at all levels of the hierarchy of behavior."[61] This view of error has entered the composition discipline through ESL (the study of English as a Second Language), where error-analysis rather than rote memorization is used to help the language learner. Error-analysis has aided composition research by offering a constructive interpretation of grammar and coherence difficulties, and what they may reveal about the writing process. It has aided composition pedagogy by helping teachers match teaching strategies to the errors students commit, and to address the source of such errors. It has been particularly useful in helping basic writers. In her seminal study of problem writers, Mina Shaughnessy relies on a version of this approach in suggesting methods for dealing with the writing difficulties of unskilled writers (See Chapter III).

Another major influence on attitudes toward inexperienced or unskilled writers is the work of Carl Rogers, whose analysis of the feelings involved in the interaction between teacher and learner is particularly relevant to hesitant or fearful writers. In *Freedom to Learn*, Rogers rejects teaching defined as "imparting knowledge or skill." Instead, he argues, teaching must be defined as the "facilitation of change and learning"; it's the teacher's responsibility to encourage the process of learning, not to pass on "knowledge" that may soon be obsolete.[62] We have seen this distinction implicit in the emphasis upon cognition as process. It appears, for example, in Bruner's distinction between the "expository mode" of teaching, in which the teacher employs "extrinsic" motivation, and the "hypothetical mode," in which the student "plays the principal role" in his learning and is "rewarded by discovery itself."[63] But Rogers' unique contribution to the composition discipline lies in his influential analysis of the affective aspects of the learning process. A "facilitating" relationship, says Rogers, involves "realness" (the facilitator's acknowledgment of his own feelings), "prizing" (the facilitator's non-possessive caring for the learner), and "empathic understanding" (a non-judgmental understanding of the learner's feelings).[64] These elements of the teacher-learner relationship will help produce a learner who is a "fully functioning person," says Rogers, adaptable to change and confident of himself as the agent of his own learning. Such qualities in the learner receive major emphasis, for example, in the NCTE's "Position Statement" on teaching composition: in learning to write the student learns to "live more fully," to "enjoy" and "control" his world, and to work toward "self-expression" and "self-realization" (219).

Classroom strategies have been influenced by Rogerian doctrine. His "methods for building freedom" for learners have been applied to the writing situation. Small-group work, simulation exercises, contract-learning systems, and student self-evaluations all have been urged upon the writing class (see Chapter V for a discussion of these methods). Two settings are particularly designed to nurture the feelings Rogers emphasizes: the writing lab and the small group. The writing lab or workshop has become an important part of many writing programs because it offers the individualized relationship usually seen as necessary to encourage poorer writers. The freedom of the workshop setting, coupled with the personal attention of the workshop instructor (who normally plays the role of "facilitator" in the Rogerian sense), offers the nurturing situation Rogers advocates. Small-group writing activity like that urged by Kenneth Bruffee and Peter Elbow (see Chapter V) is also designed to create supporting relationships among students themselves. The present popularity of the writing lab and the small group is a response by writing teachers not only to increasingly unpredictable writing preparation among students, but also to the humane influence of Rogerian psychology.

The models of mind sketched by the psychologists we have considered in this chapter have deeply influenced the way we think about writing. We have looked briefly at some of the teaching implications of these models; in later chapters we will consider other teaching applications of the writing process. We will also consider the teaching strategies that have emerged from psycholinguistics, a rapidly-growing area of psychological inquiry, and from social linguistics, a field which has helped us understand the social implications of how we teach our students about language. It seems appropriate in the next chapter to look closely at several comprehensive recent models of discourse which attempt to describe, in terms responsive to contemporary psychology and rhetoric, the forms, purposes and audiences that shape today's writing. Many recently proposed classroom strategies are derived from, or are influenced by, the discourse systems we will consider. If we are to choose intelligently among these strategies, we need to understand the strengths and also the confusion and ambiguity found in these systems.

Notes

[1] Gene Lyons, "The Higher Literacy," *Harper's,* September, 1976, p. 36.

[2] Arthur N. Applebee, *Tradition and Reform in the Teaching of English: A History* (Urbana, IL: NCTE, 1974), p. xii.

[3] Applebee, p. 138.

[4] Quoted in Evelyn Wright, "School English and Public Policy," *College English,* 42(December 1980), 329.

[5] Applebee, p. 38.

[6] Applebee, p. 106.

[7] John Passmore, *The Philosophy of Teaching* (Cambridge, MA: Harvard University Press, 1980), p. 40.

[8] D. Gordon Rohman, "Pre-Writing: The Stage of Discovery in the Writing Process," *College Composition and Communication,* 16(1965), 107.

[9] E. D. Hirsch, Jr., *The Philosophy of Composition* (Chicago: The University of Chicago Press, 1977), p. 40.

[10] For a full list see the opening sections of Richard Young, "Invention: A Topographical Survey," *Teaching College Composition: 10 Bibliographical Essays,* ed. Gary Tate (Fort Worth: Texas Christian University Press, 1976), pp. 1-44.

[11] See Wayne Booth, "The Revival of Rhetoric," *PMLA,* 80(May 1965), 8-12.

[12] Richard Ohmann, "In Lieu of a New Rhetoric," *CE,* 26(October 1964) 20.

[13] Dudley Bailey, "A Plea for a Modern Set of Topoi," *CE,* 26(November 1964), 114.

[14] Barry J. Wadsworth, *Piaget's Theory of Cognitive Development* (New York: David McKay, 1971), p. 67.

[15] John Flavell, *The Developmental Psychology of Jean Piaget* (Princeton, NJ: D. Van Nostrand, 1963), p. 151.

[16] Jean Piaget, and B. Inhelder, *The Psychology of the Child,* trans. Helen Weaver (New York: Basic Books, 1969), p. 84.

[17] Jean Piaget *Six Psychological Studies,* trans. Anita Tenzer and David Elkind (New York: Random House, 1967), p. 98.

[18] Piaget, *The Psychology of the Child,* pp. 86-7.

[19] Jean Piaget, "Comments on Vygotsky's Critical Remarks Concerning *The Language and Thought of the Child,* and *Judgment and Reasoning of the Child"* (MIT Press, 1962), pp. 4-5, published as a separate addendum to Vygotsky's *Thought and Language,* cited below.

[20] L. S. Vygotsky, *Thought and Language,* trans. Eugenia Hanfmann and Gertrude Vakar (Cambridge, MA: MIT Press, 1962).

[21] Jerome Bruner, *Toward a Theory of Instruction* (Cambridge, MA: Harvard University Press, 1966), p. 20.

[22] Jerome Bruner, et al. *Studies in Cognitive Growth* (New York: Wiley and Sons, 1966), p. 47.

[23] Alexander Bain, *English Composition and Rhetoric: A Manual.* American edition, revised (New York: D. Appleton, 1866), p. 19.

[24] Quoted by Albert Kitzhaber in "Rhetoric in American Colleges, 1850-1900" (Unpublished dissertation, University of Washington, 1953), p. 199.

[25] Quoted in Kitzhaber, p. 203.

[26] James Britton, "The Functions of Writing," in *Research on Composing,* ed. Charles R. Cooper and Lee Odell (Urbana, IL: NCTE, 1978), p. 15.

[27] James Britton, "Language and the Nature of Learning," in *The Teaching of English,* the Seventy-Sixth Yearbook of the National Society for the Study of Education, ed. James R. Squire (Chicago: NSSE, 1977), p. 33.

[28] James Britton, *The Development of Writing Abilities, 11-18* (London: Macmillan, 1975), p. 10-11.

[29] Britton, *The Development of Writing Abilities,* p. 10.

[30] John C. Mellon, *National Assessment and the Teaching of English* (Urbana, IL: NCTE, 1975).

[31] Janet Emig, *The Composing Processes of Twelfth Graders* (Urbana, IL: NCTE, 1971).

[32] John Dixon, *Growth Through English Set in the Perspectives of the Seventies,* 3rd ed. (London: Oxford University Press, 1975).

[33] Linda Flower, "Writer-Based Prose: A Cognitive Basis for Problems in Writing," *CE,* 41(September 1979), 19-37.

[34] Peter Elbow, *Writing Without Teachers* (New York: Oxford University Press, 1973), p. vii.

[35] "Teaching Composition: A Position Statement," NCTE Commission on Composition, *CE,* 36(October 1974), 219. See Appendix A.

[36] Lee Odell, "Piaget, Problem-Solving, and Freshman Composition," *CCC,* 24(February 1973), 36.

[37] Leon Festinger, *A Theory of Cognitive Dissonance* (Stanford: Stanford University Press, 1957), p. 3.

[38] Janice Lauer, "Heuristics and Composition," *CCC,* 21(December 1970), 396-7.

[39] Odell, p. 37.

[40] Janice Lauer, "Toward a Metatheory of Heuristic Procedures," *CCC,* 30 (October 1979), 268-9.

[41] Ann E. Berthoff, "Response to Janice Lauer, 'Counterstatement'," in *Contemporary Rhetoric,* ed. Ross Winterowd (New York: Harcourt Brace Jovanovich, 1975), pp. 102-3.

[42] Richard Young, "Invention: A Topographical Survey," in *Teaching Composition: Ten Bibliographical Essays,* ed. Gary Tate (Fort Worth: Texas Christian University Press, 1976), p. 23.

[43] Richard Young, Alton Becker, Kenneth Pike, *Rhetoric: Discovery and Change* (New York: Harcourt, Brace and World, 1970), p. 56

[44] Berthoff, p. 103.

[45] James Kinney, "Tagmemic Rhetoric: A Reconsideration," *CCC,* 29(May 1978), 143.

[46] Susan Wells, "Classroom Heuristics and Empiricism," *CE,* 39(December 1977), 475.

[47] Kenneth Burke, *A Grammar of Motives* (New York: Prentice-Hall, 1945), p. *xv.*

[48] Joseph Comprone, "Kenneth Burke and the Teaching of Writing," *CCC,* 29(December 1978), 336.

[49] Kenneth Burke, "Questions and Answers about the Pentad," *CCC,* 29 (December 1978), 336.

[50] D. Gordon Rohman, p. 107.

[51] Michael Paull and Jack Kligerman, "Invention, Composition and the Urban College," *CE,* 33(March 1972), 651.

[52] Published in *CE,* 40(February 1979), 641-61. Young's essay is cited above.

[53] Vivian Davis, "Toward a Model of the Composing Process," *Arizona English Bulletin,* 19(October 1976), 13-16.

[54] Britton, *The Development of Writing Abilities,* pp. 19-32.

[55] Janic Lauer, Lecture, University of Detroit, June, 1979.

[56] James Squire and James Britton, in a forward to Dixon, *Growth Through English,* 3rd ed., p. xvii.

[57] Flavell, p. 369.

[58] Flavell, p. 369.

[59] John Dewey, *Education and Experience* (New York: Macmillan, 1938), p. 38.

[60] Elizabeth McPherson, "Composition," *The Teaching of English,* p. 178.

[61] Piaget, "Comments," p. 4.

[62] Carl Rogers, *Freedom to Learn* (Columbus, OH: Merrill Publishing Company, 1969), p. 104.

[63] Bruner, *On Knowing,* p. 83.

[64] Rogers, pp. 106-12.

Chapter II
SOME RECENT DISCOURSE SYSTEMS
What They Offer Writing Teachers

Although linguistics, psychology, and philosophy have all recently contributed to our understanding of composing, rhetoric has traditionally been central to all formal discourse training. Yet in the twentieth century rhetoric has gravitated to speech departments, in the wake of the split between English departments (which took over literature and composition) and speech departments (which appropriated, by default, "oratory," or "public speaking," and the rhetorical tradition behind it). Consequently, many researchers constructing theories of written communication avoid the term "rhetoric" by labeling the object of their study "written discourse" and calling themselves "discourse theorists." Some, of course, are still willing to label themselves rhetoricians and their work "studies in rhetoric"; Kenneth Burke views his studies of symbolic action as rhetorical in important ways. But "discourse" better describes the target of the general systems we are about to examine.

The discourse theories presented below share two things: a deliberate grounding in psychology, and attention—greater in some than in others—to the relational aspects of writing. The study of writing in terms of its psychological origins and effects is not new; it has its origins in the psychological rhetorics of Campbell, Bain, and others of the earlier associationist school.[1] Interest in the relationships among elements of the writing situation—writer, text, reader, reality-reference—inheres in classical rhetoric, but has received renewed emphasis from a different source, in the "communication triangle" of scientific discourse study.[2] These influences—discussed more fully later in this chapter—have given discourse theory a new and exciting breadth in recent years.

A theory of discourse is a systematic attempt to describe the variables in human communication and the way they interact. The discourse systems examined in this chapter emphasize written discourse and fall into two major categories: those that focus on the *dynamic relations* among writer, text and reader; and those that emphasize the *static characteristics* of texts. Kenneth Burke's analyses of man's symbolic activity, including writing, provide the fullest body of recent studies on the relational aspects of human communication. Though neither James Moffett nor James Britton acknowledges Burke as a direct influence, their models of writer-text-reader interaction reflect a Burkean interest in intention and effect in discourse. The systems proposed by James Kinneavy and Frank D'Angelo tend in a different direction. Their work seeks to establish discourse categories based on the intentions embodied in them and the structures of mind implicit within their forms. The *relational* systems reflect one aspect of traditional rhetoric: the emphasis on the interactions among speakers' strategies, speech, and audience. The *categorizing* systems represent a different aspect of the tradition: the impulse to classify topics, logical strategies, forms and styles. Each kind of theoretical system has its place in our understanding of discourse, and each derives its coherence from the address it makes to vital questions raised in the act of communication.

Relational Systems: Burke, Moffett, Britton

The dynamic interrelations of speaker, speech and hearer have received attention in systems of rhetoric throughout the ages. The discourse systems of Burke, Moffett, and Britton define such interrelations in terms of the psychological functions that energize them. No modern discourse theory better exemplifies the focus on the relational nature of communication than Kenneth Burke's, nor does any other system suggest the unity of discourse elements so firmly. His work looms as a gray eminence over all contemporary studies in discourse, communication theory, and semiotics. Because of its ambitious generalizing and its intended application to all human symbolic activity, Burke's readings of language as symbolic action are as relevant to written discourse as to other communicative modes. Burke's pentad of "motives" for symbolic communication has been widely used (and somewhat misunderstood) by those attempting to devise heuristic systems for composition. (See Chapter I.) Before we examine the major aspects of Burke's discourse theory more closely, however, we need to understand why his sense of the dynamic unity of discourse appeals so widely today.

Classical rhetoricians distinguished invention from arrangement and style. They treated topics, or *topoi*, as methods for developing a discourse which was ordered and styled in accordance with its intent. Arrangement became fixed in a structure of five parts from introduction to peroration, each with its specific function. Students learned style by imitating a lush variety of sentence patterns, figures of speech, tropes, and diction. Style was seen by classical rhetoricians as "ornate form"; thoughts could be "dressed in a variety of outfits," and the speaker's role was to find the dress appropriate to the occasion.[3] This emphasis upon ornateness, the presumption of the separability of form and content, recurs in various periods of the rhetorical tradition. It seems to have been quite strong in Renaissance education, where training in speaking and writing included memorization of sentence patterns and figures of speech, and imitation of examples of ancients' writing. Even in today's writing hand-books, ornateness lurks; exercises in sentence patterns and sentence combining, diction and paragraph patterns imply that, for pedagogical purposes at least, the stylistic elements of discourse may be labored over, quite apart from their semantic importance. But the current pejorative view of rhetoric as decoration ("oh, that's just rhetoric") or persiflage is an implicit rejection of the ornate-ness which has always been one aspect of traditional rhetoric. Indeed, in the popular mind, "rhetoric" seems more closely associated with decoration now than at any time in Western culture since the Socratic attacks upon it.

The current rejection of ornateness, or stylistic dualism, stems from contem-porary understandings of language and the making of meaning. Indeed, some recent philosophers have argued that language is not merely inseparable from meaning, but constitutive of it. Language makes meaning, they have suggested. Ernst Cassirer argues that human nature is defined by its capacity to use signs and language in uniquely meaningful ways. The linguist Edward Sapir insists that the uniqueness of different cultures is a function of differing world-views inherent in their languages, the "eyes" through which a culture construes reality. And Sartre makes the constitutive power of language a central tenet of his existential philosophy, suggesting that to write is to "create" the world objec-tively for the reader, as an enactment of that freedom which Sartre sees as central to human existence.

Twentieth century psychology and philosophy have collaborated in the view that language is a source of meaning. This monistic view of language holds that since thought and verbal structure fuse in producing meaning, it is nonsense to study style and form merely as dressing for content; style and form *are* meaning. The "New Criticism" which dominated mid-twentieth century liter-ary criticism has reinforced the unitary view of discourse. Most composition teachers trained in the mid-twentieth century have been inculcated with New-Critical perceptions. From analyses of literary models, they have been taught to perceive style and form as integral with meaning. They have been made to understand that to paraphrase a verbal structure is to commit heresy. Such training has affected the teaching of writing in an important way. Since the former students of New Criticism became composition teachers out of neces-sity, their well-bred monism induced many of them to avoid exercises in style for its own sake. Interestingly, such distrust of formal exercises—paraphrase, imitation, pattern practice—has recently given way to a renewed valuing of sen-tence exercises (e.g., sentence combining), stimulated by new definitions of sentence-play emerging from transformational grammar (which we will shortly examine). Despite the increased popularity of sentence manipulation in composition pedagogy, however, the prevailing view of discourse—and writ-ing in particular—is distinctly unitary in nature.

Kenneth Burke and Dramatism

The work of Kenneth Burke has furthered the contemporary view of discourse as unitary and dynamic. Burke defines the "verbal act" as "symbolic action," emphasizing that all human utterances are "*stylized* answers" to situations which occasion them.[4] His terminology suggests how thoroughly unitary is his view of all communication, particularly discourse: "the symbolic act is the *dancing of an attitude*" (9), he suggests. For Burke a "symbolic act" is any purposive human action that communicates meaning; in devising a "grammar" of motives for any purposive act, Burke analyzes a wide range of symbolic activity, from political gestures and the making of war to the represented actions of tragedy.[5] To provide a framework for his analyses of symbolic action, Burke propounds a "dramatistic" method of analysis featuring a "pentad" of "five key terms" to analyze "what people are doing and why they are doing it" (*xv*). These terms are Act, Scene, Agent, Agency, and Purpose. But each term lacks meaning as a separate item; only the relationship, or "ratio," between them confers significance upon them, and gives them analytical force. Any symbolic action, linguistic or otherwise, contains an act, a scene wherein it occurs, an agent, an agency by which it is committed and a purpose which generates it. But because any symbolic act is by nature dynamic and relational —the structure of the pentad rests on this assumption—merely applying the individual, static terms in an attempt to define a dynamic process is meaningless. Meaningful analysis of the symbolic act can only come from a description of the relationships among the terms, relationships Burke calls "ratios" or "principles of determination." Thus, to borrow an analogy from linguistics, the pentad comprises what Burke argues is a *grammar of meaning* which, like language grammars, can describe any of the potentially infinite number of symbolic actions.

Although Burke alludes to a wide range of symbolic activity, he is primarily interested in language activity. Rhetoric, for Burke, is the art of achieving identification between speaker and listener, writer and reader, to the point of "consubstantiality," or identity of understanding about an item of experience. Rhetoric is "the use of language as a symbolic means of inducing cooperation in beings that by nature respond to symbols."[6] Cooperation emerges from consubstantiality, which in turn is achieved by a speaker or writer only by a "strategy of 'naming' in such a way . . . as to achieve identification" with the intended audience.[7] Burke understands rhetoric, then, as the art of the purposive use of language; the pentad can be used as an analytic tool for evaluating the rhetorical effectiveness of a statement, or its success in achieving identification between speaker or writer and audience. Applied to discourse, the "key terms of dramatism" can analyze the statement itself (the Act), the speaker or writer (the Agent), the medium in which the statement occurs (the Agency, or the form of the statement), the occasion in which it occurs (the Scene), and the intention which generates it (the Purpose)—but each only in the context of all the other key terms. Within this framework are two crucial assumptions which underlie rhetorical tradition from its classical beginnings, and to which Burke gives renewed emphasis: first, that human beings are capable of rational intentionality in their discourse, and second, that they have the capacities to carry out those intentions by various symbolic means. In Burke's view, any piece of discourse must be treated as an intentional seizing of an occasion to communicate something, by an actor-agent who is free to make the meaning he chooses. For "the agent is an author of his acts, which are descended from him," and the ratio between agent and act always implies a "temporal or sequential relationship."[8] Thus, the most important ratios for Burke are those between Act and Agent, Scene and Purpose, and Agency and Purpose. The dynamic interactions among these elements of discourse shape any transaction that communicates meaning.

Burke's vision of the dynamic interrelations of discourse components has been influential as a general idea, or controlling paradigm, of discourse. Unfortunately, the pentad's practical analytic value for particular pieces of discourse is given slight demonstration by Burke. He is little interested in demonstrating its utility in understanding the entire context of a discourse. After propounding the elements of the pentad in *A Grammar of Motives,* for example, Burke devotes the rest of the volume to analyzing philosophic schools and general patterns of thought in pentadic terms; he does not bring the pentad to bear upon specific pieces of discourse except in passing. His major interest in *A Grammar of Motives* is to locate underlying principles for the pentadic terms within major philosophic schools of Western culture. His primary interest in *A Rhetoric of Motives* is to establish kinds of behavior in thought or action which would achieve "identification," that is, would achieve the persuasive aims Burke identifies as rhetoric's purpose. In *A Rhetoric of Motives* Burke prescribes strategies for persuasive discourse that generally fall within Aristotle's three means of persuasion: logos or reason, ethos or character, and pathos or emotion. Burke's *Rhetoric* is tradition-oriented, that is, and does not utilize the pentadic elements developed in the *Grammar.* Thus, for many readers today the central locus of Burke's influence remains in the potently heuristic early chapters of the *Grammar of Motives* in which the pentadic terms are given their most concentrated presentation.

James Moffett's Universe of Discourse

Burke's emphasis upon the relational complexity of discourse elements has helped establish that bias in twentieth-century discourse theory. Burke, however, has been more noticeably influential in the realms of speech communication theory and practice than in the area of written discourse. The recent work of James Moffett is an example of a relational discourse theory specifically applied to written discourse. In *Teaching the Universe of Discourse,* Moffett argues that the elements of discourse—"speaker, listener, subject"—

exist meaningfully only in relation to one another: all discourse is "somebody talking to somebody about something."[9] Such a definition would have seemed sensible enough to classical rhetoricians; speaker, subject, and audience all receive attention in the canons of classical rhetoric. But Moffett turns to Piagetian psychology, rather than to the classical rhetoricians, to ground his categories of discourse. Assuming that the deepest impulse to communicate is the egocentric need to express something, Moffett places discourse along a spectrum ranging from "egocentric" expression to "decentered" statement. The process of decentering in discourse occurs, says Moffett, in different ways: it can move "from implicit embodied idea to explicitly formulated idea," "from . . . small known audience . . . to a distant unknown and different audience," or from emotion in the "there-then" to emotion in the "here-now" (57). Moffett analyzes discourse holistically, defining a given piece in relation to its larger possibilities. By contrast, classical rhetoric tends to see discourse atomistically, with each part of its content, form, and style generated by its own definitions and rules. And while classical rhetoric assumes a limited set of discourse purposes, Moffett's spectrum includes a wide range of intentions and contexts.

Moffett's scheme posits two basic relations, or (to borrow Burke's term) ratios, within which discourse may be defined:

A. The rhetorical distance between writer and listener (I-you).

and

B. The abstractive distance between writer and subject (I-it).

The "I-you" or rhetorical scale features the writer "abstracting for" an audience at varying removes from the writer. The "I-it" scale features the writer "abstracting from" "raw experience" into varying levels of generality.

Rhetorical distance between speaker and listener increases as the distance between the "I" and the "you" grows. The closest relation occurs in reflection and meditation, while the widest distance comes in addressing an unknown, general audience:

A. Reflection—intrapersonal (writing for oneself).
B. Conversation—interpersonal (speaking with intimate listener).
C. Correspondence—interpersonal (writing for intimate audience).
D. Publication—impersonal (writing for general audience).

Likewise, the abstraction between speaker and subject (the "I-it" relation) occurs as the inventing mind arranges its materials "in *hierarchies* of classes and subclasses" (19) increasingly distant from immediate experience. Thus, discourse ranges from immediate personal experience (in what sense we will examine below) to conceptual abstraction:

A. What is happening—drama—recording.
B. What happened—narrative—reporting.

C. What happens—exposition—generalizing.
D. What may happen—logical argument—theorizing.

This schematization allows Moffett to categorize all major forms of written discourse in a hierarchy which encapsules both psychological and rhetorical variables (see Figure 1). Moffett points out that his one-dimensional figure flattens the diversity of the variables he is representing. Despite this oversimplification, the schema portrays the spectrum of discourse along two axes of abstraction or distance: the "I-you" axis of rhetorical distance, and the "I-it" axis of referential abstraction. The writer-audience, "I-you," relation ranges from the child's speech for himself only, through close audiences on to the most generalized readership, rhetorically distanced from the writer. The writer-reality, "I-it," relation ranges from what Moffett takes to be the most immediate form of experiential rendering in language—drama, "what is happening"—to the generalized theorizing of metaphysics, the most abstract kind of cognitive activity. Such a scheme appears to offer teachers conceptual support in devising a coherent sequence of writing tasks.

Though he warns that his theory must not "be translated directly into syllabi" (54), Moffett's system has some pedagogical benefits. The "I-you" relationship seems to obey a rhetorical progression, from communicating with a familiar, undifferentiated audience to publication for a general, diversified audience of unknown expectations. Such a progression implies that teachers should require personal writing before setting writing tasks for more distanced or diversified audiences. Again, the "I-it" relation relies on Moffett's interpretation of Piaget's concept of decentering, which, argues Moffett, involves progression "from talking about present objects and actions to talking about things past and potential," "from projecting emotion into the there-then to focusing it in the here-now," and demands the ability to see "alternatives . . . and [stand] in others' shoes" (57). This progression implies a sequence of writing tasks moving from familiar, personal-experience topics to abstract, impersonal issues. Recent textbooks at the secondary and college level often reflect just such a progression, from diaries and personal experience essays to research papers. Moffett's system can help teachers find value in assignments outside the usual academic writing; it emphasizes the value in using language at various levels of abstraction and complexity, and for a variety of audiences. Finally, it obliges students to see that no single form of discourse is *sui generis*, a thing unto itself, but is part of a continuum of rhetorical possibilities, many of which they will need to explore in preparation for writing tasks in the future.

Moffett's system is strained by ambiguous and confusing premises, however. Some ambiguity is inevitable, of course, in any rhetorical system posited on a specific model of mind. It's hard to choose from a theory of mind the concepts appropriate to a rhetoric containing practical rules for actual language activity. For example, British rhetoricians of the later eighteenth and nineteenth centuries based their rhetorical analyses upon a mental geography whose

The Spectrum of Discourse

Interior Dialogue (egocentric speech)			P
Vocal Dialogue (socialized speech)	Recording, the drama of what is happening.	PLAYS	O
Correspondence			
Personal Journal			
Autobiography			E
Memoir	Reporting, the narrative of what happened.	FICTION	T
Biography			
Chronicle			
History	Generalizing, the exposition of what happens.	ESSAY	R
Science			
Metaphysics	Theorizing, the argumentation of what will, may happen.		Y

Teaching the Universe of Discourse, p. 47

Figure 1

poles were the "faculties" of "will" and "understanding." To make rhetoric out
of this psychology required rhetoricians to define modes of writing which
appealed separately to the various faculties—exposition relying on the faculty
of understanding, and persuasion requiring the involvement of the will. This
categorizing created narrow, rigid definitions of the "forms of discourse,"
while it also wrenched definitions of mental function. The same kind of dis-
location undermines the integrity of Moffett's categories, which are based on
several different psychological premises held together uneasily by Moffett's
skillful prose.

The ambiguity in Moffett's concept of "abstraction" severely weakens the
"I-it" portion of his sytem. Moffett begins by basing the "I-it" relationship
upon what he calls the mind's process of "abstracting *from raw phenomena*"
(18) in building concepts about experience. What Moffett is outlining here is
a theory of concept formation, which psychologists today view as an essential
part of any description of mental function. In places Moffett appears to articulate a structural theory of concept formation, based on Piaget's ideas of assimi-
lation and accommodation: the features of day-to-day experience, says Moffett,
"are not only selected but *reorganized*, and increasingly as we go up the scale
of the nervous system, *integrated with previously abstracted information*"(22).
But more often, he uses language suggestive of an empirical view of concept
formation: concepts emerge, he says, as the mind constructs "an object out of
the indivisible phenomenal world by singling out some environmental features
and ignoring others" (20). In a teaching textbook written as a companion volume to *Teaching the Universe of Discourse,* Moffett presents what appears to
be a simplistic Lockean associationism: "reason . . . operates on what the senses
represent to it of external reality, most of which has been filed away in the
memory."[10] It would perhaps be unfair to judge Moffett's discourse theory on
the basis of shifting premises, were those premises only incidental to the
theory; but Moffett makes them central to his argument by basing the "I-it"
relationship upon them. "I-it" experience is given blurred and shifting definition in Moffett's work, here as a function of cognitive structures interacting
with sense experience, there as the direct impact of sense stimuli upon "memory" and "reason."

Moffett uses the illustration of a person sitting in a cafeteria: he can record
what is happening, he can talk later about what happened, he can generalize
about what usually happens in such situations, or he can speculate about what
may happen (36 ff). Locating the beginning of abstraction in empirical experience immediately narrows the scope of the concept-forming process, implying
that all concepts begin with sense experience. This naive empiricism conflicts
with the Piagetian concept of cognitive structure which Moffett invokes elsewhere. Piaget argues that cognitive growth is controlled by universal structures
of mind *called up by*, not originating with, external experience. Thus Moffett's
assertion that recording experience as narrative is psychologically prior to
other modes of discourse (because it reflects the immediacy of empirical experience) is puzzling. What if there are modes of experience quite independent

of empirical stimuli, which form the basis of certain kinds of discourse? What if, as some psychologists argue, the mind often generalizes or theorizes independently from any empirical stimulus, immediate or original? What if, in terms of Moffett's system, the "it" of the "I-it" relationship does not always begin as a bit of sense experience recordable in the present tense, but originates as a form of deeper cognition? The mind appears to be far more complex than Moffett's associationist bias would allow; the "I-it" progression of discourse is not necessarily related in the fashion Moffett indicates.

Perhaps, then, the record of "what is happening"—whether couched in "vocal dialogue"or in journal entries—is not always less abstract, with less "I-it" distance, than theorizing about "what may happen." Consider the genre of meditative writing, for example. The *Pensées* of Pascal take the form of a series of fragments connected by certain thematic links, reflecting the drama of Pascal's probing intellect in immediate and continuous conflict with received opinion. Deeply personal in tone and address, they bear the surface marks of the self-oriented writings at the top of Moffett's hierachy. Yet the *Pensées* are profoundly abstract, theoretical, and appear aimed at a general audience of inquiring intellects. Students, too, are capable of writing personal forms containing generalizations and theorizing. Such writing may be considerably more complex than the progressions suggested by Moffett's spectrum. Another example of writing that simultaneously embodies the whole range of Moffett's spectrum is Loren Eiseley's *The Immense Journey*. These essays begin as reports of biological and anthropological lore, then generalize about the physical universe, then theorize about man's place in that universe. Extraordinarily concrete and deeply felt in tone, these essays make a drama out of Eiseley's perceptions even as they argue for a certain attitude toward the world. The experience rendered by Eiseley's presentations is as complex as it is whole; it recognizes few of the gradations outlined in the "Spectrum of Discourse"—or rather, it comprehends nearly all of them in a very unhierarchical way.

Another difficulty in Moffett's argument is his deliberate conflation of "abstraction" and "generalization." He argues that "the ranging of the mind's materials in *hierarchies* of classes and subclasses" (19)—thinking from the general to the specific—is the same activity as extending a "referent in time and space"(19), Moffett's phrase for thinking from abstract to concrete. As an example he cites "pop fly" as both more specific and more concrete than "parabolic trajectory" (20). Yet this illustration does not justify Moffett's over-extension of the term "abstraction." When we speak of something being "concrete," we mean that it exists in a form available to the senses; if it is not available to the senses, we speak of it as "abstract." But something "specific" is not necessarily concrete; it is only more particular within its class. It's true that "pop fly" is more specific and more concrete that "parabolic trajectory," because the former is a kind of parabola we can see, but, for example, the love of a parent for a child is more specific than the general concept of love, yet not necessarily more concrete; it may be enacted concretely in a hug, yet it also exists as a specific love when not enacted concretely. It's important that students understand the difference between the logic of class hierarchy and the envisioning process that renders experience concretely. They are not the same, and to confuse them is to blur the meanings of both processes and the language appropriate to each.

James Britton and Language Roles

By resting his classification of writing on the intentions implicit in it, rather than like Moffett upon the abstractedness of its content, James Britton avoids the kind of ambiguity plaguing Moffett's system. In Chapter I we saw briefly the "function categories" generated by Britton's theory; we must now look closely at the concept of "language roles" used by Britton to help distinguish among these functions.[11] Britton argues that with respect to any experience, we may either be participating in it, or evaluating it out of a desire to understand it better. When the linguistic representation of the world enables the user to *participate* in the world, then language is being used *"in the role of participant"* (80). The user employs language in the world "in order to operate in it," to "seek an outcome" in the actual world (80). However, if the user wishes to represent the world, not in order to participate in it, but in order to evaluate it "without seeking outcomes in the actual world," then he is using language *"in the role of spectator"* (80). When language is used in the role of participant, it is used to have a direct impact upon something; when it is used in the role of spectator, it strives only to represent the world.

Britton's spectator role presumes a detachment from the immediacy of experience, superficially resembling the abstractive distance at the far end of Moffett's "I-it" scale. But, in fact, Moffett's kind of experiential distance is quite different from Britton's. Moffett's "distance" measures a movement away from concrete actuality to an abstract representation of that actuality, a movement that is a continuous, automatic activity of thought. Britton's scale implies an intentional objectifying of experience through language, in order to formulate an attitude toward the experience. There is, however, a clear similarity between Moffett's abstractive scale as manifested in the hierarchy of discourse types (on the left of his "spectrum") and Britton's divisions of informative transactional writing:

Transactional Function—Informative

1. Record. Eye-witness account or running commentary.
2. Report. Account of a series of events or appearance of a place.
3. Generalized narrative or descriptive information. As above, a narration or description; but with patterns of repetition and some generalization.
4. Analogic, low level of generalization. Loosely related generalizations, not connected or made explicit.
5. Analogic. Generalizations related hierarchically or logically by means of coherent classificatory utterances.

6. Analogic-Tautologic (Speculative). Speculations about generalizations.
7. Tautologic. Hypotheses and deductions from them.

(Rear Foldout)

Britton's "functions" range from the specific to the general, with recording and reporting viewed as renderings of specific experience, followed by patterns of generalization and ultimately by hypotheses about generalizations (similar, it would appear, to Moffett's "theorizing"). But Britton avoids suggesting a hierarchy among these functions; instead he argues that each of these functions is a "stance" adopted by the writer to achieve a specific purpose for a specific audience. Generalizations and speculations are products of a deliberate approach to a topic, rather than those qualities found in the topic itself. Britton avoids Moffett's implication that "higher" levels of abstraction are likely to appear in, for example, scientific writing, but not in the younger writer's work. Britton, noting one eleven-year-old's generalization that "people get mad very easy" (97), frequently reminds the reader that abstraction is *not* a hierarchically distributed characteristic of writing, but a pattern of thought distributed among all writing functions.

Three writing functions emerge from his definitions of writing roles: "Transactional" writing comes from the participant role, "poetic" writing from the spectator role, and "expressive" writing from either role. Expressive discourse is "utterance at its most relaxed and intimate, as free as possible from outside demands, whether those of a task or of an audience" (82). Indeed, it's "free to move easily from participant role into spectator role and *vice versa*" (82). Here Britton shifts the premise of his function categories from role definition to audience awareness, an alteration he does not clearly acknowledge in his scheme of functions (Figure 2):

Participant Role--Spectator Role

TRANSACTIONAL   EXPRESSIVE   POETIC

The Development of Writing Abilities (11-18), p. 81

Figure 2

Although expressive writing may be in the role of spectator or participant, its audience is defined as a close group with shared expectations. The other two writing functions are not characterized by any particular audience. Transactional writing, in the role of participant, is "language to get things done: to inform people . . . to advise or persuade or instruct people" (88). Such writing "is an immediate means to an end outside itself" (93) and can be "contextualized" piecemeal by the reader—that is, the reader can isolate portions of transactional writing without necessarily damaging meaning in that or other portions. Poetic writing, in the role of spectator, is language used "to recount or recreate real or imagined experience for no other reason than to enjoy it" (91) or evaluate it. Poetic writing becomes "an immediate end in itself, and not a means: it is a verbal artifact, a construct" (93). Thus, poetic writing, unlike transactional writing, cannot be "contextualized"—i.e., understood in separate bits—because its meanings depend upon its formal unity. Poetic writing is not only, or even primarily, poetry; it can be any form that achieves objectivity and distance from the represented event.

Though he does not link audience directly to writing function except in the expressive mode, Britton does construct a range of writer-audience relationships to which he gives the general name "context of situation" (60). For the writer, says Britton, "context of situation" involves "writing this kind of thing in this sort of society for this sort of person" (61). But context involves more than just the nature of the writer and the reader. It also involves all the relevant assumptions within the culture they share: in order "for language to function effectively there must be 'tacit acceptance' by both speaker and hearer of all the relevant conventions, beliefs and presuppositions" (61). In written discourse, moreover, the writer does not have immediately available clues for construing the audience, as does a speaker. Rather, the writer must "represent to himself a context of situation, and this includes his readers" (61). What Moffett calls the "I-you" relationship is, in Britton's view, the reader's invention, a mind's eye representation of audience invoked continuously by the writer as he composes. The writer "must carry out a procedure of self-editing, of arresting, reorganizing and adjusting his message for his absent audience. He will be unable to do this unless he can *internalize* his audience" (62).

Britton's emphasis upon the writer's need to internalize his audience introduces a powerful new variable into his model of writer-reader relationship. Britton argues that all writers, inexperienced or mature, can "create" various audiences for themselves by inventing those audiences imaginatively, during the composing process. This deliberate "composing" of audience offers a strategy by means of which even inexperienced writers can aim their writing at what Moffett would term the more abstract writer-reader relationships. Unfortunately, Britton doesn't fully extend the idea of the "invented" audience to each category of function or audience, nor does he explore the use of the concept by other discourse theorists. Perhaps in a fuller development of the third dimension of his system—the composing process—Britton will expand this important aspect of the psychology of writing.

The audience categories as formulated by Britton appear in Figure 3 on page 46. Because their writing samples and the audiences for them were limited to school situations, Britton and his researchers were obliged to include the teacher as an audience component. In the range of readers from "self" to "unknown audience," however, a general similarity to Moffett's "I-you"

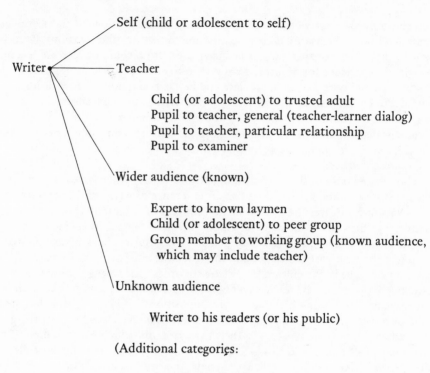

Self (child or adolescent to self)

Writer

Teacher

Child (or adolescent) to trusted adult
Pupil to teacher, general (teacher-learner dialog)
Pupil to teacher, particular relationship
Pupil to examiner

Wider audience (known)

Expert to known laymen
Child (or adolescent) to peer group
Group member to working group (known audience,
    which may include teacher)

Unknown audience

Writer to his readers (or his public)

(Additional categories:

virtual named audience
no discernible audience)

—adapted from Britton, p. 66

Figure 3

scale can be seen arising from their common debt to the concept of cognitive egocentricism. Writing for the self, says Britton, is "a written form of 'speech for oneself'" (66)—a phrase borrowed from Piaget's concept of egocentric speech, which both Britton and Moffett posit as the beginning of the child's language use. Primary audiences for school children are teachers, who can serve as "trusted adults," teachers engaged in a "teacher-learner" dialogue with the child, or teachers acting as "examiners" to whom the child reports (68-70). Within the school situation, argues Britton, children may also begin to write for a "wider audience" that includes peers and known laymen, and for an "unknown audience" which is the common target for poetic writing tasks. This range of possible audiences is presented by Britton in the same way Moffett characterizes his "I-you" scale: as a hierachy of readers requiring an increasingly sophisticated objectivity on the part of the writer.

The developmental implications of Britton's audience categories are brought out by the survey of school writings done by Britton and his colleagues. Transactional writing is the most frequent type of school writing. Expressive and poetic functions appear much less often among school writing, though the poetic function is present until the later secondary years. "The overall pattern," says Britton, "is marked by the substantial increase of writing for the teacher as examiner, together with some move towards writing for a more public audience in the fifth and seventh years" (182). Associations between audience and function appear markedly, for example, in the consistent relation between expressive writing and the "trusted adult," and between transactional writing and the "teacher as examiner." The latter audience increasingly dominates school writing in the later educational years. The teacher's monolithic control over student expectations impels Britton and his colleagues to urge that expressive and poetic functions be more consistently elicited from students, and that, if students are to be prepared for writing tasks beyond the school setting, "work in school ought to equip a writer to choose his own target audience and, eventually, to be able, when the occasion arises, to write as someone with something to say to the world in general" (192). Training in writing skills ought, in Britton's view, to allow children fuller opportunities to confront a full range of functions and audiences.

Categorical Systems: Kinneavy and D'Angelo

There is much of value for writing teachers in the relational systems we have reviewed. These systems help us see that students must be challenged with various writing situations, and must understand the various kinds of readers to whom their intentions may be directed. But another kind of discourse system is equally important: that which attempts to define types of discourse by means of their static textual characteristics. James Kinneavy by means of "aim," and Frank D'Angelo by means of "conceptual pattern," both attempt to construct a typology of discourse. Both systems appear formidably abstract, appropriate for the scholar of discourse theory but hardly (we would think) for the working teacher of writing, who has papers to read and department chairpersons to cope with. Why should teachers need to know something of the theories which appear remote from students' actual writing, and lacking in practical usefulness?

There are at least two important reasons why all writing teachers should investigate categorical discourse systems like those of James Kinneavy and Frank D'Angelo. First, an understanding of discourse types can help teachers in defining students' often incomplete writing intentions. For despite the teacher's attempts to prepare students for writing assignments, what actually occurs in students' minds as they plan and write is often neither predictable nor consistent. A typology of discourse types can help teachers become aware of the kinds of structures implicit in a piece of student writing. For, whatever the assignment, students will write with more than one motive and with various conceptual processes behind their composing. A grasp of discourse categories may enable teachers to assess students' complex and perhaps contradictory intentions. A second reason for studying discourse typology is the help a knowledge of types gives teachers in *setting* students' writing tasks. Planning appropriate and effective writing assignments is the crucial part of any composition course; teachers of writing must begin by asking what kinds of tasks will best prepare students for later writing challenges. An awareness of discourse types, framed within a coherent system that isolates the particular nature of each type, can help teachers plan more cogently. For these reasons we need to look carefully at the systems of Kinneavy and D'Angelo, two recent efforts at anatomizing discourse.

James Kinneavy's Aims of Discourse

A Theory of Discourse, the first volume of a projected two-volume series on "Aims" and "Modes" in writing, is arguably the most ambitious recent effort to build a comprehensive discourse system.[12] Kinneavy's purpose is not, like Moffett's and Britton's, to demonstrate the dynamic variables which generate a given text. Rather, it is to categorize all aspects of "an oral or written situation" (4), using the "communications triangle" that breaks down into "encoder," "decoder," "signal," and "reality." What Kinneavy attempts is an anatomy of human communication, with an emphasis on the *characteristics of its written products,* which he arranges in terms of the four aims based on the communications triangle. For the concept of the triangle Kinneavy uses the work of such early communication theorists as Weaver and Shannon, who devised the triangle to represent human communication, not as the rhetorician might view it, but as scientist might model it. "Basic to all uses of language," says Kinneavy, "are a person who encodes a message, the signal (language) which carries the message, the reality to which the message refers, and the decoder (receiver of the message)" (19). The communications triangle looks this way:

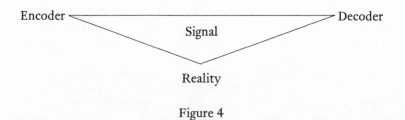

Figure 4

It has the disadvantage of being a two-dimensional model of a multidimensional entity, of course, since "reality" encompasses "encoder," and "decoder" as well as "signal." But Kinneavy's reliance on a four-point model requires him to organize his analysis upon its terms, and to invoke another four-point model later which, as we will see, is not adequately explored.

Kinneavy distinguishes two major categories of study based on the communications triangle. "Linguistics" comprehends the study of the signal (language) itself and the interaction between language and reality, both constituting the means of communication. "Discourse," of most concern to Kinneavy here, is "the study of the situational uses of the potentials of the language" (22), and is "characterized by individuals acting in a special time and place" (22). This definition of discourse seems to differ little from the situational definitions offered by Moffett and Britton; but major differences quickly appear. "Aim" is the crucial determinant of discourse for Kinneavy: "Purpose in discourse is all important. The aim of a discourse determines everything else in the process of discourse" (48). Here Kinneavy flattens out the interactive perspectives of Moffett and Britton and argues that the fundamental determinant—and thus the center of a discourse sytem—is "aim." But by "aim" Kinneavy does not mean the intent of the speaker or writer, or the purpose with respect to the hearer or reader.[13] Instead, he defines "aim in discourse" as that "aim which is embodied in the text itself—given the qualifications of situation and culture" (49). "Aim" and "text" are coterminous entities, the one a part of the other. Text is a "totality of effect" which is "generated by the things talked about, the organization given the materials, the accompanying style" (49). Text includes the notion of "effect" as "a reaction of some kind of acceptance or rejection" generated by the interaction of textual elements. What happens in the writer's mind as he works, or in the reader's mind as he reads, is of interest to psychology, Kinneavy says, but not to discourse analysis.

Kinneavy's system differs from the dynamic, relational systems in its assumption that the text itself contains or bodies forth purpose, and that this purpose, or "aim," determines all other elements of a discourse. Aim determines discourse in four possible ways: by representing the sender, the receiver, the reality being presented, or the form of the text itself:

> In literary discourse the [textual] artifact is present; in informative and scientific discourse the reality is represented; in expressive discourse the reaction of the [sending] self is displayed . . . [and] in persuasion, the acceptance [by the receiver] is implicitly or explicitly requested in the text (60).

The majority of texts, Kinneavy acknowledges, have more than one aim. But the possibility of multiple aims in one discourse does not, in Kinneavy's view, weaken his system, for he argues that, however singular or combined, it is still *aim* that is the basic determiner of discourse. Thus, Kinneavy's purpose is to create an anatomy of discourse (see Figure 5) which abstracts "the different norms" of each aim, "and consider[s] them in isolation" (63). These norms "are distinct from the various aims of discourse"; they are respectively "the distinctive nature, the distinctive logic, the characteristic organizational patterns, and the stylistic features" (63) of texts representing each aim.

A cursory examination of one of the four "aim" categories reveals how

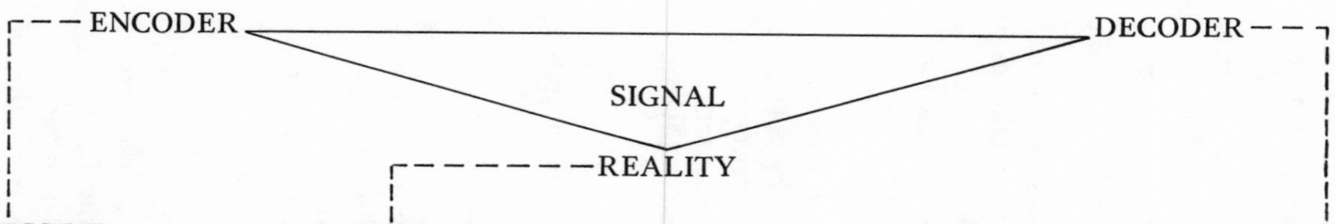

ENCODER — — — DECODER

SIGNAL
— — REALITY

EXPRESSIVE

Examples:

Of Individual
Conversation
Journals
Diaries
Gripe sessions
Prayer

Of Social
Minority protests
Manifestoes
Declarations of inde-
  pendence
Contracts
Constitutions of clubs
Myth
Utopia plans
Religious credos

REFERENTIAL

Examples:

Exploratory
Dialogues
Seminars
A tentative definition of . . .
Proposing a solution to problems
Diagnosis

Scientific
Proving a point by arguing from accepted premises
Proving a point by generalizing from particulars
A combination of both

Informative:
News articles
Reports
Summaries
Nontechnical encyclopedia articles
Textbooks

LITERARY

Examples:

Short Story
Lyric
Short Narrative
Limerick
Ballad, Folk Song
Drama
TV Show
Movie
Joke

PERSUASIVE

Examples:

Advertising
Political speeches
Religious sermons
Legal oratory
Editorials

Figure 5

Kinneavy's anatomizing works. Reference discourse is that whose aim is "to designate or reproduce reality" (39). There are three kinds of reference discourse, each characterized by a different attitude toward reality. *Informative* discourse is one of these; it assumes that reality is understood and that "the facts about it are simply relayed to the decoder" (39), so that "factuality, content comprehensiveness and informative surprise value" (129) are the hallmarks of informative logic. Informative organization and style will also reflect the characteristics of comprehensiveness, factuality, and surprise value. Logic in informative discourse consists in the building of an implicit "universe" or "system" of facts whose completeness is validated by the coherence of the system, in terms of its own internal principles. Factuality must always be verified; if the facts are established inductively, then they must be verified empirically. If the facts rely on assumptions not empirically verifiable, then they must verify themselves according to deductive logical patterns. As practical measures of factuality, the "credibility of the source" and the integrity of the medium in which the discourse occurs also come into play (131-2). The organization of informative discourse, continues Kinneavy, may rely on the principle of "comprehensiveness," or "surprise value," or "importance," or "logical ordering principles of deduction and induction" (161). Kinneavy uses journalistic writing as his main source of examples in discussing informational discourse, so that the "inverted triangle" news presentation and the "5 W's" of comprehensiveness appear as his salient points. As for style, informative discourse involves three issues most often: "readability, avoiding dullness, and pacing" (181). Informative diction tends to be jargon-free, denotative, and concrete; about informative syntax, Kinneavy has very little to say.

Kinneavy's analysis applies the same norms of logic, organization, and style to two other kinds of referential discourse, *scientific* and *exploratory,* and to persuasive, literary, and expressive discourse. He discusses the theoretical antecedents of his concepts, criticizes the weaknesses in previous theory and methodology, and indicates needed study. Indeed, the sections entitled "The Nature of . . . " under each of the four primary discourse types are valuable reviews of contributory theories and concepts. The essay on persuasive discourse, for example, contains a concise review of rhetorical theory from Aristotle to Burke. The chapter on literary discourse summarizes literary theory in terms of the four-part model offered by M. H. Abrams and others, in which literature is seen in terms of the writer, the audience, the universe it represents, and the text itself:[14]

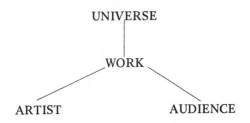

This schematization is similar in its components to the communications triangle Kinneavy cites at the beginning of his study. Unfortunately, he does not pursue the implications of the similarity. His discussion of style in literary discourse reviews several modern theories of style and analyzes several types of literature. Beyond the wide range of Kinneavy's eclecticism, however, another point of interest claims our attention: the striking similarity between Kinneavy's "aims" and Britton's "functions."

In defining "function," Britton says that he combines "intention," "purpose," "effect," into a defining question, "Why are you writing?" (75). Kinneavy attempts a similar reduction of epistemologically difficult terms (writer's intention, effect upon reader) to an apparently simpler definition of aim, as that "which is embodied in the text itself" (49). Thus Britton's "transactional" writing shares some of the features of Kinneavy's "referential" and "persuasive" writing, Britton's "poetic" function is very similar to Kinneavy's "literary" aim, and their joint use of the "expressive" category reveals similar purposes:

KINNEAVY	*BRITTON*
A. Referential discourse	A. Transactional (informative)
1. Informative	1. Recording, reporting, narrating, describing events and places.
a. presents facts	2. Analogic, analogic-tautologic, tautologic writing
b. strives for completeness	a. objective
c. relies on surprise value	b. increasingly speculative and generalized
2. Scientific discourse	3. Analogic (low-level), analogic writing
a. impersonal	a. personal or impersonal
b. demonstrates hypotheses	b. informal generalization
c. strives for certainty	
3. Exploratory discourse	
a. creates hypotheses, does not prove them	
b. often personal	
B. Persuasive discourse	B. Transactional (conative) writing
1. Focuses on decoder	1. Regulative writing
2. Induces to belief or action	a. instructs, demands, imposes authority
3. Deals with probable or plausible	2. Persuasive writing
	a. attempts to influence behavior or action
	b. attempts to change attitudes
C. Literary discourse	C. Poetic writing
1. Emphasis upon internal structure of text	1. Emphasis upon "phonic substance of language itself" (90)
2. Organic unity in structure	2. Pattern of arrangement crucial
3. Logic of developing probability	3. Writer's feelings as subject

D. Expressive discourse
1. Focuses upon encoder, the "speaking self" (398)
2. Self discovers its identity through expressive discourse
3. Self formulates a "Being-for-the-World" (406) in expression
4. Style is linguistic expression of these selves

D. Expressive writing
1. Writing for the self
2. Intimacy between writer, audience
3. Meaning often assumed as shared contexts

The most obvious similarities lie in the poetic and expressive categories of discourse. Britton's "poetic" writing is concerned with the shape and sound of language rather than its impact. The function of poetic writing, Britton continues, is to allow the evaluation of experience, or its re-creation for pleasure. Any poetic text exists as an object of contemplation, not as a means to achieve an effect upon the reader or a release for the writer, though these functions may contribute secondarily to the making of the work. Kinneavy's "literary" discourse has an identical feature: it emphasizes the structure and unity of the text, which must develop an aesthetic purpose. Kinneavy goes beyond Britton in developing the idea of "the primacy of structure" (348) in literary discourse. Structure is dominant in literature, says Kinneavy, because "the logic of literature is the internal probability of its structures, the structures are patently the organization, and the style is achieved by the distinctive patterns of organizations" (348). Britton, on the other hand, emphasizes the autonomous self-sufficiency of poetic writing. Because the spectator role is the basis of poetic language, Britton argues, such language intends nothing outside itself, aiming rather at a self-contained wholeness. Britton urges the importance of poetic writing tasks in the early years of the school curriculum, since such writing rapidly loses ground to transactional writing tasks at higher educational levels. Britton brings audience into his consideration of poetic writing—an element that does not interest Kinneavy in literary discourse—by pointing out a possible association between the fading of poetic writing and the replacement of the "teacher-learner dialogue" with the "pupil-to-examiner" audience type in later school years.

Britton and Kinneavy also use the term "expressive" to denote a certain kind of writing. But Kinneavy's concept of expressive writing has little in common with Britton's. Kinneavy's definition catches the flavor of his influences: "expressive discourse is . . . psychologically prior to all other uses of language" because the "expressive component . . . involves a man with the world and his fellows to give him his unique brand of humanity" (396). The phenomenological tone of this assertion is developed in the analyses of "selfhood" which follow. Tracing the influence of Heidegger and the phenonemologists upon the existential thought of Sartre, Kinneavy employs the categories of Being-for-oneself, Being-for-others, and Being-in-the-world to discriminate kinds of self-identity which can be expressed by controlled methods of style. Kinneavy anayzes the Declaration of Independence to show the interplay among these elements of identity, as conceived in terms of national (rather than personal) selfhood. Kinneavy's example removes the personal element from the idea of expressiveness, and defines it as a purpose inherent in the subject matter rather than in the mind of the writer.

Britton's analysis of expressive writing reflects a very different influence, the Piagetian concept of cognitive egocentricity. Expressive writing is a written-down version of "speaking for oneself," the form of discourse typical of young children who have not learned to use language beyond shared contexts and personal meanings. Britton is interested in the psychological context of expressive utterance, the shared meanings upon which it depends, and, in particular, its primacy in a child's growth. Kinneavy treats the concept of expression from a philosophical point of view, focusing not, like Britton, on practical questions of writer-audience relations, but on what he perceives to be the textual characteristics of the expressive aim, its forms and styles.

Kinneavy's analysis of expressive writing is considerably more abstract than Britton's, and, unlike Britton's, offers little of value for pedagogy. Britton's handling of expressive writing focuses on its developmental nature. By means of student protocols, Britton demonstrates the importance of the expressive function in the efforts of young writers and concludes that such writing should be a major part of schoolchildren's language experience. Kinneavy's philosophical analysis of expressive discourse offers a general perspective on the place of expression in human discourse. Britton's handling of expressive writing offers more immediate teaching benefits by illuminating its functions and audience relationships in terms of language growth processes.

Unfortunately, Kinneavy's work is a victim of its own aspirations. Its most obvious flaw is the inconsistent treatment accorded different kinds of discourse. Persuasive discourse gets a thorough introduction through his review of traditional and modern rhetorical systems, yet the subsequent analysis of Roosevelt's first inaugural address is framed almost exclusively in Aristotelian terms. It would appear that although Kinneavy analyzes the theoretical force of such twentieth-century analyses as Burke's, he is unable to *synthesize* Burke with other rhetorical approaches or suggest how useful Burke might be, along with Aristotle, in a genuinely fresh approach to persuasive discourse. Perhaps the most incomplete portion of *A Theory of Discourse* is its largest section, attempting to classify various kinds of referential discourse. Informative discourse is held by Kinneavy to be one type of referential discourse. From the elaborate framework of categories and norms adduced by Kinneavy in preparation for the chapters on major discourse types, the reader is led to expect a thorough analysis of each type of referential discourse, and of each example. He does not get it. The examples of informative discourse are so divergent in context and content that Kinneavy is unable to clarify the norms of organization and style. And, because his analysis is incomplete, he fails to present a genuine synthesis or new understanding of informative discourse. It's inevitable that any system attempting to build a hierarchy of categories for all writing will overlook some types of writing. But the real disappointment in Kinneavy's study is that, for all the information it amasses, it does not offer the genuinely fresh "theory" of writing its title promises.

Frank D'Angelo's Conceptual Theory of Rhetoric

Frank D'Angelo postulates in his *A Conceptual Theory of Rhetoric* that rhetorical forms derive from mental processes. but weakens his case by relying on the familiar categories of school-text rhetoric to define the major portions of his system.[14] And while his methods of analysis offer useful strategies for helping students perceive structure in prose, the theoretical framework for these strategies is underdeveloped and ultimately unsatisfying.

D'Angelo argues that all discourse forms and styles are embodiments of thought patterns: "conceptual patterns in discourse are symbolic manifestations of underlying thought processes," he argues (33). Such processes manifest themselves at the sentence, paragraph, and discourse level, as expressions of mind: "similar conceptual structures" are " 'topics' when they serve a heuristic function . . .'patterns of arrangement' when they are used to organize discourse" and " 'stylistic' when they inform sentences" (35). Implicit here is the idea of a deep structure analogous to the linguistic universals of transformational grammar: "What are the innate organizing principles, the deeper underlying mental operations, the abstract mental structures that determine discourse?" he asks (26). Acknowledging the influence of gestalt and cognitive psychology, D'Angelo says he seeks to describe "innate structural patterns" underlying all language use (26), patterns presumably generated by an underlying process of mind which D'Angelo does not identify. D'Angelo argues deductively, from the principle of innate conceptual patterns, that "if the same innate structural patterns underlie all languages, then discourse patterns in different languages, regardless of surface differences, must be basically alike in many ways" (26). And, he concludes, if "common structural features of discourse can be identified, then "discourse universals" may be said to exist (26).

D'Angelo begins with an analysis of the "topics" he finds inherent in the process of invention. A traditional view of the topics is that they are "content-laden," he suggests, "pre-fabricated arguments" to be used wherever appropriate in the discourse (38). This view of the topics is represented in the commonplace books, for example, so popular with classical and Renaissance scholars. But, he argues, topics may be abstract rather than content-laden, consisting of a process bearing a "psychological reality" which allows them to "probe any subject whatever" (38). It is this view of the topics that D'Angelo illustrates in the scheme represented in Figure 6, which contains many forms of discourse traditionally termed "modes," "expository methods," and the like. The hierarchical arrangement of the diagram reveals the generative assumptions of the

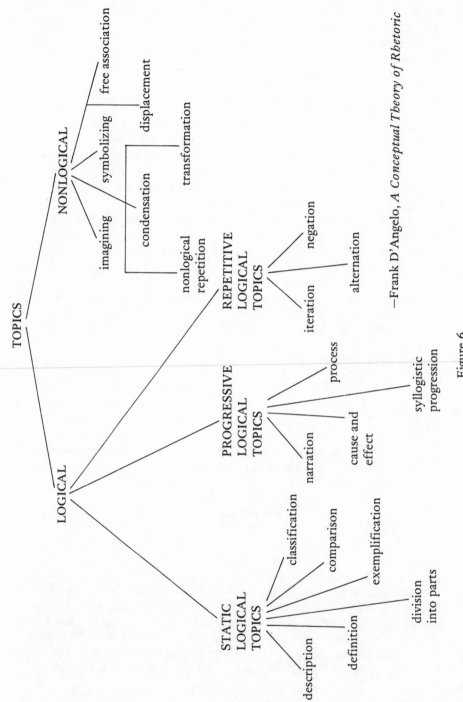

Figure 6

—Frank D'Angelo, *A Conceptual Theory of Rhetoric*

scheme: each kind of category ("static," "progressive," "repetitive," and "non-logical") controls a range of topics which embodies the major characteristic of its class. Few discourses are purely one type; most combine two or more of the conceptual patterns represented by the topics. D'Angelo's claim of generative power for his topics rests on his argument that they signify activities of mind. Unfortunately, many of his categories, especially those in the group labeled "static logical topics," have customarily described rhetorical patterns rather than cognitive processes. As we shall see, the conventionality of his categories undermines his claim that his system offers uniquely generative potential.

Patterns of "arrangement" and "style" in D'Angelo's system are identical with the topics, since according to him, conceptual strategy (the topic) *becomes* the form of the written product (the arrangement). "The concept of arrangement is closely connected to that of invention," says D'Angelo, because "the writer begins with a mental image or plan of the discourse" which "corresponds roughly to the order of the discourse itself," in the same sense in which the Aristotelian efficient cause, "extrinsic to the discourse," corresponds to the formal "intrinsic" cause (56). The abstract topical categories become incarnate as observable patterns of organization; they undergo this reification only because they are identical in conceptual essence. They are "dynamic organizational processes" which manifest themselves as "conventional, static patterns" (57). They appear in any discourse, in various combinations, and they may be clarified by two analytic methods: "syntagmatic analysis" and "paradigmatic analysis." Each of these strategies represents a way of distilling out the organizational essence of a discourse.

Syntagmatic analysis is sentence-level scrutiny of the logical and grammatical progression of a text. It owes a major debt to the Christensen paragraph model (examined later in this chapter). Syntagmatic analysis, says D'Angelo, "follows the linear order of elements from one sentence to another and from one paragraph to another. Thus, if a discourse consists of five paragraphs, containing a total of 250 [sic] sentences, then the structure of the discourse is described in terms of this order" (60). Syntagmatic analysis depends upon two assumptions crucial to the Christensen method: that paragraphs have a lead or topic sentence, and that logical progression from sentence to sentence is primarily a matter of of varying levels of generality. If all paragraphs could be shown to have a topic sentence, D'Angelo's premise would be convincing. But since topic sentences aren't universal in paragraphs, D'Angelo's first premise lacks credence.[16] Variation in generality levels is also difficult to interpret in some types of paragraphs, but frequent enough to give it more credence. D'Angelo demonstrates syntagmatic analysis by using Christensen's method of numbering sentences according to their generality, with 1 signalling the most general level. D'Angelo shows, for example, how the logical structure of a news article may be represented by numbering the total sentence-by-sentence progression (as though the article were one "macro-paragraph"). Though D'Angelo does not clarify how this procedure may be "generative" for a writer, his illustration offers a useful method of analyzing sentence progression in a written text.

Syntagmatic analysis reveals logical movement in the sentence. Paradigmatic analysis focuses on the structural movement of a text beyond the sentence level: it is the "analysis of a text in which certain sentences or other linguistic elements are extracted from the sequential order and placed in a schematic pattern or paradigm" (60). The paradigms emerging from such analysis have no preconceived categories or labels in D'Angelo's system; each text will yield up its own unique pattern. To demonstrate, D'Angelo analyzes a sequence of paragraphs to illustrate a classification progression:

1. The motives which lead people to seek college education divide the students into *three types.*
2. The *first type* are *the few* who love learning.
3. The *second type* are *the many* whose motive is preparation for a professional career.
4. The *third type* are *the majority* whose parents are "putting them through college because it is the expected thing to do" (97-98).

Stylistic paradigms constitute the last portion of D'Angelo's system, for "style in the theory of conceptual rhetoric is inseparable from form" (104). To illustrate at length the "relationship that exists between style and structure" (109), D'Angelo analyzes a five-paragraph sequence from Thomas Wolfe, emphasizing syntactical repetition, parallelism, and alternation of structures. Wolfe's syntax, says D'Angelo, achieves a rhythm of "alternation and progression" (120) based primarily on the parallel repetitions of noun, prepositional and participial phrases, which amplify the polarities of life and death, permanence and change. After analyzing style within the sentence, D'Angelo focuses on "intersentence relationships." Stylistic features at this level parallel intrasentence structures. Repetitions of parallel structures link most of the passage's sentences and paragraphs together in a progression of assertions about life and death, permanence and change. "Progressions in sentence and paragraph length" are a "constant feature" of the passage, with the first paragraph the shortest and the last paragraph the longest (129).

After lengthy consideration of the grammatical and semantic features of individual sentences, D'Angelo summarizes syntagmatic and paradigmatic schemas of the passage. Figure 7 depicts the various levels of analysis D'Angelo applies to the last three (and longest) paragraphs of the passage. D'Angelo argues that "patterns of alternation and repetition" create the basic rhetoric of the passage": "the pattern of negative-positive alternation" (140). Syntagmatic analysis emphasizes the semantic repetitiousness of the passages, all the sentences maintaining the same level of generality. Paradigmatic analysis emphasizes the duality in the passage, which emerges as a tautology: "some things will never change," "these things will always be the same." D'Angelo repeats his claim that the patterns discovered in the text are "formal principles of repetition and alternation" which are "deeply rooted in the nature of man and in the world around him. They are universal patterns of experience exemplified in particular works" (145).

The glitter of sunlight on roughened water,
the glory of the stars, the innocence of morning,
the smell of the sea in harbors, the feathery blur
and smoky buddings of young boughs, and something
there that comes and goes and never can be captured,
the thorn of spring, the sharp and tongueless cry—
these things will always be the same.

All things belonging to the earth will never change—
the leaf, the blade, the flower, the wind that cries
and sleeps and wakes again, the trees whose stiff arms
clash and tremble in the dark, and the dust of lovers
long since buried in the earth—all things proceeding
from the earth to seasons, all things that lapse and
change and come again upon the earth— these things will
always be the same, for they come up from the earth that
never changes, they go back into the earth that lasts
forever. Only the earth endures, but it endures forever.

The tarantula, the adder, and the asp will also
never change. Pain and death will always be the same.
But under the pavements trembling like a pulse, under
the buildings trembling like a cry, under the waste
of time, under the hoof of the beast above the broken
bones of cities, there will be something growing
like a flower, something bursting from the earth
again, forever deathless, faithful, coming into
life again like April.

—D'Angelo, pp. 109-10

Figure 7

and repetition:

2 The glitter of sunlight on roughened water, (NP)
2 the glory of the stars, (NP)
2 the innocence of morning, (NP)
2 the smell of the sea in harbors, (NP)
2 the feathery blur and smoky buddings of young
  boughs, and
2 something there that comes and goes and never can
  be captured, (NP)
3 the thorn of spring, (NP)
3 the sharp and tongueless cry— (NP)
1 these things/will always be/the same.

    —D'Angelo, pp. 109-10

1 All things belonging to the earth/will never change.
2 the leaf, (NP)
2 the blade, (NP)
2 the flower, (NP)
2 the wind that cries and sleeps and wakes again, (NP)
2 the trees whose stiff arms clash and tremble in the
  dark, (NP) and
2 the dust of lovers long since buried in the earth—(NP)
2 all things proceeding from the earth to seasons, (NP)
2 all things that lapse and change and come again
  upon earth— (NP)
1 these things/will always be the same,
2 for they come from the earth that never changes
2 they go back into the earth that lasts forever. (SC)

    —D'Angelo, pp. 114-15

D'Angelo's syntagmatic analysis.

1 The glitter of sunlight on roughened water, the glory of the stars, the innocence of morning, the smell of the sea in harbors, the feathery blur and smoky buddings of young boughs, and something there that comes and goes and never can be captured, the thorn of spring, the sharp and tongueless cry—(NP) these things will always be the same.

1 All things belonging to the earth will never change—the leaf, the blade, the flower, the wind that cries and sleeps and wakes again, the trees whose stiff arms clash and tremble in the dark, and the dust of lovers long since buried in the earth—all things proceeding from the earth to seasons, all things that lapse and change and come again upon the earth—these things will always be the same, for they come up from the earth that never changes, they go back into the earth that lasts forever.

1 Only the earth endures, but it endures forever.

D'Angelo's paradigmatic analysis:

these things will never change

these things   will always be the same

All things belonging   will never change
to the earth

all things
proceeding from the
earth to seasons

all things
that lapse and change
and come again upon
the earth
these things   will always be the same
Only the earth   endures
it   endures forever

D'Angelo's syntagmatic analysis.

1 The tarantula, the adder, and the asp will
  also never change.
1 Pain and death will always be the same.
1 But under the pavements trembling like a
  pulse, under the buildings trembling like
  a cry, under the waste of time, under the
  hoof of the beast above the broken bones
  of cities, there will be something growing
  like a flower, something bursting from the
  earth again, forever deathless, faithful,
  coming into life again like April.

                        —D'Angelo, pp. 137-8

D'Angelo's paradigmatic analysis:

The tarantula,   will also never change
the adder, and
the asp

Pain and death   will always be the same

something
growing like
a flower

something
bursting from
the earth again.

forever deathless   coming into
                        life again
                        like April

                        —D'Angelo, pp. 138-9

Figure 7 (cont.)

D'Angelo's categories of analysis—syntagmatic and paradigmatic—offer a useful framework for analyzing the logical and rhetorical structures of prose. They deserve to be more widely known than they are, as tools both for research into the textual characteristics of rhetoric and logic, and for illustrating these characteristics in the classroom. One or two intensive classroom exercises using his analytic strategies could help students see the connectedness that marks all good writing. D'Angelo's analyses offer useful ways of studying the written product.

D'Angelo's categories do *not* add up to a convincing "conceptual theory" with generative power. Repeatedly, D'Angelo affirms the universality of his conceptual patterns, yet he is offhand and cryptic in supporting his claims. Of the conceptual topics, for example, he remarks that they lend themselves "to easy memorization" in order that students may "internalize these topics (and the questions which they suggest) so that they can be used for subsequent invention" (47). But he gives no illustration of how this may work for a specific subject matter (as the tagmemic theorists illustrate their proposal, for example, in Chapter I of this book). Again, when D'Angelo insists that paradigmatic analysis is designed "not only to reveal the underlying principles that inform discourse, but also to make them generative (in the sense of actually producing discourse)" (86), he does not clarify how paradigms might actually serve a heuristic purpose for student writers. Indeed, D'Angelo ignores the fact that his "conceptual paradigms" *have* no conceptual life apart from a particular discourse, since they are not explicit patterns but only paraphrases of discourse. His paradigmatic analysis is a method of extracting concise summarized meaning by isolating internal patterns; it is not a system of delineated paradigms (like the tagmemic system or Burke's pentad). Thus, a student must first master the ability to penetrate prose structure on his own, recognizing the internal patterns there, before he can convert them into the paradigmatic scheme used by D'Angelo. This is not a generative pedagogy; it's a method for helping students organize their own perceptions of prose structure.

Moreover, the conceptual categories themselves are not adequately defined or developed. In separating the progressive logical topics from the static logical topics, for example, D'Angelo asserts that "narration (What happened? When did it happen?) is related to process (How did it happen? How does it work?), to cause and effect (Why did it happen? What caused or produced it? What are the results or consequences?) and to syllogistic progression (If certain things happen, then what must follow?)" (45). Yet he does not develop the ways in which these relationships might actually exist or what forms of logic may be unique to "variation," "process," or "cause and effect." In asserting, for example, that "narration is related to enumeration (a narrative is a recounting in time), to exemplification (examples can be *exempla*), and to process (a narration, like a process, is a succession of actions)" (45), D'Angelo posits similarities between processes of mind that perceive static characteristics, and those that perceive the dynamic elements of reality. But he does not make clear what understandings he rests this linkage upon, nor why, having separated dynamic and static topics, it's logically coherent to claim that the dynamic and the static are "related" in some other mode.

Perhaps the fundamental problem is methodological: D'Angelo's system is presented deductively, as a series of classes and subclasses derived from head-classes of conceptual process. But in describing the classes of his system, D'Angelo often uses the language of probability suited to an inductive system, rather than the language of universality that a deductive system would require. "Iteration," he says, "*may be* the repetition of the same idea for emphasis or it *may be* a restatement of the same idea" (46); "principles of repetition," he continues, "are *more often* related to form than to invention" (46) [italics mine]. Having argued initially that conceptual patterns exist, D'Angelo offers his categories without sufficient development for the universality he appears to invest them with. The "conceptual rhetoric" offers a useful method for classroom analysis of texts; as a theory of mental process it demands more reasoned support than D'Angelo's slim volume permits.

Micro-Rhetorics: The Sentence

The systems discussed so far are primarily concerned with the categories and processes of whole discourse. Some micro-rhetorics, however, focus on paragraphs and sentences. Macro-discourse (or whole-discourse) theory has remained the province of rhetoricians, but the linguists have moved boldly into micro-discourse analysis; increasingly, analysis at the sentence and paragraph level has blended traditional rhetoric with linguistics.

Francis Christensen's Generative Rhetoric of the Sentence

In the mid-1960s Francis Christensen proposed two "generative rhetorics"—one on sentences and another on paragraphs—which have influenced the development of current micro-rhetorics.[17] Confessing his weariness with the philological basis of sentence models in many texts (consisting mostly of loose-balanced-periodic designations), Christensen argues that this traditional division of sentence patterns is no longer relevant in English prose. Instead, he suggests, "the typical sentence of modern English, the kind we can best spend our efforts trying to teach, is what we may call the *cumulative sentence*" (2). Invoking a rather simplistic version of transformational grammar, Christensen posits that the essence of sentence formation is "a process of *addition*" (2) which adds to a "main clause" modifiers that, depending upon their position with respect to the main clause, may move forward or backward in direction of modification. His own sentence best illustrates this paradigm:

> The main clause, which may or may not have a sentence modifier before it, advances the discussion; but the additions move backward, as in this clause, to modify the statement of the main clause or more often to explicate or exemplify it, so that the sentence has a flowing and ebbing movement,

advancing to a new position and then pausing to consolidate it, leaping and lingering as the popular ballad does (2).

He appears to be arguing that the major propositions in a sentence are always expressed in a "main clause," and are extended and particularized by additional clauses and phrases placed before or after the main clause. This proposition is intriguing but weakened by the ambiguity in the term "addition." It's not clear whether Christensen means "main clause" in the sense of "kernel sentence" (NP + VP), the basic propositional form of a sentence in versions of transformational grammar. If "main clause" does mean "kernel sentence," Christensen does not clarify the relationship between transformational rules and his principles of addition and direction of movement. But if "main clause" is simply a term for that surface structure happening to contain a substantive and a finite verb, such an outmoded parts-of-speech definition of a sentence weakens Christensen's system by its failure to address recent linguistic models of syntax.

Despite its ambiguous linguistic definition, Christensen's system offers a remarkably practical model of sentence-building. In its three major principles— addition, direction of modification, and level of generality— the Christensen paradigm illuminates the potential flexibility and complexity of the English sentence in a way that permits inexperienced writers to analyze sentences and to generate their own within the formula. It allows students to recognize the major propositions of a sentence, as contained in a definite syntactic unit—the independent clause. It encourages their recognition of optional structures for modifying and particularizing these propositions. And it requires writers to be aware of general-and-specific differentials among their sentences. The major objection to Christensen's model, which he anticipates, is that such a model best fits descriptive and narrative aims in writing. The examples he uses reflect this bias:

1 The flame sidled up the match,
  2 driving a film of moisture and a thin strip of darker grey before it.
    —Faulkner

1 He could sail for hours,
  2 searching the blanched grasses below him with his telescopic eyes,
  2 gaining height against the wind,
  2 descending in mile-long, gently declining swoops when he curved and
    rode back,
  2 never beating a wing.
    —Walter van Tilburg Clark

These sentences, and most of the others he uses as illustrations, exhibit a single independent clause followed or preceded by modifying structures—often participials—which add concreteness to an essentially visual event. The independent clauses are numbered 1, and the modifying phrases (participials, absolutes, prepositionals) are numbered in descending numerical order depending on whether they modify the main clause or one of the subordinate elements of the sentence. Christensen does not deny that the cumulative pattern is most appropriate to narrative-descriptive purpose. Indeed, he defends the pedagogical value of such writing as the best teaching vehicle for student writers who must ultimately write "utilitarian prose": "We can teach diction and sentence structure far more effectively through a few controlled exercises in description and narration than we can by starting right off with exposition" (6). One reason Christensen's system has seemed so workable in teaching sentence-building is that it anticipated the methodology of sentence combining.

Sentence Combining

The most prominent development in sentence rhetoric is sentence combining, a method of manipulating syntactic elements that has become widely popular in the last decade. Sentence combining had its beginnings in the early years of transformational grammar; it arose from a conception of the sentence which appeared directly appropriate to the classroom application of the new linguistics. The key is the idea of the "kernel sentence" and its transformations, the core of early transformational theory. According to this theory, all sentences begin as "simple, declarative, affirmative, indicative sentences" that are "kernels" comprising the "deep structure" of a sentence.[18] By means of various transformations creating negatives, questions, passives, and relatives, and by means of morphemic changes denoting tense, these kernels emerge as complex "surface structures" whose efficiency is measured by the information packed within the embedded structures. This description of syntactic complexity attracted teachers looking for ways to improve on the conventional, static categories of traditional grammar. If it could be claimed that the most "mature" sentences were those containing the largest number of transformations, then a pedagogy could be devised based on exercises intended to improve the writer's "transformational" ability, as measured on a quantified basis.

Such a promise proved seductive to researchers interested in composition pedagogy. The concept of the kernel sentence offered an attractive foundation for a sequence of sentence-building tasks characterized by repetition and variation. However, as transformational theory evolved, the idea of the kernel sentence dwindled in importance as new versions of deep structure were devised. New "base rules" of phrase structure and lexical insertion were posited, and heretofore optional transformations were made part of deep structure. The widened concept of deep structure which emerged has been accompanied by a more complex version of transformations generating surface structures. "Singulary transformations" (involving only one clause) account for questions, negatives, passives, and imperatives. "Generalized transformations" (involving more than one clause or "sentence string") involve embedding: adjective, appositive, possessive, relative, and absolute structures result. These generalized transformations have become the basis of current sentence combining techniques. Singulary transformations play little part in most sentence combining texts. The concept of embedding, crucial to generalized transformations, has become the central element in "syntactic maturity," a measure of sentence skill based on the observable increase in sentence length and number of embedded structures in mature writing. A new pedagogy of style has emerged, featuring the conversion of choppy, unmodified base clauses into complex, embedded structures, by means of exercises in generalized transformations.

Crucial to the development of a transformational-based pedagogy of style is Kellogg Hunt's proposal of what he terms the "T-unit" (or terminable unit) as the best gauge of progressive age-level differences in writing.[19] A T-unit he defines as an independent clause plus all its subordinate structure, phrasal or clausal; he argues that syntactic maturity is a condition best indicated by T-unit differentials. Influenced by Hunt's work and using his T-unit as the primary measure, John Mellon proposed that "growth of syntactic fluency can result only from increased use of sentence-embedding transformations."[20] Thus, "embedding transforms, together with measures of depth of embedding, cluster size, and unique nominal patterns, constitute the appropriate criteria for describing . . . syntactic fluency" (20) and comprise the basis for a pedagogy of sentence-making. His program of sentence combining, and those of other researchers extending his early proposals, have targeted embedding transformations as the core of transformational pedagogy.

One current text features a series of combining exercises that teaches generalized transformations first by introducing the syntactic forms they take (relative clauses, participles, appositives, absolutes, prepositional phrases), then by introducing combining strategies ("rearrangement," "repetition," "emphasis").[21] The text's authors attempt to minimize the a-rhetorical nature of sentence combining by developing series of kernel strings which, when combined into individual sentences, may then be structured into a unified paragraph or multi-paragraph discourse. The sentence-building skills targeted by the exercises emerge primarily as structural skills, representing the writer's ability to build grammatical, varied sentences. The "strategies" emphasized in the later portion of the text focus on rhetorical rather than grammatical skills. Students are urged to learn strategies of repetition, emphasis, and coherence that contribute to the rhetorical power of writing; long, often multi-paragraph passages of kernel strings and of pre-combined sentences are featured, the former requiring lengthy combining activity at various discourse levels, the latter requiring analysis and recombination for additional rhetorical effectiveness.

Another recent sentence-combining text embodies a different approach: it de-emphasizes syntactic categories, taking students instead through programmed exercises in embedding modifiers and in adding coordinating and subordinating structures to kernel sentences.[22] This text assumes that requiring students to learn units of syntax is counterproductive and unnecessary at the outset of sentence-combining work. Rather, students are asked to combine sentences in response to general coordinating and subordinating signals, so that they may gain confidence in their basic sentence competence. Only in the second portion of the text are syntactical units named as targets for combining activity; in the later portion also, longer kernel strings and multi-paragraph exercises are introduced, on the principle that students cannot build longer units of discourse until they develop skills and confidence at the single-sentence and single-paragraph level.

Sentence combining flourishes in composition pedagogy today, despite the changes in transformational theory which have de-emphasized the concept of the kernel sentence. One reason for its flourishing is its demonstrated success in helping students write more complex sentences. Seldom has a specific kind of writing drill been so intensively measured by quantitative methods, most of which have indicated that it does produce measurable gains in sentence complexity at all age levels from elementary through college. One group of researchers reports that students doing sentence combining in a one-semester course made greater gains than students not doing it, both in measures of syntactic maturity and in overall quality as evaluated holistically.[23] Other research has tended to show that gains produced by sentence combining are real enough, but limited in terms of level of improvement and persistence of gain after combining activity ceases.[24] Perhaps the strongest contribution of sentence combining to writing pedagogy is its substitution of a creative, sentence-*building* activity for the sentence-*repairing* drills traditional to writing texts. Correcting fragments, dangling modifiers, and agreement problems through drills appears useful to error-prone students. But making sentences from given parts is helpful to all students, in allowing them to experience the flexibility and range of sentence structure.

Teachers using sentence combining should remember that it's not a panacea and should not be emphasized over the crucial activies of mind that *create* writing. Making sentences from given parts does *not* require inventive thinking, does *not* help students learn focus and organization, does *not* help them control voice and tone, and does *not* sharpen editing for mechanics and usage. Sentence combining is like making model airplanes out of labeled parts; genuine inventiveness has no part in it. Though any sentence-combining problem has (unlike a problem in math or chemistry) more than one "right" solution, the limits of the problem control solutions students may "discover." A problem may, for example, illustrate how relative clauses may be shortened to modifier status. But here, as in the most complex combinations, the pathways are confined to the syntactical direction desired by the problem-setter. Such limitations are useful only for inexperienced writers and only for a short time. As we have already seen, writing is an "open" activity, infinite in the processes of mind it requires. Any artificial reduction of this continuous openness diminishes the need for students to think and write inventively—a diminishing no writing teacher should tolerate.

Micro-Rhetorics: The Paragraph

Francis Christensen's Generative Rhetoric of the Paragraph

Francis Christensen expresses a distaste for textbook models of the paragraph that parallels his distaste for text models of the sentence. Citing the bewildering variety of paragraph principles found in writing texts, Christensen proposes a model based on the same "generative" principles contained in his sentence rhetoric: addition, direction of movement, level of generality, and texture.[25] The first sentence is "nearly always" the topic sentence, he argues; when it is, it begins the logical movement of the paragraph, as "the sentence whose assertion is supported or whose meaning is explicated or whose parts are detailed by the sentences added to it" (22). Though he doesn't say so directly, he appears to define the topic sentence as the most general sentence in the paragraph. Two types of sequence are related to the topic sentence, he says: coordinate and subordinate. In a coordinate sequence the topic sentence is developed by other sentences using repetition and parallel structures. In a subordinate sequence the topic sentence is developed by other sentences at various levels of generality, using a variety of structures.

Seldom however, do coordinate or subordinate sequences occur in pure form in paragraphs; the mixed form, says Christensen, is the most common, with a blend of coordinate and subordinate sentences. As in his sentence rhetoric, Christensen here illustrates the working of his paradigms by breaking each paragraph into its constituent sentences, numbered and placed by means of their relation both to the topic sentence and to the immediately preceding sentence. Christensen offers the following examples of coordinate and subordinate sequences:

Coordinate Sequence

1   He [the native speaker] may, of course, speak a form of English that marks him as coming from a rural or an unread group.

2   But if he doesn't mind being so marked, there's no reason why he should change.

3   Samuel Johnson kept a Staffordshire burr in his speech all his life.

3   In Burns's mouth the despised lowland Scots dialect served just as well as the "correct" English spoken by ten million of his southern contemporaries.

3   Lincoln's vocabulary and his way of pronouncing certain words were sneered at by many better educated people at the time, but he seemed to be able to use the English language as effectively as his critics.

(Bergen Evans, *Comfortable Words,* in Christensen, 24)

Subordinate Sequence

1   The process of learning is essential to our lives.
2   All higher animals seek it deliberately.
3   They are inquisitive and they experiment.
4   An experiment is a sort of harmless trial run of some action which we shall have to make in the real world; and this, whether it is made in the laboratory by scientists or by fox-cubs outside their earth.
5   The scientist experiments and the cub plays; both are learning to correct their errors of judgment in a setting in which errors are not fatal.
6   Perhaps this is what gives them both their air of happiness and freedom in these activities.
(J. Bronowski, *The Common Sense of Science*, in Christensen, 23)

The mixed sequence is by far the commonest paragraph arrangement, says Christensen, citing a wide range of examples with varying coordinate and subordinate patterns indicated by progressive and regressive numbering. The analytical power of the mixed-sequence model may be measured by applying it to an expository paragraph at random: for example, to the first paragraph underneath the heading above, "Micro-Rhetorics: The Paragraph":

Mixed Sequence

1   Francis Christensen expresses a distaste for textbook models of the paragraph that parallels his distaste for text models of the sentence.
2   Citing the bewildering variety of paragraph principles found in writing texts, Christensen proposes a model based on the same "generative" principles contained in his sentence rhetoric: addition, direction of movement, level of generality, and texture.
3   The first sentence is "nearly always" the topic sentence, he argues; when it is, it begins the logical movement of the paragraph, as "the sentence whose assertion is supported or whose meaning is explicated or whose parts are detailed by the sentences added to it."
4   Though he doesn't say so directly, he appears to define the topic sentence as the most general sentence in the paragraph.
3   Two types of sequence are related to the topic sentence, he says: coordinate and subordinate.
4   In a coordinate sequence the topic sentence is developed by other sentences using repetition and parallel structures.
4   In a subordinate sequence the topic sentence is developed by other sentences at various levels of generality, using a variety of structures.

The first sentence is certainly the leading sentence here, the most general sentence of the paragraph and the indicator of its drift. But it's not really the topic sentence; the second sentence actually announces the topic of the paragraph (the Christensen paragraph model) and is therefore more specific in its content than the first sentence. The third sentence is more specific yet (thus is numbered at the "3" level) because it begins a description of the principles named in sentence two. Sentence four is even more specific than sentence three because it defines one of its terms ("topic sentence") more thoroughly. Sentence five returns to level 3 generality because it further defines the principles named in sentence two. It is less general than the fourth sentence, but more general than the last two sentences, which return to the "4" level because each further defines one of the terms in sentence five.

It appears that the structure of this paragraph fits generally into the pattern identified in Christensen's paradigm. However, the first sentence is not the topic sentence as Christensen defines it; indeed, Christensen's system does not appear to offer a way of describing what the lead sentence actually does in this paragraph. It introduces (though does not set out) the paragraph topic by reminding the reader of what Christensen has already done with sentence rhetoric. The problem lies in Christensen's ambiguous handling of the concept of the topic sentence itself. In the introduction to his system he asserts that the "top sentence" in the paragraph—i.e. the most general sentence—is "nearly always the first sentence of the sequence" (22), a generalization that would appear to allow very few exceptions. Yet later he cites several examples of paragraphs with no topic sentence, or with sentences as general as the topic sentence, but unrelated to what appears to be the paragraph's main focus. Though Christensen suggests that many such "false" topic sentences probably tie into the discourse at a level beyond the paragraph, his system functions best as a descriptor of structure at the single-paragraph level (see note 16 for this chapter).

A. L. Becker's Tagmemic Paragraph Analysis

Another influential set of paragraph models has been proposed by A. L. Becker, one of the proponents of the tagmemic grammar that generated the nine-point heuristic discussed in Chapter I.[26]

To adduce the tagmemic model, Becker surveyed many student paragraphs, rather than those of professional writers as Christensen did. As a way of "partitioning discourse," says Becker, tagmemic analysis generates "grammatical markers of paragraph slots" that are "nearly identical for all types of paragraphs" (34). Becker agrees with Christensen that levels of generality are crucial in paragraph structure. But various "lexical" (word-related) elements are needed, he continues, to account for the ways in which levels of generality are made "explicit" in paragraphs (34). Thus, the tagmemic model of expository paragraph structure offers two kinds of "slot arrangements" which represent varying levels of generality, and two major categories of lexical (word and phrase) indicators of these levels of generality. One expository model relies on the TRI pattern: "in the T [topic] slot the topic is stated, in the R [restriction] slot the topic is narrowed down or defined, and in the I [illustration] slot the topic, as restricted in R, is illustrated or described at lower level [sic] of generality" (34). These slots can be filled by various "rhetorical types of sentences." The T slot "can be filled by a simple proposition, or a proposition implying a contrast, comparison, partition, etc." (35), while the I slot can contain examples, analogies, or comparisons. The slot order may be reversed, so that an IRT pattern controls the paragraph in a specific-to-general sequence. Lexical markers of paragraph structure fall into two categories, what Becker calls "equivalence classes," and transitional markers. Equivalence markers are parallel words and phrases, linking pronoun references, synonymous words and phrases, and other lexical devices for echoing and repeating key terms. Transitional words are conjunctions, conjunctive adverbs, and phrases that imply logical movement (*for example, in other words*). Other elements of paragraph structure—indentation, verb sequences, and phonological (oral) markers—are mentioned by Becker, but given little emphasis.

Thus, the structure of a given paragraph may be delineated primarily in terms of grammatical slots and lexical markers, according to the tagmemic system. The usefulness of this model can be briefly illustrated by applying it to the same paragraph used to test the Christensen model, the first paragraph under the heading "Paragraph Rhetoric" above:

(T) Francis Christensen expresses a distaste for textbook models of the paragraph that parallels his distaste for text models of the sentence. (R$_1$) Citing the bewildering variety of paragraph principles found in writing texts, Christensen proposes a model based on the same "generative" principles contained in his sentence rhetoric: addition, direction of movement, level of generality, and texture. (I) The first sentence is "nearly always" the topic sentence, he argues; when it is, it begins the logical movement of the paragraph, as "the sentence whose assertion is supported or whose meaning is explicated or whose parts are detailed by the sentences added to it." (I) Though he doesn't say so directly, he appears to define the topic sentence as the most general sentence in the paragraph. (R$_2$) Two types of sequence are related to the topic sentence, he says: coordinate and subordinate. (I) In a coordinate sequence the topic sentence is developed by other sentences using repetition and parallel structures. (I) In a subordinate sequence the topic sentence is developed by other sentences at various levels of generality, using a variety of structures.

The T sentence indicates Christensen's readiness to offer an alternative to textbook paragraph models. R$_1$ narrows the disapproval into a specific proposal. The following two "I" sentences amplify elements of R$_1$, including "direction of movement" and "level of generality." R$_2$ is another restriction of the "T" sentence, at approximately the same level of generalization as R_1, introducing the term "sequence" as a way of summarizing the four principles in R_1 and giving a heading for specific structural types. The final "I" sentences illustrate types of sequence. Equivalence and lexical markers also figure in the paragraph's structure. The terms "paragraph" and "principles" link the first two sentences, "topic sentence" the middle two, and "sequence" the last three. The initial parallelism in the last two sentences emphasizes the equivalent generality of each sequence named. Transitional devices include repetition of Christensen's point of view in rejecting outworn paragraph models and proposing his own in their place: "Christensen expresses a distaste," "Christensen proposes," "he argues," "he says."

Becker identifies the other expository paragraph arrangement as P-S or Problem-Solution: "the P slot, often in question form, is the statement of a problem or an effect which is to be explained, and the S slot states the solution or cause of P. If it is extended, the S slot states the solution or cause of P. If it is extended the S slot very often has an internal structure of TRI (an example of embedding at the paragraph level)" (35). Interestingly, a quick look at the Christensen paragraph above reveals what could be termed a Problem-Solution pattern. The utility of textbook paragraph models, called into question by Christensen, is the problem, and the solution is the proposal of "generative principles" that govern all paragraph structure. The solution portion of the paragraph is further subdivided in terms of a restriction-and-illustration pattern which amplifies the nature of the solution. It seems clear from this example and from the single example of the P-S pattern offered by Becker that the P-S category itself is potentially redundant to the TRI pattern. The problem which heads a P-S pattern will inevitably be followed by a listing or an analysis of the items involved in a solution, in the presentation of which varying levels of generality in the R-and-I pattern will normally occur. Without more examples from Becker, it's hard to know whether he wishes to present the P-S model as a true paradigmatic alternative to the TRI model, or simply as a kind of shadow paradigm for describing what may also be seen as a TRI sequence. The present analysis indicates that the TRI pattern is more universal in its applicability, because it accounts for a more complex interrelation of generality and logic.

Paul Rodgers' Discourse-Centered Rhetoric of the Paragraph

A third paragraph model is termed by Paul Rodgers a "discourse-centered rhetoric of the paragraph."[27] Citing Christensen's reluctance to claim descriptive universality for his model, Rodgers argues that "piecemeal inductive observations" have failed to generate a set of descriptors sufficiently broad and complex to account for all paragraphs. What's needed, says Rodgers, is "a concept of the paragraph that will comprehend *all* paragraphs," "a flexible, open-ended *discourse-centered* rhetoric of the paragraph" (41). Rodgers offers a set of paragraph descriptors that, he implies, suggests better than less complex systems the actual conditions governing paragraph choices. In asserting that "all we can use-fully say of *all* paragraphs at present is that their authors have marked them off for special consideration as *stadia of discourse*" (42), Rodgers evidently relies on an intuitive common sense to achieve a complex accounting of paragraph constituents. He rejects Christensen's model because, in striving for generative simplicity, it omits crucial elements. He argues, for example, that neither induc-tive nor deductive patterns actually account for most paragraph divisions. "Both types of movement exist at all levels of discourse, in units smaller than the sentence and larger than the paragraph," he points out, and while "indenta-tion frequently does mark" breaks in levels of generality, "other considerations" often take precedence over logical movements (42). Indeed, he says, "logical, physical, rhythmical, tonal, formal, and other rhetorical criteria, set off from adjacent patterns by indentations," (43) all may govern a stadia of discourse that takes paragraph form. "A tight deductive formula" can never account for these complex factors; only an "inductive study of the art of paragraphing" can begin to define the diversity of paragraph elements (43).

Rodgers does not wish to propose a universal paradigm for the paragraph, only to adduce elements he has noticed in the paragraphing practice of skilled writers. He chooses a sequence of paragraphs from Walter Pater's difficult essay "Style" to illustrate the complex interplay of factors affecting a skilled writer's paragraph choices. In the first three paragraphs of Pater's essay Rodgers finds characteristics which would defy "a strict traditional paragraph analysis" (45). These paragraphs could by conventional description be condensed into one large paragraph, for the first two have no topic sentences, says Rodgers, and seem to lead logically into the third paragraph, which is all one sentence and the topic sentence for all three paragraphs. Thus, he argues, these paragraphs form "a single synthetic logical stadium broken into three paragraphs . . . for physical or editorial reasons" (45), not for any reason related to internal structure. Rodgers identifies another "stadium of discourse" lying athwart paragraphs four through six. The break between paragraphs four and five seems arbitrary, keyed by the three final sentences of the fourth paragraph that apparently frac-ture that paragraph, and introduce material belonging to the next two para-graphs.

Traditional paragraph analysis, Rodgers reiterates, would find Pater's strategy baffling. The explanation, says Rodgers, lies in Pater's sensitivity to the pivotal role of the third-from-last sentence in paragraph four. It culminates issues raised in earlier portions of the paragraph, and is simultaneously a topic sentence for a parallel series of clarifications which follow it in the two succeeding para-graphs. It cannot therefore be separated from its preparatory sentences in para-graph four; and it must be succeeded by a parallel series too long for an entire, continuing paragraph. Thus, Pater must break up the series of clarifying state-ments following it; these breaks must indicate the parallel nature of the state-ments; and they must obey some size limitations. Pater, argues Rodgers, simply chooses to divide his clarifying series into two more paragraphs whose topic sentence is at the end of a preceding paragraph: "rhetorical criteria in P4-6 take precedence over logical . . . and a stadium of thought is allowed to straddle two paragraph breaks" (46).

Pater, "Style" (1888)

P4 [Pater begins this paragraph by focusing on "the line between fact and something quite different from external fact"; a writer, he says, will inevitably strive to express, not fact, but "his sense of it, his peculiar intuition of a world." Pater continues by illustrating various ways in which a "sense of fact" is more compelling than fact itself, even for historians.]

> For just in proportion as the writer's aim, consciously or unconsciously, comes to be the transcribing, not of the world, not of mere fact, but of his sense of it, he becomes an artist, his work *fine* art; and good art . . . in proportion to the truth of his presentment of that sense; as in those humbler or plainer functions of literature also, truth—truth to bare fact, there—is the essence of such artistic quality as they may have. Truth! there can be no merit, no craft at all, without that. And further, all beauty is in the long run only fineness of truth, or what we call expression, the finer accommodation of speech to that vision within.

> P5 The transcript of his sense of fact rather than the fact, as being preferable, pleasanter, more beautiful to the writer himself. In literature, as in every other product of human skill, in the moulding of a bell or a platter for instance, wherever this sense asserts itself, wherever the producer so modifies his work as, over and above its primary use or intention, to make it pleasing (to himself, of course, in the first instance) there, "fine" as opposed to merely serviceable art, exists. Literary art, that is, like all art which is in any way imitative or reproductive of fact—form, or colour, or incident— is the representation of such fact as connected with soul, of a specific personality, in its preferences, its volition and power.

> P6 Such is the matter of imaginative or artistic literature—this transcript, not of mere fact, but of fact in its infinite variety, as modified by human preference in all its infinitely varied forms. It will be good literary art not because it is brilliant or sober, or rich, or impulsive, or severe, but just in proportion as its representation of that sense, that soul-fact, is true, verse being only one department of such literature, and imaginative prose, it may be thought, being the special art of the modern world. That imaginative prose should be the special and opportune art of the modern world results from two important facts about the latter: first, the chaotic variety and complexity of its interests, making the intellectual issue, the really master currents of the present time incalculable—a condition of mind little susceptible of the restraint proper to verse form, so that the most characteristic verse of the nineteenth

century has been lawless verse; and secondly, an all-pervading naturalism, a curiosity about everything whatever as it really is . . . .[28]

By means of this analysis, and through analyses of other unusual paragraph strategies elsewhere in Pater's essay, Rodgers demonstrates that often in Pater's writing "other legitimate criteria have overridden the tug of logic" (47). That is, Pater's paragraphs are not always—or even usually—informed by a specific rhetorical or logical pattern identifiable as a paradigm. Rather, his reasons for indenting to make a paragraph are as various as his structural and rhetorical variety require. Rodgers does not defend all of Pater's choices for paragraphing, nor is he able to show convincing reasons why some of them were made. But Rodgers succeeds in demonstrating how diverse the bases of paragraph choice may be for a skillful writer. By implication, he suggests that attempts to formulate "generative" paragraph models must account for more than levels of generality, logical movement, and syntactical structure. Rodgers' analysis of Pater's style demonstrates how extraordinarily subtle and various is Pater's strategy, which takes into account not only logical development and coherence but also many other factors: reader expectation, paragraph size and readability, rhythm within and across the "stadia," parallelisms and juxtapositions within the stadia, and, Rodgers concludes, "tonal fluctuation" and "Pater's unusual penchant for underplaying important ideas grammatically while stressing them rhetorically" (48). The art of paragraphing emerges from Rodgers' analysis as an intuitive process of choice among a range of possibilities far too diverse for any single paradigm to explain.

Compared with Rodgers', the proposals of Christensen and Becker have a seductive simplicity about them. Christensen, for example, never clearly explains why he chooses levels of generality as the crucial variable in his generative paradigm. He says only that "the structural relations I have disclosed are real (they were discovered by induction)" (32), without explaining how they were induced, and how the controversy concerning the topic sentence was confronted as he devised his model. His range of examples suggests that he perused the published work of contemporary professional writers for paragraphs to illustrate his paradigm, criticizing a few which deviate too far from his principles as illogical or erroneously punctuated (30). Rodgers, on the other hand, argues that "inductive study of the art of paragraphing has an immense neglected potential" (43) which, he appears to suggest, may lead to "a concept of the paragraph that will comprehend *all* paragraphs" (41). But Rodgers' tone is tentative, and unlike Christensen, Rodgers avoids citing a wide range of paragraphs to illustrate his definition of a paragraph as a "pattern in prose discourse, identified originally by . . . logical, physical, rhythmical, tonal, formal, and other rhetorical criteria, set off . . . by indentations . . . as a noteworthy stadium of discourse" (42-3). Rodgers illustrates this capacious definition only by his lengthy analysis of Pater's paragraphs. The effect of this extended but narrowly conceived exemplification is twofold. It calls into question Rodgers' stated aim of positing a paragraph model "that will comprehend *all* paragraphs." At the same time, it usefully subverts the models of Christensen and Becker, to the extent that these models are based on less complex assumptions about paragraph constituents. After reading Rodgers, it's difficult to accept that other models have sufficiently taken into account the complexities of paragraphing.

Other differences among these paradigms are also clear. While both Becker's and Christensen's systems are confined to explaining relationships within the paragraph, Rodgers' "stadia" comprehend interrelations among paragraph sequences that constitute whole discourses. Becker restricts his analysis to the partitioning of paragraphs, without addressing the relationships that bind paragraphs together into discourse. Nor does Christensen make an attempt to show how his sequences illustrate discourse-level relationships; it is D'Angelo's application of Christensen's patterns (in "syntagmatic analysis") that actually shows the larger potential of Christensen's system. Rodgers alone emphasizes the need for a comprehensive model to account for the place of paragraphing in a whole discourse. Another difference lies in the stated or implied applicability of the models to various forms of discourse. Only the tagmemic model is overtly limited to expository paragraphs, although Becker argues that paragraphs in other forms or modes embody the same "markers of paragraph slots" (34). Christensen does not actually state limits to his model, yet his primarily expository examples suggest that exposition is the mode he envisions as most appropriate to his T-R-I model. Although Rodgers does not explain the relevance of his definition to stadia in other than expository prose, its sensitivity to the many variables of paragraphing make it a plausible choice for further exploration.

Only Christensen claims that his model is "generative": "my justification for the term generative lies here. The teacher can, with perfect naturalness, suggest the addition of subordinate sentences to clarify and of coordinate sentences to emphasize or to enumerate" (24). Christensen does not appear to be using "generative" in the linguistic sense, as the power of a rule-system to permit abstract patterns accounting for all utterances. He seems to claim a more limited potential for his pattern, as a self-limiting set of choices which are not put forward as all the choices paragraphing may require. But neither the tagmemic nor the stadia-of-discourse model is put forward as generative in this sense. The tagmemic system, says Becker, is not concerned with "the point of view of the writer" as he makes choices about forming paragraphs: it is "concerned with *the reader's recognition* of certain linguistic units as paragraphs" and thus is a "reader-oriented approach" based on the way Becker believes readers recognize paragraphs.[29] Designed primarily as a pedagogical tool to help students discover paragraph structure as they analyze prose discourse, it offers a useful gross anatomy of paragraph organization. Rodgers' more complex analysis is intended in the same spirit, as a way of revealing "what a paragraph *can* be, not what it must be" (48). It would appear most useful as a way of helping experienced student writers recognize just how various and subtle the organization of discourse may be.

Despite Christensen's claim of generativeness for his paragraph model, it's clear that paragraphing is not the same kind of activity as sentence combining. Wisely, Becker and Rodgers claim only analytical value for their models. Formulating paragraphs from a given model misrepresents the actual paragraph composing situation. It is not like sentence combining, in which certain syntactic elements fit together in specific ways within a sentence unit. Paragraphs are responses not only to cues within a certain group of sentences, but to signals from everywhere in the discourse of which they are a part; the significance of a paragraph draws from the whole of which it is (or ought to be) an integral unit. Sentence form is governed by a grammar. But there is no "grammar" of the paragraph, for paragraphs emerge from a diverse and somewhat arbitrary set of customs perceived differently by different writers. Requiring students to generate paragraphs in response only to a given internal structure oversimplifies the number and diversity of clues writers actually take into account in forming paragraphs. Writing teachers should be wary of single-paragraph exercises, therefore, because such exercises suffer even more than sentence combining from the same disadvantage: a lack of rhetorical context. While lack of context does not strip sentence combining of its limited value, paragraph choices mean virtually nothing unless they emerge from a whole-discourse context. Students may be asked to compose a single paragraph on some topic, but what emerges is not a paragraph but a mini-discourse. Paragraphs have genuine life only as units within a discourse. And the integrity of a paragraph within a discourse is more likely to appear in revision than in other composing stages, for many of the clues that generate paragraphs are available to the writer only in a draft of the whole piece. Like sentence combining, paragraphing as an isolated exercise forces contextless composing upon students. Teachers should require single-paragraph exercises (such as can be found in many texts) only from inexperienced writers, and only as a means of introducing the nature of paragraphs themselves to students. Such exercises should never replace longer writing tasks and should be used only to make students aware of the basic fact that paragraphs are discourse units. Students can only learn to shape effective paragraphs by composing them within contexts that give them significance.

Notes

[1] For background on the rhetorics of the eighteenth and nineteenth centuries, look first at Wilbur Samuel Howell's *Eighteenth-Century British Logic and Rhetoric* (Princeton, NJ: Princeton University Press, 1971). For a schematic placing of eighteenth and nineteenth century rhetoric in Western culture, see Douglas Ehninger's "On Systems of Rhetoric," *Philosophy and Rhetoric*, 1 (Summer 1968), 131-35. The most important figures of this period are George Campbell, Hugh Blair, Richard Whately and Alexander Bain; for recent editions of these rhetoricians see the bibliography for this chapter.

[2] For background on the communication triangle, see Claude Shannon and W. Weaver, *The Mathematical Theory of Communication* (Urbana: IL: University of Illinois Press, 1949) and Wilbur Schramm, "How Communication Works," in *The Processes and Effects of Communication* (Urbana: IL: University of Illinois Press, 1954), pp. 3-26; and for a summary of the scientific approach to communication, Wilbur Schramm, "Communication Research in the United States," in *The Science of Human Communication* (New York: Basic Books, 1963), pp. 1-16.

[3] Louis T. Milic, "Theories of Syle and Their Implication for the Teaching of Composition," *College Composition and Communication*, 16(May 1965), 66-9, 126.

[4] Kenneth Burke, *The Philosophy of Literary Form* (New York: Vintage 1957 [1941]), p. 8.

[5] Kenneth Burke, *A Grammar of Motives* (New York: Prentice-Hall, 1945). All subsequent textual references to this work are taken from this edition.

[6] Kenneth Burke, *A Rhetoric of Motives* (New York: Prentice-Hall, 1950); p. 43.

[7] Virginia Holland, *Counterpoint* (New York: The Philosophical Library, 1959), p. 68.

[8] *Rhetoric of Motives*, p. 16.

[9] James Moffett, *Teaching the Universe of Discourse* (Boston: Houghton Mifflin, 1968), p. 10. All subsequent textual references to this work are taken from this edition.

[10] James Moffett, *Student-Centered Language Arts and Reading*, K-13, 2nd ed. (Boston: Houghton Mifflin, 1976), p. 8.

[11] James Britton, et al., *The Development of Writing Abilities* (11-18), Schools Council Research Studies (London: Macmillan Education, 1975). All subsequent textual references to this work are taken from this edition.

[12] James Kinneavy, *A Theory of Discourse: The Aims of Discourse* (Englewood Cliffs, NJ: Prentice-Hall, 1971). All subsequent textual references to this work are taken from this edition.

[13] Note Kinneavy's debt to the arguments of William Wimsatt, particularly "The Intentional Fallacy" and "The Affective Fallacy," collected in *The Verbal Icon: Studies in the Meaning of Poetry* (Lexington, KY: University of Kentucky Press, 1954).

[14] See, for example, M. H. Abrams, *The Mirror and the Lamp: Romantic Theory and the Critical Tradition* (New York: W.W. Norton, 1958), pp. 6 ff.

[15] Frank D'Angelo, *A Conceptual Theory of Rhetoric* (Cambridge, MA: Winthrop, 1975). All subsequent textual references to this work are taken from this edition.

[16] The existence of the topic sentence as a major component of paragraphing has been challenged by Richard Braddock, "The Frequency and Placement of Topic Sentences in Expository Prose," *Research in the Teaching of English*, 8(Winter 1974), 287-302; and by Arthur A. Stern, "When Is a Paragraph?" *College Composition and Communication*, 27(October 1976), 253-257.

[17] Francis Christensen, "A Generative Rhetoric of the Sentence," *CCC*, 14 (October 1963), 155-61; and "A Generative Rhetoric of the Paragraph," *CCC*, 16(October 1965), 144-56. These articles and the others cited below on paragraph rhetoric are collected in *The Sentence and the Paragraph* (Urbana, IL: NCTE, 1966).

[18] Jeanne Herndon, *A Survey of Modern Grammars*, 2nd ed. (New York: Holt, Rinehart and Winston, 1976), p. 126.

[19] Kellogg Hunt, "A Synopsis of Clause-to-Sentence Length Factors," *English Journal*, 54(April 1965), 300, 305-09.

[20] John C. Mellon, *Transformational Sentence-Combining* (Urbana, IL: NCTE, 1969), p. 18

[21] Donald A. Daiker, Andrew Kerek, Max Morenberg, *The Writer's Options* (New York: Harper and Row, 1979).

[22] William A. Strong, *Sentence Combining and Paragraph Building*, Teacher's Edition (New York: Random House, 1981).

[23] See Warren G. Combs, "Sentence-Combining Practice: Do Gains in Judgment of Writing 'Quality' Persist?" *Journal of Educational Research*, 70(July/ August 1977), 318-21, and Donald A. Daiker, et al., "Sentence-Combining and Syntactic Maturity in Freshman English," *CCC*, 29(February 1978) 36-41.

[24] Mary Ann Jones, "Sentence Combining in Freshman English: Measuring the Rate of Syntactic Growth," paper delivered at the Conference on College Composition and Communication 1981 annual meeting in Dallas, TX.

[25] See Christensen, "A Generative Rhetoric of the Paragraph," note 17 above. Page numbers cited in text are from the NCTE reprint.

[26] A. L. Becker, "A Tagmemic Approach to Paragraph Analysis," *CCC*, 16 (October 1965), 144-56, as reprinted in *The Sentence and the Paragraph*. NCTE, 1966. Page numbers in text are cited from this reprint.

[27] Paul Rodgers, "A Discourse-Centered Rhetoric of the Paragraph," *CCC*, 17(February 1966), 2-11, as reprinted in *The Sentence and the Paragraph*. NCTE, 1966. Page numbers in text are cited from this reprint.

[28] From "Style," in *English Prose of the Victorian Era*, ed. Harrold and Templeman (New York: Oxford University Press, 1938), p. 1426.

[29] A. L. Becker, "Symposium on the Paragraph," in *The Sentence and the Paragraph*, pp. 58-59.

Chapter III
PRESSURE POINTS
Social Differences in Language, Testing, Remediation

Scene: Early in the fall semester, two English instructors are sitting in the departmental lounge furnished with castoff chairs and sofas. Between bites of tuna salad and bologna sandwiches they drift into a discussion of their respective sections of freshman composition:

Bill: Good grief, my eleven o'clock section is really bad. Half of them must be conditionals and the other half jocks. I mean, you know, there's hardly one of them that can write a complete sentence. I gave them an impromptu on "My First Day at College" and one of them wrote, "That is really an interesting topic. I want to take it home and maul it over in my mind." The rest of them wrote things like "Once fully assembled, the orientation director introduced himself to us," or, "I was forwarded from his class to another freshman English class." I'm gonna get lots of laughs from this bunch, if nothing else.

Jane: Well, they probably got a snicker from the topic you assigned them, too. I'll have to admit mine wasn't a lot better, though: you know, "Describe Something You Learned Recently." Isn't that terrific? One kid wrote a theme around the topic "What Goes Around Comes Around"; another one talked about "human sufferage" and political debates that are "seeping us back into dark ignorance." One said that TV was a lot of "fantastic grabble" and another said he was tired of reading so much "satirism" where people were "casting dispersions" on one another.

Bill: I'm telling you, students these days are really bad. Some of the kids in my class didn't write more than ten minutes before they just quit and left. When I was in college I would've been embarrassed not to do my best. The other kids in my classes at least tried too. We didn't dare not try, you know, we felt as though we were lucky to be in college and we knew the professors wouldn't take any garbage from us.

Jane: Yeah, right, I remember in my class the instructor was a TA who really had high standards. He would take up students' papers and then read the worst ones aloud, with all the misspellings and everything, so the kid who wrote it would just cringe with embarrassment. I mean nobody dared hand in a paper that wasn't absolutely perfect. You'd see some of the kids the night before really working on their papers, really sweating them, not just handing in some sloppy first draft like the kids today do. You know what would happen in my classes now if I read some of the bad papers aloud? The kids would just laugh, you know, just get a kick out of hearing other people's dumb mistakes and their own. They wouldn't care. I asked one girl why her first out-of-class paper was worse than her first impromptu, and she said she didn't really have time to work on it; she had to go through sorority rush and she was really busy. Can you believe that?

Bill: It must be the way kids are raised these days, or the way they're just passed through school without having to do any work. When I was in high school I really had to work hard; my English teacher was a demon. He'd tell my parents if he thought I wasn't doing enough work. Schoolteachers these days really coddle the kids, and their parents don't care either. Just want the kid to come to school, get a degree, and get a good job. They think they pay good money, why shouldn't their kid do well?

Jane: Right. Something has happened to students these days. They just aren't like we were in school. Maybe I should go to work for the government; you know, a day's work, a day's pay, who notices?

Maybe Bill and Jane were tired of tuna and bologna, or had stayed up too late the night before, reading student papers. Or perhaps they were simply articulating an academic deteriorationism, the usual counterpoint to an optimistic faith in human progress. Should our instructors' plaints be viewed in the long perspective of cultural cycling, or even in the short view of a day's dyspepsia? Have students changed since our instructors were in college a decade or so ago? Are there any objective correlatives for the unhappiness of our brownbag philosophers?

Our teachers' sense that *something* has changed in American education cannot be gainsaid; things are not as they were in school when they were there, and the students they confront in college classes now are not the same kinds of students *their* teachers confronted in earlier generations. The evidence for this may be found, for example, in statistical comparisons between the number and kind of college students in earlier decades and in recent years. These comparisons reveal important differences in enrollment sizes and the socioeconomic and racial makeup of student populations.

The most visible change in postsecondary education in recent decades is the vast increase in numbers of students finishing high school and going on to college. Since the early 1960s many academic communities have grown into cities, with dormitories rising on every available acre of ground. The construction boom in academic housing during the last two decades has resembled the frantic building of barracks during the mobilization years of World War II. The numbers show why such haste was necessary: for example, of every 1000 students who entered fifth grade in 1942, only half graduated from high school and only one-fifth went on to college; of 1000 fifth-graders in 1956, two-thirds graduated from high school and one-third went on to college. The last set of numbers is astounding: of 1000 fifth-graders in 1966, three-fourths graduated from high school and almost half went on to college.[1] By the mid-1970s there were more than twice as many students going to college as there were in 1950. Most of this increase has been absorbed by public institutions. Major state universities multiplied and divided into many smaller satellite institutions, some limited to accepting undergraduates not acceptable to the parent institution. It has been at these newer four-year universities, and at the increasing number of two-year community colleges, that the issue of literacy and its pressure upon writing instruction has been most acute. That's because, in addition to the leap in enrollments in higher education, significant changes have occurred in the composition of student populations.

One Census Bureau statistic suggests the alteration in racial makeup of the college-going population. In 1950, of all whites aged 25 to 29 in the United States, only 8% had completed four or more years of college; by 1975, 23% had completed four college years. Contrast this increase with that shown by non-whites: in 1950 only 2.8% had completed four or more college years, but by 1975, 15% had completed college.[2] While the number of whites finishing college increased three times during that twenty-five year period, the number of non-whites finishing college increased five times. This does not mean, of course, that the minority students have gained full educational equality in America, or that the numbers of black and other minority students have increased on all campuses. Of all students enrolled in public four-year colleges in 1966, for example, about 11% were minority students; by 1972 this percentage had risen to 16%. In the same year the figure for minorities at private colleges was only 5% of their total student populations.[3] This increasing proportion of minority students is not equally distributed among all colleges and universities. The relatively few black academic institutions account for some. But the urban public universities, some operating on an open-admissions basis, have absorbed the great part of minority students, who in earlier decades might not have considered going to college. The language problems associated with these students' academic efforts have posed several unprecedented challenges to composition teachers untrained in the needs of their universities' new constituencies.

These challenges are all related to the central problem of literacy. First, the appearance in many composition classes of nonstandard-dialect speakers has obliged teachers to ask what constitutes literacy: does ability with nonstandard dialects of English constitute literacy? Is it possible to be a literate writer and still use a minority dialect like Black English? Second, the widespread use of standardized tests to evaluate language skills raises the question of how literacy may fairly be measured: are such tests a true measure of students' language ability? And third, the increasing numbers of educationally disadvantaged students in schools and colleges have forced teachers and their institutions to develop, quickly and often without adequate instructor training, crash programs in rudimentary literacy instruction. Each of these challenges will be considered separately later in this chapter; first, however, we need to review the relationship between them, with respect to the underlying question, what constitutes literacy in an academic setting?

Customarily, literacy is defined as the ability to read and write standard English, not a nonstandard variety used by a minority group. And standard English is normally defined as the language of the "educated middle class," that heard in classrooms, public offices, and on radio and television.[4] Conversely, illiteracy is often defined as the inability to use language appropriate to such settings, or as the inability to make a "competent" score on language aptitude tests or armed forces entry tests.

The customary linkage between literacy and standard English has been sharply challenged in recent years. Sociolinguists have argued that defining illiteracy as the inability to read or write standard English is simplistic and illogical. Their arguments center on the "deficit-difference" distinction about language use. If a student's low score on an aptitude test can be said to result from inadequacy in language skills (whether from native inability or from environmental deprivation), then that student may be said to have a language *deficit.* If, however, it can be shown that the student's language "inadequacy" is merely the inability to use standard English, and if it can also be shown that the student can use a nonstandard variety of English quite functionally within a particular racial or cultural subgroup, then the low test score or poor school performance may reflect a language *difference,* not a deficit. Those who take the latter view argue that "what are referred to as deviations or errors or substandard features of language are in reality marks of consistent, well-ordered, grammatical systems exercised within the norms of some particular subgroup of speakers."[5] As we will see later in this chapter, such criticisms of traditional conceptions of literacy have made the task of defining literacy considerably more difficult than in the past.

Because the tests which purport to measure language ability are couched in standard English, the definition of literacy as the inability to score adequately on the tests has been challenged. The nationwide, standardized tests determine, by the very form they take, the nature of the language skills they are intended to gauge. In the view of many educators the customary connection in the public mind between test scores and literacy levels is potentially damaging to minority students. These students, more numerous than white students in the lower socioeconomic ranges, consistently score lower on verbal aptitude tests than white, middle-class students. This pattern, according to those advocating the "difference" view of language, does not indicate inferior language ability, but only minority students' unfamiliarity with the standard dialect of English. For these advocates, the question of literacy is actually a question of measurement intention: tests designed to reveal control over a standard dialect will not reveal other forms of linguistic control, indeed will interpret such control negatively, since it will not show up on the tests. And if the tests' rationale is faulty, are not the received opinions of what constitutes literacy also open to question?

The relationship between literacy, testing, and nonstandard dialects is only one facet of the controversy over testing and standards of literacy. The noisiest phase of the controversy has emerged from the public notice given the SAT score decline which began in 1963 and continued into the 1980s. One of the first major notices of this decline appeared on 1972 in the impeccably restrained *Change: The Magazine of Higher Learning:* "The Decline of the SAT's," it gently labeled the issue, offering an analysis of the by-then decade-long decline and the persistent correlations between socioeconomic status and test scores.[6] By 1976, however, the decline had become a national disaster in the headlines: *Change* billed it as "THE DECLINE OF LITERACY" in inch-high capitals; a Midwestern newspaper proclaimed an "academic debacle" in reporting on the decline; and *Newsweek* bemoaned the "appalling statistics" which were proving that "the U. S. educational system is spawning a generation of semiliterates."[7] In response to this unwelcome media attention, the ETS called out a search-and-rescue party in the form of a panel of educators, psychologists, and statisticians to discover reasons for the decline. Their conclusion was that different proportions of nontraditional, lower-scoring students in the test-taking population from 1963 to 1970 accounted for some of the drop.[8] For the continuing decline after 1970 many culprits were named: larger classes in schools and colleges, more TV, lower student motivation, and linguistic confusion in teaching methods, among others. The panel admitted it could not identify any root cause and suggested that the decline may indicate a major shift in the way young people learn in an increasingly media-dominated age. (The recent leveling-off will probably bring a spate of rethinking.)

The score decline is only one issue in the testing controversy. A more important issue is the nature and use of the tests themselves. Administrators, pressed to admit and place large numbers of students in colleges and universities, have argued that test scores offer a more equitable way of judging admissions applications than any other available means. Their argument—and that of ETS— is that because the SAT measures "developed abilities" for academic success, and because academic success is officially defined in terms of gradepoint average, SAT scores can predict moderately well a student's potential for academic success.[9] As we will see later in this chaper, the statistical basis for confidence in SAT prediction is open to question; close examination of the figures has provoked scepticism, even outrage, from many researchers. As a result, academic testing, often mystifying to those unfamiliar with its jargon, has become more visible and more vulnerable in recent years.

The National Education Association, the national PTA, and Ralph Nader's research group have all set upon the Educational Testing Service, accusing it of creating culturally biased tests which foster the tyranny of the white middle class in educational decision-making. Because it has attracted considerable attention nationwide, however, the Nader report deserves particular consideration. Two main criticisms of the SAT emerge from this report: first, that its predictive potential is far lower than most users realize (a point we will consider later), and second, that it measures socioeconomic status much more clearly than verbal aptitude—"class in the guise of merit."[10] Citing the fact that as the socioeconomic status of the test-taker increases, so does his chance of scoring well on the test, the Nader-Nairn report argues that the SAT is an instrument of class oppression manipulated by the educational establishment. The ETS itself is portrayed in the report as an interlocking directorate of class privilege, economic advantage, and academic elitism. The whole matter of the SAT would seem tangential to the concerns of writing teachers were it not that the SAT: Verbal test and its sister, the ACT: English Usage exam, are used in many institutions for exemption and placement in composition courses. Because these tests are often at the heart of institutional judgments about student writing, we should consider briefly what educators have long known about the relationships between class, race, and test achievement in educational testing.

Scores on aptitude tests have traditionally correlated with income and race. Students from low-income families do tend to score lower on such tests than students from higher-income families. There is also a racial aspect to score patterns: black students tend to score lower on standardized tests than white students.[11] Of course, socioeconomic level and race are themselves correlated, since there are larger numbers of racial minorities at the lower socioeconomic levels than at the higher. But the relationships between academic achievement, income levels, and race are not limited to test scores; they hold for other aspects of education as well. Students from lower-income levels don't stay as long in secondary school as other students, fewer of them graduate from high school, and fewer of them go to college. Students from lower-income levels and minority students score lower on IQ tests.[12] These statistics do not "explain" why such students score less well on standardized tests; they simply suggest that for any number of reasons, a student's class, income, and race have some influence on that student's academic achievement. Most psychologists reject the claim by a few researchers that the heritability of intelligence is proven by such statistics. They also reject the corollary claim that academic attainment is largely determined by one's socioeconomic level because that, in turn, is "inherited" by virtue of some dominant genetic factor of mental ability. The majority tend to favor, in Christopher Jenck's words, "environmental explanations" for observed differences in cognitive skills.[13]

Indeed, the educational establishment's faith in environmental intervention has provided the rationale for the enormous increase in writing remediation in recent years. Low test scores are often taken by schools as primary evidence for remedial need. Remediation is thus directly correlated with testing; both may be seen as systematic responses to the changes in student population in recent decades. While most colleges and universities have added some remedial elements to their writing programs, the largest programs have emerged in places with the most disadvantaged students—i.e., in urban universities with students who score poorly on the tests couched in standard written English. Remediation, in other words, is a function of the growth of testing, which in turn is partly a result of the increased numbers of students who require careful placement in a remedial program. All these related developments have their source in the changes noted above in the kinds of students completing secondary education and going on to college. In the rest of this chapter we'll look more closely at three major aspects of contemporary writing instruction: the problem of nonstandard dialects in writing classrooms, the role of language tests in judging language ability, and the nature of remedial programs.

Literacy and Dialect in Composition

Educators generally define literacy as the ability to understand and use standard written English in school and college work. This is not an entirely stable definition, however, for it has been argued that students required to take a test or write a paper in a standard form of English unfamiliar to them are placed at a disadvantage that masks their actual literacy. Can the concept of literacy be expanded to include writers working in nonstandard dialects? How may we judge the quality of literacy in written forms of English?

The question of linguistic performance within different social and ethnic groups has been addressed in two important ways. Researchers in Great Britain have approached sociolinguistic differences through the idea of *code,* which may be defined as a particular form of language use governed by the user's psychological outlook, as determined by class status. American linguists have preferred the more traditional concept of *dialect* to distinguish between "standard" language forms practiced by the cultural majority, and those "nonstandard" forms used by different minority groups. Codes are not dialects; the differences between them help account for the fact that code research has made little headway in the United States. The idea of code depends on the availability of clear distinctions between working class and middle class social contexts, distinctions more readily found in European than in American culture. But although code research has gained little acceptance in America, a review of its main outlines may clarify some of the complex social dimensions of language use for composition teachers.

The concept of code developed by Basil Bernstein contains two pairs of definitions: two types of family structure—"positional" and "personal"—are said to evoke two types of language code—"restricted" and "elaborated."[14] The typical working-class speaker, says Bernstein, gains identity in a family governed by strong "boundary maintenance," in which family roles are clearly delineated by age and sex. In working-class families "the authority structure is based upon clear-cut, unambiguous definitions of the status" of each family member (184). This family structure produces a restricted code of language use, featuring reduced syntactic alternatives, reduced vocabulary range, and "communalized" language contexts which depend upon shared acceptance of speech roles among speakers and listeners. Users of a restricted code also rely on what Bernstein calls "particularistic meanings," which depend upon localized relationships and shared assumptions about society and work. In Bernstein's view, the class system has produced the restricted code for the working class by limiting the "distribution of knowledge" and the opportunity to explore concepts outside a rigidly defined social position (175).

The middle class embodies a family structure Bernstein terms "personal." In families with flexible authority relationships, "differences between persons," rather than age or sex differences, govern individual identity, resulting in "person-centered families" in which verbalization itself helps formulate individual differences (185). Children in such families gain "a strong sense of autonomy" which allows them to exploit an elaborated code of language use (185). Attributes of an elaborated code include grammar and usage carefully edited to conform to standard English, wide vocabulary, and most importantly, "universalistic meanings" which are context-free and flexible because the speaker has the individual freedom to use language as a means of exploration and growth (79). One of the empirical evidences adduced by Bernstein for code differences is "hesitation phenomena"; middle-class children were observed to hesitate more often and for longer durations than working-class children in closely-observed discussions (87). Bernstein takes this phenomenon to mean that because middle-class children value language as an expression of individual uniqueness and authenticity, they tend to select and edit their language more carefully than working-class children, whose restricted code does not encourage such language play.

The correlation between code and class has gained some research support in Britain, but has generated scepticism among researchers in the United States.[15] The basic obstacle to the acceptance of code research in America is the difficulty in assigning clear-cut differences in class to separate groups of students. Bernstein defines his working-class subjects as those educated on a vocational track outside the grammar school, and his middle-class students as those with a grammar school preparation (82-3). Since American students cannot be categorized in this way, the research premised on such categories has not been persuasive to American linguists. Yet Bernstein's "codes" should be better known to all teachers of language arts, for they reflect certain rhetorical considerations discussed in the first two chapters of this book. The importance of context-based meanings for the restricted code, for example, is analogous to Britton's emphasis upon context in his definition of "expressive" writing. All children, he postulates, begin their mastery of speaking and writing by exercising language competence within the context of "close relations" between speaker or writer and audience. Britton defines linguistic growth, in fact, as the child's progress from contextual language to language for generalized, distanced audiences, a capacity Bernstein associates with the elaborated code of the middle class. The issue of context may also be found in *Teaching the Universe of Discourse,* where Moffett argues that "rhetorical distance between speaker and listener" is a crucial determinant of the level of complexity in a communication situation. Britton and Moffett associate the ability to go beyond limited-context communication with individual cognitive growth; Bernstein attributes it to the impact of class status upon the individual.

Class divisions do not appear appropriate as a way of understanding differences among varieties of American English. Language differences in the United States are usually approached in terms of ethnic differences in correlation with socioeconomic rank. For these variables dialect seems a more appropriate concept of language differentiation than the concept of code. Dialect "means a variety of language spoken by a distinct group of people in a definite place"; it "varies in pronunciation, vocabulary, and grammar from other varieties of the same language."[16] Composition teachers are more interested in written than spoken language, of course, and standardized tests and writing samples require command of written, not spoken, English. But dialectal differences in spoken language do carry over into writing. This is especially true of the most visible nonstandard dialect in the schools, the one receiving the most attention from linguists: Black English. In different versions it is used by blacks in urban ghettoes and the rural South, serving as the main form of oral communication for them. Black English differs in pronunciation, syntax and vocabulary from standard English. Some of its most frequent markers are:

A. Lack of the copula *be:* the use of the invariant *be.*
    He going home.
    He be going home.
B. Lack of *d* and *ed* as past tense inflection.
    She talk about him yesterday.
    She walk home by herself.
C. Lack of *s, es* as third person singular present tense inflection.
    He want to read the book.
D. Lack of suffix *s* as possessive inflection.
    Mary dress be pretty.
E. Use of multiple negation.
    I ain't got no tickets.

These markers are not the only characteristics of Black English syntax; they are simply the most visible differences between black dialect and standard English.[17] Nor are such dialectal variations limited to black speakers. The loss of the final *r*, for example, is characteristic of both Southern and New England regional dialects used by the general population. And double negatives are as typical of nonstandard speech in working class and rural white populations as they are of Black English.

It's no longer possible for any writing teacher to adopt a simple prescriptive approach to usage, and insist that certain ways of speaking are by nature "better" than other ways. In the words of some recent linguistic researchers, it is now "axiomatic that language is one form of cultural behavior," reflecting varieties of that culture within its whole language community.[18] Thus "usage" is today a far more flexible concept than it was in the earlier eras of American education, when correctness of speech was a major definer of status. As we have already seen in earlier chapters, audience, setting and purpose are considered the important variables in judging language appropriateness.

Nowhere has this linguistic relativism been more evident than in the controversy over "bidialectalism," the policy of encouraging nonstandard speakers to learn standard English dialect without abandoning their own dialect. As a way of mitigating nonstandard speakers' difficulties in reading and writing in school, bidialectalism has been encouraged by some educators and damned by others. That Black English is a functional dialect for a large minority of American school children, particularly in urban areas where the minority is often a majority, has made the traditional "deficit" view of nonstandard dialects difficult to defend. Most educators no longer attempt to eradicate Black English in the schools by insisting upon standard English in the classroom; black children often cannot cope with school materials or relate their own experience to schoolwork in standard English. Yet, although "the majority of sociolinguists who have studied social dialects advocate the bidialectalist position," there are great differences among linguists and educators about how standard and nonstandard dialects can actually coexist in schools.[19] The majority of researchers subscribe to Dwight Bolinger's call for "helping teachers to see that, when students come to be limited to . . . a nonstandard dialect, what they need is not to be corrected in supposed mistakes but to be introduced to a new and in many ways different but related system, no better and no worse than the old one but more useful in their new contacts."[20] Texts and teaching materials in standard and Black English have been introduced in some schools in attempts to help students understand both the linguistic validity of their native dialect and the value of learning the standard dialect also. Such efforts have frequently been perceived as failures, due in part to the great difficulty in teaching literacy (in whatever dialect) to students who do not value literacy itself.

One viewpoint hostile to bidialectalism asserts that Black English is best put aside by any speaker of a nonstandard dialect who wishes to become part of the social and cultural mainstream. In this argument, essentially a version of the "deficit" view of dialect, Black English is a corruption of standard English precluding the user from full participation in society: Black English "doesn't lend itself to clear expression," for it is "an idiom of fettered minds, the shuffling speech of slavery," as one commentator suggests.[21] The political and moral aspects of the dialect question are central to another group of opponents of bidialectalism. In their view, requiring minority students to learn standard English is tantamount to forcing their repudiation of their own culture and self-identity. It's an act of oppression, a "false promise to put black people up, while in fact putting them on and keeping them down."[22] It's a way of telling black students they must learn the majority dialect because it *is* the majority, and because that majority is not going to accommodate itself to a minority dialect. "Standard English," says another opponent of bidialectalism, "is a principle means of preserving the existing power structure, for it builds the system of class distinctions into the most inward reaches of each child's humanity: the language."[23] The premise of this argument is that schools—and society in general—ought to nurture individuality, linguistic and otherwise, and encourage communication among dialect groups, not impose a standard dialect upon all groups.

The most controversial argument for bidialectalism comes in the form of a pamphlet entitled "Students' Right to Their Own Language," published in 1974 by NCTE. Its authority derived from its official sanction by the umbrella organization of all English teachers in the United States; yet the ranks of the NCTE were split by varying degrees of opposition to the document (see Appendix B for some of its crucial sections). After discussing the insights of dialect research mentioned earlier, the pamphlet argued, among other things, that dialectal differences are always superficial and never meaningful, that students ought to be permitted to write in nonstandard dialects, and that students ought to be offered "dialect options" to increase their "self-esteem." Teachers were also urged to acquire a wide range of knowledge about language in order to better grasp the nature of language differences, and to tolerate them as expressions of speakers' individual and cultural identities. "Students' Right to Their Own Language" is an expression of the new relativism in the concept of usage, a brief for linguistic tolerance on the part of teachers and the society they represent.

Unfortunately, but perhaps inevitably, some of the document's statements blur issues that require clear discrimination by writing teachers. One of its major premises is naive: i.e., that sociolingistic insights into nonstandard dialects, particularly Black English, carry over nicely into composition, and have as much relevance to written as to spoken English. This argument has encouraged composition teachers to believe that, if only their attitudes toward nonstandard dialects could change, writing instruction in schools and colleges could include both standard and nonstandard dialect forms. The difficulties of this position, standing against the moral and social justness of dialect tolerance, may not be easily recognized or admitted by supporters of "Students' Right." But they are real and they must be examined closely.

The research precipitating the liberalized attitudes toward dialectal differences has been carried forward by linguists, who by trade are not concerned with writing pedagogy. Teachers of writing may understandably fail to notice what research linguists accept as a given—the fact that Black English in the United States is a spoken, not written, language. Indeed, linguists prefer to rely on speakers of any dialect under investigation because only spoken language is used by all members of the dialect group. Written dialect, where it exists, may often be a codification of oral forms based on the writer's ear for phonetic-scribal equivalence. It's therefore less trustworthy for the linguist interested in the present state of the dialect. Such is the case of Black English. It's true that in tracing the history of Black English linguists have had to rely on written transcriptions of dialect; but since most of these are contained in works of imaginative literature, and were produced by writers laboring without the aid of the phonetic alphabet, most written versions of Black English lack sufficient authenticity for linguistic research. Efforts to establish the rule-governed basis of Black English today focus on speech patterns; little research in linguistics has been devoted to any written—as compared with spoken—versions of Black English.[24]

The actual relationship between spoken and written forms of Black English has never been clearly established, either in terms of the possible differences between oral and written markers or in terms of the percentage of oral markers carried into writing. It's easy to assume that oral characteristics are simply reproduced in written dialect, so that the latter may be measured in terms of its faithfulness to the oral form. But there's no research into written Black English comparable to the great body of work on its oral form. There's a sound reason for that: most written versions of Black English are intentional transcriptions of the spoken dialect. Major American black writers have written most of their work in standard English. There are plays, poems, and novels written in dialect by black and white writers, but these are deliberate renderings of spoken Black English. Most fiction couched in Black English involves first-person narration by a dialect-using narrator; Black English poetry artfully renders the voice of black consciousness expressing itself in its own vernacular.

What cannot be found in American culture is written Black English put to the purpose of transacting the business, politics, and education of our society. Standard written English has been established by the middle class, black and white, as the "transactional" (Britton's term seems apt) written dialect of the United States. Black English has no comparable written form. It's an oral dialect, serving the colloquial purposes that vernacular dialects serve in many languages. E. D. Hirsch has made clear the distinction between dialects (related to region, ethnic culture, occupation, etc.) and a "grapholect," which he defines as a "national written language" that is "transdialectal in character" and "normative" precisely in its "very isolation from class and region."[25] Standard written English is a grapholect; Black English has never been established as one. This fact, unacknowledged by the committee which prepared "Students' Right" and of minor interest to linguists, has major importance for composition teachers, who must use imaginative prose whenever written models of Black English are desired for classroom use. The dearth of transactional Black English prose severely restricts the availability of prose models for instructors attempting to teach black students "the fundamental skills of writing in their own dialect."[26]

This limitation is compounded by another problem for the teacher of writing, inherent in the "Students' Right" admonition that students should be encouraged to write in the dialect comfortable to them. When students attempt to write in a nonstandard dialect like Black English, they will violate some rules of standard written English by using Black English conventions. Such violations will be permissible in a "Students' Right" environment because they will be rule-governed choices resulting from dialect habits. However, students will also make errors in syntax, idiom, diction and mechanics which will not be dialect-related. These will not be acceptable because they will not be rule-governed dialect choices. When the differences between dialect choices and non-dialect errors are systematic and clearly attributable to their respective sources, students may be made to see with moderate ease the differences between these two kinds of nonstandard usages, the one acceptable and the other not. But because Black English does not have a normative written form, and because oral variations among regions and social groups may cover a wide range of nonstandard usages, efforts to separate acceptable usage from unacceptable can easily bring confusion for student and teacher alike. Where is the line to be drawn between dialect usage and freshman-English garbling? Does freeing students to use "their own language" mean that students so freed will produce "clear, forceful writing" ("Students' Right," 8) authenticated by the markers of their personal dialect?

Before some tentative answers to these questions are explored, another related difficulty posed by "Students' Right" should be mentioned. Its authors assert that "differences among dialects in a given language are always confined to a limited range of *surface* features that have no effect on what linguists call *deep structure,* a term that might be roughly translated as 'meaning' (6)." Here the "Students' Right" Committee draws upon the familiar distinction made by transformationalist grammarians between deep structure—the latent propositional meaning of a statement—and surface structure—the explicit grammatical form of the statement. But in phrasing their statement, the authors have oversimplified the relationship between deep and surface features of language. One linguist defines deep structure as "a system of propositions that express the meaning of the sentence," and surface structure as "these propositions in sentences as they are actually spoken."[27] Another defines deep structure as "the basic meaning of a sentence," and its surface structure as "the form of a sentence." Moreover, says the latter, "transformations do not alter the basic meaning of sentences, [but] they do affect the surface meaning."[28] Cognizant of such reluctance on the part of many linguists to assign *all* meaning to deep structure, William Labov suggests that differences among dialects "are *largely confined* to superficial, rather low-level processes which have *little effect* upon meaning [italics added]."[29] However, where Labov suggests that dialectal differences are "largely confined" to surface features, the authors of "Students' Right" claim that those differences are "always confined" to surface features. Where Labov suggests that dialect features have "little effect" upon meaning, the "Students' Right" authors insist that such features have "no effect" upon deep structure, which they apparently equate with the complete meaning of any statement. It appears they have read Labov and have carefully altered the qualifiers, as though to suggest that meaning is not to some extent inherent in the rhetorical and stylistic elements—surface features, certainly—of writing.

While such changes are neither wide nor deep, they do blur an important truth. All composition teachers confront writing in which dialect markers are randomly embedded in non-dialect errors. Students will readily accept the

"Students' Right" position that dialect markers are not meaningful, but this acceptance may block their recognition of an equally important counter-truth: that non-dialect-related deviations from standard syntax and mechanics *do* obscure meaning. To afford a closer look at the ambiguous task of dealing with dialect and nondialect variations from standard usage in the same writing, let's examine a piece of transactional writing with just such a blend. Here is an excerpt from an essay comparing Bigger Thomas of Richard Wright's *Native Son* with Maggie of Stephen Crane's *Maggie: A Girl of the Streets:*

> Bigger Thomas is able to show some freedom of action, while Maggie really
> 1a   1b   2a
> haven't no control of her course in society. (What give you a feeling that Big-
> 2b   3b   3a
> ger is more determined than Maggie) is shown threw Bigger drive to find his
> 4b   4a 5b   6b
> idenity in society. Both protagonist are naturalism, (that both are seen as
> 5a   7b   6a
> product of their environment.) With this, Wright show Bigger being caught up
> 8b
> in this society where blacks have no identity. (Where this is so evident that
> 7a   9b   8a
> Wright try somewhat to Bigger seem as a hero,) because even tho he is doom
> 9a
> Bigger end up finding his identity.

Clearly this writer understands the basic distinctions he wants to make between these two protagonists, with reference to the concept of naturalism, which is the basis of the comparison. He has control of the literary works and of the concept in whose terms he is analyzing the literature. He is, in other words, an excellent example of the student whose dialect habits have not precluded his understanding literary works written in standard English, or kept him from grasping lectures and discussions about naturalism conducted in standard English. Thus, this student may find it hard to understand why his prose is unreadable, particularly if he has taken to heart the "Students' Right" approval of "vigorous and thoughtful statements in less prestigious dialects" (9), and its disapproval of "finicky correctness in 'school standard' " (8) writing. This student knows that he has understood the material moderately well and that he has made a decent attempt to relate the specific to the general. When the instructor suggests that certain sentences do not communicate meaning, how can the instructor work around the student's predictable assumption that his dialect usage is what's responsible for the teacher's criticism? How can the student be made to see that blurred meaning is a direct result of syntactical strangulation?

Instructors in such situations must maneuver students into seeing themselves first as writers, not as representatives of a particular culture. Students must be encouraged to free themselves from the ethnocentricity implicit in "Students' Right." Students must be made to see that a temporary neutralization of cultural identity is a necessary first step to any real communication of meaning, and that style (here in the form of syntactical choices) is profoundly related to meaning. In the situation of the sample above, the instructor could begin by numbering the clearly definable dialect markers "1a, 2a, 3a," etc., until all such markers are included in the series.[30] Then the non-dialect errors may be numbered in a different series: "1b, 2b, 3b," etc. Then the instructor may show the student the causes of the nonstandard usages for each series; such a demonstration clearly will require time, patience, and tact. If the course is remedial, an individualized laboratory setting may be available; if the student is "mainstreamed" into a class of mixed abilities and cultural backgrounds, the instructor must find the time to individualize the situation.

The sequence of black dialect markers occurs as follows:

1a. Multiple negation; leveling of present tense inflection ("have" for "has").
2a. Lack of suffix -s as third person singular present tense inflection.
3a. Lack of suffix -s as possessive inflection.
4a. Lack of suffix -s as plural inflection.
5a. Ditto.
6a. Lack of suffix -s as third person singular present tense inflection.
7a. Leveling of present tense inflection ("try" for "tries").
8a. Lack of suffix -ed as past participle inflection.
9a. Lack of suffix -s as present tense third person singular inflection.

The authors of "Students' Right" are correct that these dialect-related usages do not interfere with the passage's meaning. Whether the student is urged to learn the inflections appropriate to standard English depends upon the task and intentions of instructor and student. Proponents of bidialectalism might ignore the dialect markers, on the premise that they are a normal part of the writer's usage, and concentrate on the obvious syntactical difficulties. Those believing in the need for standard English might require the student to revise the dialect markers before going on to sentence structure. What is clear is that while the dialect-related surface features of this passage do not interfere with its meaning, other surface features—sentence order and idiom—seriously block its meaning.

Non-dialect problems may be summarized as follows:

1b. The noun clause "What . . . Maggie," while acceptable as the subject of "is," does not fit idiomatically, because the construction "What gives you [one] . . . " is normally followed by the copula plus a nominative construction, not a copula plus a participle making a passive predicate. Idiomatic English does not permit double predicate constructions linked in this fashion. Traditional handbooks recommend labels like "awk" or "shift" for such errors.

2b. "Determined" is misused here in a semantic not a syntactical sense. Trying to display his grasp of the concept of determinism, the student uses the word in a modifying sense that is not idiomatic. This kind of error results from the student's attempt to apply a regular rule of conversion (from noun of quality to adjective of quality) to a word meaning that cannot be so converted.

3b. A phonetic rendering unrelated to dialect.

4b. A misspelling that could be attributed to any poor speller. It could also be related to the phonological marker of Black English involving lack of final -*t*, or -*d* sounds in consonant clusters.

5b. Linking a count, animate noun with a noncount, abstract noun seems outrageous, until we realize that the verb (a form of *be*) is the source of the error. Substitue "exemplify" for "are" and the construction is acceptable; it's the student's lexical poverty that causes the difficulty.

6b. The relative clause "that . . . " dangles incoherently and would be so marked by traditional editing. But an "in" inserted before "that" converts the whole phrase to an acceptable structure. Here the student's partial control over a complex, formal idiom ("in that both . . . ") suggests a struggle to express a complex understanding with an inadequate command of standard idiomatic phrases.

7b. The unattached demonstrative pronoun is a common error in all student writing.

8b. The attempted clause "Where . . . hero" is incoherent for several reasons. Again the student leads off with an apparently nominative clause (as in "What give you . . . " earlier), but the verb for which the clause is the subject is absent. The relative "that" attempts to link the initial "where" clause with "Wright try," but fails to do so. The "to" is part of an infinitive whose verb component is also omitted. The student is trying to say that Wright makes Bigger a hero, and that this enhancement of Bigger's stature illustrates (in an "evident" fashion) by contrast the oppressive nature of white society. But the complexity of this literary perception eludes the student's capacity to predicate it.

9b. "Tho" is a colloquial, perhaps phonetic, spelling unrelated to dialect.

To show the student the irrelevance of the dialect markers to the passage's meaning would not be difficult. How extraordinarily difficult it is, by contrast, to clarify the syntactical problems of the passage! Told that he may write "in his own language," the student will be astonished to discover how little "his own language"—defined as his dialect—has to do with meaning. It's "his own language" that blocks the meaning of the passage. It may be argued, that is, that there are elements of two languages in this passage: Black English and what may be called the "interlanguage" of a basic writer trying unsuccessfully to achieve the target language (here, formal written English). Some of the surface nonstandardisms in the passage follow the rules of Black English. Systematic error-analysis (see Chapter I) may well reveal that many of the deeper errors also follow certain consistent patterns—rules, if you like—which govern the writer's attempts to approximate standard English. Error-analysis could also show which of the syntactical difficulties not related to Black English are accidental slips in spelling, usage or mechanics, and which are deeper intentions gone awry during the writing process.

Error-analysis can help teachers remediate the work of basic writers; but what of the causes of such writing? The transcription of meaning, not the meaning itself, is the source of the syntactical confusion in this passage. The student

knows what he wants to say: he has a grasp of the way the literary text embodies the abstraction "naturalism" he seeks to define. The basic propositional
meanings of the passage are accessible; the syntactical configuration of those
meanings is incoherent. However, the quality of literacy is not just a function of
propositional meaning, however clearly worked out; it also depends upon the
syntactical realization of that meaning. The passage yields no examples of black
dialect markers themselves blurring the passage's meaning; the paragraph is not
disabled by its dialectal characteristics. Yet it is syntactically disabled, even illit-
erate in the context of college-level writing. It's not close enough to its target of
standard written English to communicate its meaning in that standard dialect.
Whatever error patterns or interlanguage "rules" may govern the syntax, they
are not adequate approximations of the rules of standard written English.

We may say, then, that a passage with Black English characteristics may be
perfectly literate, *if* all syntactical elements not related to Black English follow
the rules of standard English. It's misleading to students to tell them they may
use their own language; they may, but only if that language obeys the rules of
the standard dialect in all usages except those related to common, well-defined
dialectal markers. Unfortunately, simultaneous obedience to the rules of both
standard and nonstandard English dialects—easy enough for the talented or professional writer—is not possible for most student writers. In particular, a student
striving for basic literacy should not be encouraged to use dialect as a dodge for
violations of the basic syntactical rules which govern all written English.

Measuring Writing Skills

Much of the fuel for the controversy over student literacy has been provided
by scores on the standardized verbal aptitude tests (the SAT:Verbal and ACT:
English Usage) given to high school juniors and seniors, which claim to measure
general verbal facility, not writing ability. There are other standardized tests, of
course, which do claim to measure writing ability, most produced by the Educational Testing Service, and we will consider these in some detail shortly. But because scores on the verbal aptitude tests are used in many institutions for placing
students in composition courses, we must take a closer look at them.

The SAT:Verbal and the ACT:English Usage are heavily oriented toward
vocabulary control and error recognition. Many questions ask students to recognize synonyms, antonyms, and matched pairs of words closely related in meaning. Here are some fabricated examples of typical test questions:

Here is a related pair of words, followed by five lettered pairs of words or
phrases. Select the lettered pair that expresses a relationship closest to that
of the original pair.

1. DAZZLE: SHIMMER

(A) bright: dull

(B) confuse: clarify

(C) polish: glisten

(D) glow: gleam

(E) brilliant: tremulous

This question typifies what verbal aptitude tests tend to measure: students' control of a vocabulary available only from written sources. Because many of these words are not commonly used in colloquial speech, because several are rather literary, only well-read students will be able to answer this question; non-readers will be nonplussed by it. The target pair of words describes the production of light; they are descriptions of opposite kinds of radiance. "Dazzle" means to shine directly and brilliantly, while "shimmer" means to shine softly and waveringly. Only E suggests a similar relationship, although between adjectives rather than verbs. A is wrong because what "shimmers" is not "dull"; B is wrong because although "dazzle" may imply brilliance that confuses, "shimmer" does not imply clarification. C is wrong because its predications are logically dissimilar. And D is incorrect because "glow" and "gleam" represent radiances more alike than those suggested in the original pair of verbs.

Other questions require students to recognize violations of standard written English; here's a typical question of this kind:

> Some parts of the following sentence are underlined and lettered. One of these underlined passages may contain an error in grammar, usage, diction, or idiom. Identify the passage that contains the error.
>
>   1   2   3   4
> If I *had known* how much you *wanted* to go roller skating, I *would of let*
>   5
> you *come with us* last night.

The right answer of course is "3," a choice many students might miss, since young writers often use the spoken colloquialism "of" in writing as a substitute for "have." That does not mean they misunderstand the tense itself; it means that "of" seems, to many students unaccustomed to standard written English, an acceptable substitute for "have." And indeed, those same students might think "1" the right choice, under the impression that there ought to be an "of" after "had." "2" might seem right to others who envision a "would of" before "wanted," to match the same conditional in the main clause. This question requires students to sense the difference between the colloquialism of spoken English and the formality of standard written English. Many of the questions are similar: they test awareness of literate prose or sensitivity to *written* language. So do the vocabulary questions; they test students' command of words they will only have seen in writing. Both kinds of questions will tend to detect students who are readers, able to recognize word function within the context of standard written English.

The SAT and the ACT verbal aptitude tests do not include in the error-recognition sections any questions using nonstandard dialect markers as errors. These tests cannot be said, therefore, to discriminate against minority students in any overt way. Yet these students do not score as well, on the average, as other students on these tests. A number of reasons may account for this fact. Minority students may lack familiarity with the vocabulary and idioms of standard English in which the test questions are couched. Students may lack factual knowledge of mainstream culture, from which test questions are drawn. Or perhaps minority students suffer more test anxiety than test-hardened white, middle-class students.[31] In other words, the tests' discriminatory potential derives from the culture reflected in their language and content. To the extent that speakers of Black English, for example, score poorly because of these factors, white culture exerts *de facto* bias through tests. But testing is only one form of such discrimination; the entire educational process discriminates similarly, through the books, lessons, and even the cultural bacgrounds of its teachers educated in standard English. This, of course, is just the situation addressed by both advocates and critics of bidialectalism. Advocates argue that speakers of Black English need to learn standard English in order to surmount cultural discrimination expressed in language. Opponents argue either that a minority dialect is culturally disabling and must be totally set aside; or that the standard dialect is a tyranny which society itself must disavow by fully accepting minority dialects. The problem of bias in verbal aptitude tests is ultimately not a question of language but of cultural forces embodied in language.

To a limited extent the standardized admissions tests measure those variables active in the educational process itself. That is why the test scores and GPA's correlate to a modest degree, although it's impossible to give a categorical name to these variables. Testmakers fudge their descriptions with phrases like "developed ability," "learned responses," and "academic development"; what the real cognitive equivalents of these phrases are no one can say, any more than one can really say what "intelligence" is. By themselves ACT and SAT scores can account for 10 to 20% of the variation in college GPA. Test scores and high school grades together can, at best, account for one-third of GPA variation, according to some studies.[32] The other two-thirds of the factors affecting academic performance are beyond the ability of any test to measure.

Composition teachers might normally be concerned about SAT and ACT scores only to the extent of their interest in academic admissions policies *per se*. But because some colleges and universities use admissions test scores to place or exempt students in writing courses, writing teachers need to understand what such tests can and cannot say about writing ability itself. These tests do not give students an opportunity to write anything. Students who can make accurate choices about sample problems in vocabulary, usage, idiom, and mechanics may not necessarily be able to generate these same choices in the composing process. They may lack the developed ability to structure a series of paragraphs into a discourse. They may create a voice inappropriate to their audience. They may be able to detect illogic in a test question, but they may not be able to generate a coherent series of sentences on a given topic. Any attempt to use standardized verbal aptitude tests to measure writing skill is inappropriate to the real (and limited) purpose of such tests.

There *are* standardized tests designed to measure the ability to manipulate language in sentence or longer contexts. These tests, of which the ETS' CLEP composition tests are a familiar example, are also used for composition placement and exemption; they are far more appropriate to this purpose than are aptitude tests like the SAT and ACT series. Such tests are specifically designed to "avoid items solely devoted to error recognition." Instead, they are said by their designers to "measure students' competency in expository writing skills, following the conventions of standard written English," or to measure the "ability to recognize and apply principles of good writing."[33] That is, they are intended to measure not only the recognition of good writing but the ability to compose it. Certain types of questions occur in these tests that cannot be found in the SAT or ACT:

Questions requiring the building of a sentence from given parts.
    I am an atheist.
    I question the existence of a god.
    I also question the varying forms of religion.
    If you were to combine all the sentences above into one, what is the best way for that sentence to begin?
    A. Because I am an atheist, I question the existence of
    B. The existence of a god and the varying forms
    C. As an atheist, I question both the existence
    D. My being an atheist
    E. Since atheism is my belief, I question

From the test-makers' point of view "C" is the best choice since it most efficiently combines the information of the three base sentences. "A" is wrong because a beginning clause is unnecessary when a phrase will do as well; "B" because it clearly leads nowhere; "D" because the idea of atheism is not the subject here, but the writer's embrace of it; and "E" because the parallel nouns "atheism" and "belief" create needless redundancy.

Questions requiring the analysis of logic and tone at the sentence level.
    Which of the following sentences suggests that the speaker thinks she has improved as a writer?
    A. My English teacher made me do so much writing that I hardly had time to study for other classes.
    B. I worked hard on my writing because I knew I needed more practice than most students.
    C. All the writing I did for my English teacher helped me to understand just how hard it is to write well.
    D. My English teacher liked most of my writing so much she didn't ask me to revise it.
    E. After so much criticism from my English teacher, I don't write papers as carelessly as I used to.

This is a difficult question because it asks students to judge meaning through a combination of tone and factual statement. Choice A is clearly neutral in tone and reveals no value judgment; B suggests the speaker's awareness of her short-comings but not of any improvement; C suggests a gain in understanding but not in writing skill. D sounds self-congratulatory, as though the speaker is convinced she doesn't need to improve. Only E suggests the speaker's genuine sense of growth as a practicing writer.

Questions requiring the ability to perceive and manipulate paragraph structure.
[1] Recent films have set new precedents in explicit anatomical horror. [2] Other films recently have offered their cringing audiences limb amputations by saws, dental surgery with chisels unaccompanied by anesthesia, and mutations of facial features into scarred lumps. [3] The popcorn's not the only thing causing indigestion in theaters these days. [4] One movie offers a blood-spattered close-up of an exploding stomach.
What should be done with sentence 4?
A. It should be left as it is.
B. It should be combined with sentence 2.
C. It should be placed first in the paragraph.
D. It should be placed between sentence 1 and sentence 2.
E. It should be lengthened to include more explicit detail.

This question is intended to test students' ability to perceive structural coherence in a paragraph of a given number of sentences. They must first perceive that the logical pattern of this paragraph moves from the general to the specific back to the general. They are then expected to sense that, first of all, sentence 4 does not belong at the end or the beginning (choices C & A) since those positions should be occupied by generalizations. They are expected to see also that it has enough detail already (Choice E), and that such detail requires that it go with the other detail sentence. That leaves choices B and D; but students are also expected to see that sentence 2 is already long enough, rendering any combination with sentence 4 impracticable. Finally, they are expected to see that the transitional phrase "other films" beginning sentence 2 indicates that sentence 4 has already offered one film example, and should therefore precede sentence 2 (choice D).

Questions like these make the writing ability tests more than just exercises in error recognition (although there are such questions in them). Students must be able to recognize efficient syntax, logical coherence in sentences and paragraphs, nuances of tone and meaning, and from a limited number of options select the most effective rendering of these qualities. Making such choices does not require generating language; it requires the skilled editing of language. We might say, then, that a high score on such multiple-choice tests demonstrates that the student is a capable *editor* of writing.

Editing, of course, is not writing. It is manipulative skill brought into play in what Britton terms the "rule-governed" phases of the composing process, which Britton suggests follow the "non-rule-governed" earlier phases of "conception" and "incubation" (see Chapter I for Britton's model of the composing process). As editors, student test-takers are showing that they can implement the "rules" of syntax, usage, logic, and mechanics which control the actual transfer of meaning from writer to reader. They are not, on multiple-choice tests, able to demonstrate the capacity to select and narrow down a topic, structure paragraphs around specific points within the topic, or develop those paragraphs with ample supporting detail. In recent years test-makers, aware of this gap in their tests' range of evaluation, have added essay questions which students may write on in addition to the multiple-choice questions. These essays are returned to the institution for evaluation, their scores to be combined with those on the multiple-choice section.

But this convenient adjustment leaves a crucial question unanswered: What exactly do *we*, the teachers of writing, want to measure? When we try to judge language ability, do we want to find out primarily how well our students can manipulate given parts of language, or do we want to discover how well they can control the whole writing process, from invention through editing? If we are content to judge their ability to manipulate language, then multiple-choice questions will do the job. But if we want to test students' mastery of the entire writing process, then something more than the manipulation of given parts is required. We can't see what's happening in our student's minds as they compose; nor in a mass testing program will we have the leisure to observe the stages of writing behavior by means of the structured empirical observation used by researchers. What we can insist on is a complete written product—a lengthy piece of writing (not just one or two paragraphs) that represents the breadth of the student's writing process.

An extended writing sample is the most *valid* measure we can get of writing-process mastery. To see why this is so, we need to consider two terms directly related to testing. One is *validity*, the appropriateness of a test to the skill or ability it purports to measure. A writing sample is obviously the most valid measure of whatever the phrase "writing ability" actually denotes; a piece of writing is the only fruit of writing skill. However, judging writing samples is not always a completely reliable process. *Reliability* is the consistency with which the same test will yield similar scores for the same test-takers over successive testings. Reading samples of student writing involves some unpredictable variables. On a given day a student may suffer testing strain, may not think clearly because of fatigue, may not find the topic congenial, or may be trapped in a composing deadend only to discover there is not time to start over. Reliability is also affected by variation in the standards of those evaluating the writing. But there are ways of reducing these differences, as we will see later in this chapter; with such measures, evaluators can make fairly consistent judgments across a wide sprectrum of student writing.

On the whole, extended writing samples are a far more *valid* measure of composing ability than multiple-choice tests, though sometimes less reliable in evaluation than the machine-scored tests. And if a measure of something is not fundamentally valid, no amount of reliability in the testing process can enhance its usefulness. Nor do the standardized scores and percentile ranks offered by national multiple-choice tests give any useful information about the strengths and weaknesses of individual writers or the test-taking population. If they are scored on a particularized scale by institutional readers, writing samples can reveal much about the writers' skills. Even if the samples are scored only by general-impression marking, readers can form judgments about the skills of the test group as a whole. In some large institutions, of course, enough readers to undertake writing-sample evaluation may be hard to find; evaluating large numbers of writing samples requires many hours of exacting, repetitive labor. For this reason many schools find it expedient to use standardized tests. Yet in so doing they yield control over the testing process to the impersonal standardized programs, and lose the advantages institutionally evaluated writing samples can offer. There are methods by which institutional evaluation can be accomplished.

Evaluating Writing for Placement or Exemption

The first step is to establish a setting for administering the writing samples. Since most placement and exemption decisions concern incoming freshmen, some arrangement must be made to require all students to write for the same amount of time, on the same topic (or on very similar topics), under the same conditions, and with the same test instructions. Enough time must be allowed for students to exercise their skills in focusing, organizing, developing supporting detail, styling, and editing. Several paragraphs (300-500 words) are necessary for this purpose, and at least one hour; if true editing and revision are expected, two hours should be allowed. Topics should assume no prior knowledge of a particular subject matter, nor, to be safe, any awareness of current national affairs. The only fair topic, when a display of writing skill is the only measurement goal, is one appealing to general adolescent experience: family relationships, peer relationships, education, or a specific issue calling for an evaluative response which a teen-ager could reasonably be expected to formulate. All students should be told what standards will be used to judge the writing, how it will be judged, and what the consequences of the evaluative process will be.

Two methods of evaluating writing for placement or exemption have emerged as the most workable for writing teachers in schools and colleges. The *general impression* method relies on a scale consisting of numbers—1 through 4, for example—each of which represents a level of writing quality. On a four-point scale a 1 would be given any paper appearing to the rater to belong in the lowest fourth of all papers in the group; a 4 would be given any paper belonging to the highest fourth in the group. What is invoked here is the "holistic" method of evaluation, in which raters read each paper rapidly and make an intuitive judgment about the place of that writing among all similar writings from that particular group of students and that particular writing task. No marks are made on the paper, and raters make their judgments with reference only to the direct, general impact the writing makes upon them. No specific descriptions of characteristics appropriate to each score level are needed; instead, all raters must sit down together and collectivize, or "calibrate" their judgments so that they will consistently give writing samples similar ratings on the basis of intuitive judgment alone. The larger the range in the scoring scale, the finer the discriminations that can be made. If the only purpose in the process is to select students for exemption, a relatively narrow rating scale will suffice. If placement within two or more composition courses is desired, then a wider scale capable of finer discriminations may be needed.

The process of holistic reading requires a very specific procedure:

1.The writing samples should be randomized (alphabetizing them is one way of accomplishing this) so that those turned in early and late in the test period, or those collected from early-morning and late-afternoon test administrations, or those from different classroom sections which may have had some unknown selectivity in their forming are all mixed randomly together. No trend or disproportion within the group being tested should be obvious to raters, since either may cause bias.

2. All raters should be convened in one place and their judgments "calibrated." This requires that a number of writing samples exactly like those about to be read be given to each reader, evaluated individually in terms of the scale to be used, and the results compared and openly discussed. The purpose of this exercise is to enhance reliability in evaluation by reducing differences among readers' standards of judgment. Calibration is a crucial first stage in any holistic reading; without it, the scoring may result in some widely scattered numbers that could moot the results and make the affair a waste of time.

3. After calibration, readers should immediately begin their work. Each sample should be read by two different readers and the scores added or averaged so as to produce a single total score for each student. If two readers diverge too far (more than two points on any scale with four to eight points), a third reading should be given and the closest two readings counted. If all three scores are equidistant then the mid-point of the three should be designated as the score. If there are too many samples to be read in one sitting, each successive reading should be preceded by further calibration to keep readers mindful of collective standards. Readers may want to disperse or take tests home for more convenient reading, but these temptations should be resisted because they can introduce variations of setting and mood into a process whose reliability depends on consistent, unmolested judging.

The other scoring scale appropriate to placement, though not to exemption, is an *analytic scale,* which permits a breakdown of writing elements on each paper. Two kinds of scales may be devised: one that permits only a "yes" or "no" checkoff for each element, and one that requires a numerical rating for each standard. The two-way ("dichotomous") scale might look like this:

	Yes	*No*
Topic clearly focused		
Organization clear and logical		
Generalizations supported with specific or concrete details		
Sentence structure free of awkwardness and errors		
Spelling and punctuation mostly error free		

A numerical scale could be constructed as follows:

	High		Middle		Low
Topical focus	5	4	3	2	1
Organization	5	4	3	2	1
Support for generalizations	5	4	3	2	1
Sentence structure	5	4	3	2	1
Punctuation and spelling	5	4	3	2	1

TOTAL

Although the standards of judgment are spelled out in the analytic scale, there is a need for calibration and joint reading. Still, the benefits of collective reading for all writing teachers in a department—enhanced awareness of common expectations and standards, strengthened confidence in individual judgments—make such readings very desirable. In *Evaluating Writing* (NCTE, 1977) Charles Cooper describes the various purposes and advantages of the methods just described and other less widely used evaluative procedures.

Evaluating Writing for Other Purposes

Writing samples administered for the purpose of diagnosing areas of weakness or strength within a classroom group need not follow all the steps outlined above. But any writing sample (a first-day impromptu, for example) assigned for the purpose of diagnosis should result from a topic students can be expected to handle extemporaneously, and should be evaluated with clear standards in mind. If, for example, reassignment to a remedial class may follow upon the evaluation of an initial impromptu, that sample should allow students to fully demonstrate the skills they do have, and it should elicit the elements of writing that are to be used as a basis for judgment.

When writing samples are used to measure learning progress or the relative efficacy of several teaching approaches, testing procedures must follow specific, well-established guidelines if they are to produce useful information. A group of instructors may, for example, want to compare the writing growth of students in their classes based on certain distinct teaching approaches the instructors have agreed to try. The most important task is to fit the study method to the study goal. Perhaps the effect upon writing growth of two different ways of teaching invention, one "innovative" and the other "traditional," is to be measured, or the effectiveness of two different ways of using grammar in the classroom. An experimental group and a control group should be established, the same instructors teaching one of each if possible, with the experimental group using the "innovative" method and the control group using the "traditional" pedagogy. Comparisons of the writing done by each group of students at the beginning and the end of the semester or quarter (the "pretest" and the "posttest") could provide a means of measuring comparative writing growth. Writing samples, not tests of content knowledge, should be used to measure results, because it's the impact of innovation upon the development of skills that is the measurement goal. We're not interested, for example, in how much grammar each group learns but the effect of different presentations of grammar upon writing behavior. Nor are we interested in how well students learn a particular discovery method, but what effect each method has upon the inventive fullness of student writing.

In other words, the project must minimize the variables we do not want to measure: in the cases just mentioned, differences in student attitudes and ability, variations in instructional settings, and differences among instructors' standards and personalities. The effect of various settings may, in another instance, be measured in terms of *its* impact on student writing; but because that variable is not our present interest, it must be equalized for all students. Suppose we have collected pretests and posttests; how should we proceed? Three different methods of evaluation may be used, two of them already discussed earlier in this chapter; each will provide different information about the writing samples under evaluation. All require two steps essential to trustworthy results: the randomizing and the blind reading of all tests. Tests should be coded and entered on a master sheet so that all scores can be collated and results totaled, and all traces of name, class and other information covered up on the tests themselves. They must then be put into random order to eliminate any pattern discernible to readers. When these steps have been taken, samples may be read by one of these methods:

1. *General Impression* marking, as described earlier, will produce mean pretest and posttest figures for each group, figures that can reveal any mean difference in writing achievement between experimental and control groups. If, for example, the experimental group in the invention project showed an average gain of .7 on a 1-to-4 rating scale, while the control group showed only a .2 mean improvement, that might suggest that the experimental method did result in greater improvement in overall writing achievement than the traditional method. But the general impression method measures only the overall impact the writing makes upon the rater; it does not permit distinctions about organization, development, use of supporting detail, or other features which might be a func-

tion of inventive activity. Nor does it allow the stylistic and syntactic distinctions that might be appropriate to a change in grammar awareness in students.

2. The *analytic scale* could allow readers to mark each element of the writing sample, singling out changes in a specific element. The scale would have to enumerate the various elements of writing in a way that reflected the perceptions of the raters and the goals of the course. With this method the total score could be computed for each separate element and for the whole test, and comparisons made between pretests and posttests.

3. *Primary trait* scoring could be used. This evaluative method, first widely used in the National Assessment of Educational Progress program, is a way of measuring specific "traits" (not the traditional elements of organization, style, and mechanics) seen as desirable in terms of a preconceived rhetorical framework. For example, in the first round of the NAEP writing assessments "Imaginative Expression of Feeling through Inventive Elaboration of a *Point of View*" was designated a primary trait.[34] The main advantage of primary trait scoring is that it allows such things as point of view, voice, and other aspects of rhetorical context usually difficult to define, to be targeted in a testing situation. The disadvantage of primary trait scoring is the complex, time-consuming preparation necessary to its success; lengthy training is necessary to prepare readers to recognize and evaluate the trait(s) being measured. An NCTE publication, *National Assessment and the Teaching of English,* by John C. Mellon, reports on the first round of this nationwide evaluative effort; in the volume *Evaluating Writing* Richard Lloyd-Jones describes the scoring scale and rating methods appropriate to primary-trait scoring.

Strategies for Basic Writers

A corollary to—in some ways a result of—the widespread emphasis on writing measurement has been increased attention to unskilled, or remedial, or "basic" student writers. The social and educational changes noted earlier in this chapter have required schools and universities to develop programs to help inexperienced writers on a systematic and continuous basis. Such programs involve intensive, often individualized instruction in writing and reading standard English. The pressures felt by schools and colleges as they have formed these programs, however, have generated mutual recriminations. College teachers blame secondary teachers for inadequately preparing students, while secondary instructors in turn often accuse elementary teachers of failing to send them literate twelve-year-olds. All teachers join in accusing administrators of failing to support standards of learning and discipline in the classroom; administrators suggest that parents and the community—in the guise of the school board—won't give administrators the money and support needed to run the schools properly. Commentators outside the educational community tend to return the favor by blaming "spineless" administrators and "lazy" teachers: "We, and most especially our educational system, have accepted an anti-language culture. The young do not learn their language simply because they are not taught."[35] No one sees fit to argue that the young are not wasted illiterates; all seek convenient targets, depending on the direction of their self-interest.

Blame implies guilt, which in turn implies responsibility. A rational view of the literacy question, however, suggests that no segment of our society—family, educational institutions, community—has single responsibility for something as complex as literacy. Even if literacy is defined as narrowly as the ability to use standard written English in a school or college setting, it is obviously a function of cultural background, socioeconomic advantage, intensity of preparation, and individual motivation and talent. Although the decline in SAT scores has caused alarm about a "literacy crisis," the small percentage (10 to 20%) of overall college performance actually predicted by the SAT scores suggests that *whatever* the SATs measure (and which has obviously declined) is not crucial in college writing. This university reports enrollment in basic composition up 50% from a few years ago; that college claims more of its students need remediation than ever before. What is usually not advertised is that ten years ago *this* university abolished freshman composition as a way of denying support to politically active teaching assistants, while *that* college ten years ago had no remedial program at all. What *has* changed in education is the *perception* of increased writing problems. And this general public awareness results in part from the pressures created by placing vast, diverse student populations in writing courses in schools and colleges.

Whether in response to new needs or to longstanding ones newly perceived as important, remediation has become a vital part of writing programs in many institutions. And identifying "basic" writing students has become a far more sophisticated and complex process than counting sentence fragments, just as helping such students is now perceived as requiring more than drills on complete sentences and correct punctuation. In the next few pages we'll examine ways in which students with remedial needs may be identified, strategies for answering those needs, and settings and methods for implementing those strategies.

The traditional image of the basic writer centers on the large, unbright athlete laboring with a stubby pencil to form a simple sentence on a crumpled piece of paper, like Thurber's football player who cannot name a common mode of transportation until someone whispers "choo-choo." The equally traditional view of remediation for this student includes requiring him to diagram "The boy and his dog ran up the hill" and write twenty-five times, "A sentence expresses a complete thought and ends with a period." This student and his peers sit together in "bonehead English," herded into the non-credit dungeons of the composition curriculum and taught by an instructor struggling with four sections of the remedial course. Underlying this attitude toward the basic writer is the assumption that such students can't write because they haven't learned "grammar" and because they can't think clearly, since it's self-evident that in order to write well one must think straight. Little is expected from such students and often less is gotten, since (in this view) they come to college with such severe disabilities (the fault of previous teachers) that they cannot realistically be expected to do more than scrape by. The athlete has come because of the athletic pressures at the university, and the minority student because of the open admissions policy.

While such caricatures exaggerate the attitudes of any single institution, they reflect a well-entrenched conviction in academia that remedial students, like the poor, will always be with us, and that institutions should do what they can without hoping for too much. With the coming of open admissions, however, the needs of basic writers have pushed most institutions far beyond the piety of benign neglect. Basic writers in many universities now must be brought to competency in writing because they *are* the student population. Necessity has generated remedial strategies which have gone far beyond earlier attempts at building writing skills.

New remedial strategies differ from the traditional attacks on writing problems by virtue of their attitude toward error. The traditional sentence-and-punctuation-drill strategy assumes that basic writers are those who make more errors than others, and that their improvement requires the correction of errors through repetitive drilling. In this view—behaviorist if you like—writing is a making of choices, some proper and some improper and remediation is the extinction of improper choices through conditioning for proper choices in each writing situation. The cause of errors is not as important as the *fact* of them, which is the point of attack. However, in recent remedial research, inspired by the ESL strategy of error-analysis (see Chapter I) and best represented by Mina Shaughnessy's *Errors and Expectations* (New York: Oxford, 1977), this proposition is reversed. The *cause* of writing errors is more important than the fact of each error, because when teachers discover *why* students make errors, they can help students eliminate habits that cause errors.

As some recent researchers have pointed out, these contrasting views of error reflect the contrast between process and product in writing: instead of simply training basic writers to replace the product errors with "correct" usages in writing, "the composition teacher as error-analyst *investigates* error (to discover how a student arrived at the mistake) and then *applies* these insights."[36] This focus on the conceptual causes of error reflects in yet another way the pervasive influence of cognitive psychology. Psycholinguists argue that since *all* language-making is rule-governed, the making of errors must reflect the same systematic behavior as the making of correct utterances. The most important task of the basic writing teacher, in this view, is to help students define for themselves those concepts, or "rules," which create errors, and which if isolated can be changed to generate better writing patterns.

In this definition, the "basic writer" is one who writes poorly because of inadequate concepts or rules of encoding. Arguing that forming sentences is the basic activity in generating writing, Shaughnessy identifies several categories of erroneous sentence formation, each reflecting a well-meant intention gone wrong. One category she terms "blurred patterns," which includes sentences "that erroneously combine features from several patterns, creating a kind of syntactic dissonance" (49). A second source of errors for Shaughnessy is basic writers' efforts to "consolidate": "that is, to subordinate, syntactically, some elements of an idea or statement to others and to conjoin other elements that are clearly of equal semantic weight" (51). Errors may occur, for example, as students try but fail to join parallel elements in a complete sentence:

> The war in Vietnam was a vast waste of human resources. Also an undeclared war and the United States had no business there.

Here the student is tying to make two judgments (the war as waste and as politically illegitimate) and to connect them both with an ultimate judgment. Sensing that it's inappropriate to link all three propositions in one independent clause, the student chooses to separate the two initial judgments and connect the second with the culminating judgment. This creates what would traditionally be called a sentence fragment; Shaughnessy's "consolidation error" is more accurate because it suggests what the student has actually done—i.e., failed to hold together a series of statements related by a common predicate and an underlying single intention. "Coordinate consolidation" errors include the traditionally-named fragments, nonparallelisms, and run-on sentences (actually often a punctuation misjudgment).

Another major source of error, identified by Shaughnessy as "subordinate consolidations," includes the traditional dangling and squinting modifiers, pronoun reference, and faulty subordination. For example:

> These men left the country of their own accord which I think they should have to face the consequences.

Here the *which* links what is essentially a cause-and-effect sequence (because they left . . . they should have . . .), as the student attempts to yoke the cause to the effect with a relative pronoun which cannot provide the desired connection. A traditional diagnosis of this sentence might result in a marginal "coh" for "coherence," or perhaps a "ref" with the *which* underlined in hopes of making the student see where the connection breaks. Neither emendation would help the student, of course; Shaughnessy's description helps us see that what the student needs is an explanation of why the chosen form of subordination does not suffice. Although Shaughnessy identifies other varieties of syntactical errors, they do not differ markedly in the examples she offers from the major "consolidation" errors listed above.

Of central interest in Shaughnessy's book is her profile of the basic writer. Her three "causes of syntactic errors" offer a convincing characterization of this kind of writer. First, says Shaughnessy, basic writers lack the "command of the language" needed to "bring off the consolidations that are called for in writing" (73). This formulation embodies a radically nontraditional understanding of error-prone student writers. They are not, in this view, careless and lazy scofflaws with sentences, but well-intentioned learners struggling to make inadequate sentence strategies bear the weight of complex perceptions. Part of their difficulty is a lack of vocabulary control; they often do "not know the word that would enable [them] to consolidate" sentences (76), or they do not know the appropriate "grammatical form" of the word required by the syntax. Second, continues Shaughnessy, such students do "not know how writers behave" (79). In this assertion we can see again the influence of recent interpretations of mental processes in writing, particularly in the composing process which, she claims, basic writers cannot control because they do not understand it. Unless students understand how to develop ideas, organize them at discourse, paragraph, and sentence levels, and, most importantly, shape them for others' eyes, they will continue to produce ineffective, error-laden work. Especially important to Shaughnessy is the basic writer's need for a sense of audience, the capacity to create "reader-based prose."[37] The third characteristic of the basic writer, in Shaughnessy's view, is "that the student lacks confidence in himself" and fears writing as exposure (85). "Writing anxiety" has been shown in several studies to have a distinctly dampening effect upon the production of well-developed and well-edited writing; Shaughnessy suggests that such anxiety is not just an incidental problem of basic writers, but is a central, disabling trait in them.[38]

A significant number of remedial writers are minorities accustomed to black or Hispanic dialects, who must alter their oral dialects into the forms of standard written English. As we saw earlier in this chapter, however, often only a minor part of these students' writing difficulties is dialect-related; most of their errors result from problems in sentence formation and vocabulary. Thus, dialect-using basic writers bring a special pedagogical challenge: motivation. Helping these students learn standard English requires teachers who can make them *want* to learn unfamiliar usages and idioms. Students nurtured in minority dialects will be prone to see school and college not as enhancement of their own basic language skills, but as an intimidating, unfair struggle to meet arbitrary standards. This challenge to composition teachers has produced a wide range of instructional responses.

The most common method of writing remediation is based on the alteration of the usual settings for writing instruction. The most common settings for remediation—the writing lab and the small (usually fifteen or fewer) remedial class—both represent efforts to isolate and individualize basic writing instruction. Yet institutional decisions to single out basic writers in individualized settings have been based more upon writing teachers' instincts than upon proven differences in results between individual settings and traditional classroom instruction. Relatively few studies have compared, for example, the results of writing laboratory instruction with those of classroom remedial efforts. One study early in the history of large-scale remediation compared multiple-choice test performances (not writing samples) of students in classroom and laboratory settings: "the experimental group [writing laboratory students]," it reports, "showed statistically significant change as measured before and after instruction on vocabulary, mechanics, grammar, controlled composition, and free composition."[39] This study showed students in regular composition classrooms performing about as well as writing lab students in mechanics, but much less well on vocabulary, syntax, and organization, as measured by multiple-choice tests. A more recent study (which also avoided writing samples as the means of measurement) used grade-point average comparisons to conclude that "the highly individualized instructional methodology employed in the Writing Laboratory had a significantly beneficial effect upon the future English grades of students," and a positive relationship with "overall grade-point average."[40] What neither of these studies measures is whether individualized laboratory experience helps basic writers produce better *writing*, as compared with more traditional classroom approaches. Nor does either study measure what may be the most important consequence of individualized settings: the enhancement of students' self-confidence as writers and as learners in general. These attitudinal changes derive from several important advantages for basic writers of the individualized laboratory approach.

The frequent contacts between student and instructor in the laboratory arrangement can give students feedback on all stages of the composing process. Whereas in most composition classes students get feedback on their writing only when final drafts are submitted (when that feedback is mostly evaluative rather than advisory), in writing labs students may get instruction on each stage of composition. Teacher intervention throughout the composing process helps clarify that process for basic writers, addressing precisely that need for understanding "how writers behave" which Shaughnessy identifies as characteristic of basic writers. Writing labs also provide a noncompetitive atmosphere important for those students suffering from writing anxiety. Shaughnessy's diagnosis of the basic writer's "fears that writing will not only expose but magnify his inadequacies" (85) suggests that poor writers fear not only the writing process, but the intellectual inadequacies which their writing may reveal.

Remedial methodology reflects the same division between process and product that characterizes composition pedagogy in general. Whether it's conducted in classrooms or in writing labs, the product-oriented approach tends to emphasize what are usually referred to as "basic" or "fundamental" writing skills. This normally entails a workbook-based, mastery-learning sequence of lessons that in most texts begins with the study of parts of speech and sentence elements, continues with work on simple, compound, and complex sentences, and includes many drills in error recognition and sentence analysis. Most such texts also cover spelling and punctuation along with drills to drive home these formal mechanics. The emphasis on sentence formation and mechanical control marks the product-oriented view that what basic writers most need to learn is "correctness" of expression at the sentence level before they are challenged with larger prose units. The majority of basic writing texts devote their space to sentence elements, usage, and mechanics; in most, paragraph-length or longer discourse gets little coverage, and the composing process itself almost none. This emphasis upon sentence-making and punctuation forces basic writers to labor almost entirely with discrete, a-rhetorical writing tasks. Such an approach is frequently defended as necessary if students are to learn to write error-free prose.

Yet especially for unskilled writers, language is not a set of pieces they are anxious to assemble more effectively. It's an open process of meaning-making, significant to them *only* as it has relevance to their struggle to communicate experience. If basic writers are limited to workbook drills, their experience will be "streaked with reductive and discontinuous qualities that cancel the promise of the students' own full literacy."[41] The piecework approach may seriously underestimate the capacity of basic writers, for as Shaughnessy points out, it's not their experience or intelligence but their language inadequacies that separate them from their more competent peers. "Writing," she says, "is not simply the sum of a number of discrete skills but an expanding work of competencies that interact and collide and finally merge" (289). In recent years, a number of techniques have been developed for improving the composing (as opposed to the editing) skills of basic writers and their ability to structure sustained writing even as they learn to master basic elements of syntax and usage.

Perhaps the common denominator of process-oriented techniques is their reliance upon sensory experience as the stimulus for basic writers. As one proposal suggests, basic writing students usually fail to grasp the difference between abstraction and concreteness in language: "our students had lost their 'ability to look at the world directly,' " and could not see that language "often forced them to look at the world through the veil of overly generalized concepts."[42] This proposal recommends such writing exercises as "Happenings," in which students concentrate on some immediate sensory experience while composing journal entries. Another basic writing instructor suggests the use of a very concrete personal experience, narrated in one paragraph, as a way of applying "sensory language to real experience" in a controlled rhetorical framework.[43] Another instructor, urging that "the image as stimulus" is "the sole kind [of experience] effective on the basic writing level," suggests writing exercises based on uncaptioned cartoons or other visual material.[44] Students first write a descriptive paragraph in simple sentences, then revise it into compound sentences, and finally work it into complex sentences with appropriate devices for coherence and transitions. This process offers several pedagogical advantages over workbook drill methods: it requires invention from students, it paces them through a hierachy of syntactical structures, and it requires them to develop a rhetorical framework within which these sentence-making skills are exercised. One disadvantage is the arbitrariness of a staged sequence from simple to complex sentences; students may be led to conclude from such exercises that subordinate structures are "better" than simple or coordinate syntax.

Still another—but often over-used—remedial method is sentence combining. Shaughnessy defends it as "perhaps the closest thing to finger exercises for the inexperienced writer" (77). But as we discovered in Chapter II, sentence combining is only a sophisticated type of a-rhetorical drill that does not engage the crucial inventive and organizational phases of composing. Andrea Lunsford proposes a type of sentence exercise that she argues engages both analytic and synthesizing efforts.[45] Students should first be asked to combine given kernels into specified patterns, then to put their own kernels into patterns which imitate the originals, and then to generate each pattern themselves. She also advocates assignments that build "inferential reasoning" by asking students to compose a paragraph or longer discourse from a list of "data" from which students must infer generalizations that will, in turn, provide the organizational framework for inclusion of the original information. These techniques have the advantage of creating rhetorical contexts within which students must devise tone, voice, and a consistent pattern of meaning for an audience.

It's often difficult for instructors to determine which students need remediation badly enough to warrant placing them in remedial courses, which may not carry credit and are taken before the regular composition requirement. The evaluative strategies described earlier in this chapter will diagnose obvious remedial needs. But often student writers need remediation only in specific areas; some will be able to organize and develop writing but will lack mechanical skills, while others may write error-free prose but be unable to organize coherent paragraphs or develop and support chosen topics. In establishing a successful remedial program, then, instructors must agree on what consitutes remedial need in their school or college. They must define competence and incompetence in the context of their own program and the writing challenges students will face in other parts of the curriculum. And, of course, they must accept the unavoidable responsibility of the writing teacher to deal individually with many kinds of remedial needs. Only in this way can students with specific but not overwhelming difficulties make progress within the regular writing courses which provide the foundation for a liberal education.

Notes

[1] *Digest of Educational Statistics* (Washington, DC: National Center for Educational Statistics, 1975), p. 14.

[2] *Digest of Educational Statistics,* 1975, p. 14.

[3] Hunter M. Breland, *The SAT Score Decline: A Summary of Related Research.* (Princeton, NJ: Educational Testing Service, 1976), p. 19.

[4] Walt Wolfram and Ralph Fasold, *The Study of Social Dialects in American English* (Englewood Cliffs, NJ: Prentice-Hall, 1974), p. 21.

[5] Frederick Williams, ed., *Language and Poverty,* Institute for Research on Poverty Monograph Series (Chicago: Markham Publishing Co., 1970), p. 7

[6] *Change,* "The Decline of the SAT's" (November 1972), p. 17.

[7] *Change,* November 1976; *Des Moines Register,* August 1, 1976, 2B; *Newsweek,* Dec. 8, 1975, p. 57.

[8] *On Further Examination: Report of the Advisory Panel on the SAT Score Decline* (New York: College Entrance Examination Board, 1977), pp. 44-8.

[9] "Memo to the Members," CEEB, June 1980, p. 1.

[10] *The Reign of ETS: The Corporation That Makes Up Minds,* Allen Nairn and Associates (Ralph Nader Report, 1980), p. 219.

[11] *On Further Examination,* p. 15.

[12] See *Digest of Educational Statistics* (1975), p. 14; and Christopher Jencks, et al., *Inequality: The Reassessment of the Effect of Family and Schooling in America* (New York: Basic Books, 1972), pp. 77-78.

[13] Jencks, p. 83.

[14] Basil Bernstein, *Class, Codes and Control: Theoretical Studies Towards a Sociology of Language* (London: Routledge and Kegan Paul, 1971), p. 1.

[15] See, for example, Diana Davis, "Language and Social Class: Conflict with Established Theory," *Research in the Teaching of English,* 11(Winter 1977), 207-17.

[16] Jean Malmstrom, "Dialects—Updated," *Black Language Reader,* ed. Robert Bentley and Samuel Crawford (Glenview, IL: Scott, Foresman, 1973), p. 13.

[17] For fuller descriptions of Black English see Joan Baratz, "The Language of the Ghetto Child," in *Black Language Reader;* William Labov, "Language Characteristics: Blacks," in *Reading for the Disadvantaged,* ed. Thomas D. Horn (New York: Harcourt Brace Jovanovich, 1970); and J. L. Dillard, *Black English: Its History and Usage in the United States* (New York: Random House, 1972).

[18] Wolfram and Fasold, p. 15.

[19] Wolfram and Fasold, p. 181.

[20] Dwight Bolinger, *Aspects of Language* (New York: Harcourt Brace Jovanovich, 1968), excerpted in *Reading and Writing About Language,* ed. Stephen Tollefson and Kimberly S. Davis (Belmont, CA: Wadsworth Publishing Company, 1980), p. 166.

[21] J. Mitchell Morse, "The Shuffling Speech of Slavery: Black English," *The Irrelevant English Teacher* (Philadelphia: Temple University Press, 1972), as excerpted in *Exploring Language,* ed. Gary Goshgarian (Boston: Little, Brown, 1980), p. 276.

[22] Wayne O'Neil, "The Politics of Bidialectalism," *The Politics of Literature,* ed. Louis Kampf and Paul Lauter (New York: Random House, 1972), as excerpted in *Black Language Reader,* p. 190.

[23] James Sledd, "Doublespeak: Dialectology in the Service of Big Brother," *CE,* 33(January 1972), p. 454.

[24] See the above articles by Labov and Baratz, for example.

[25] E. D. Hirsch, *The Philosophy of Composition* (Chicago: The University of Chicago Press, 1977), p. 44.

[26] "Students' Right," p. 8. See Appendix B for partial text.

[27] Wolfram and Fasold, p. 6.

[28] Roderick Jacobs and Peter Rosenbaum, *Transformations, Style, and Meaning* (Waltham, MA: Xerox, 1971), p. 20

[29] William Labov, *The Study of Nonstandard English* (Urbana, IL: NCTE, 1977), p. 40.

[30] This is the strategy recommended by Wolfram and Fasold, p. 205.

[31] Nairn, *The Reign of ETS*, pp. 113-117.

[32] "Memo to the Members," CEEB, February 1980, p. 3.

[33] These specifications appear in the following ETS publications: "Announcing a New CLEP General Examination in English Composition," ETS, 1977, p. 5; and "CLEP General and Subject Examinations," ETS, 1979, p. 58.

[34] Richard Lloyd-Jones, "Primary Trait Scoring," in Charles R. Cooper and Lee Odell, *Evaluating Writing* (Urbana, IL: NCTE, 1977), p. 48.

[35] Vermont Royster, "Cheating Our Young Out of the Tools of Thought," *Des Moines Register*, December 22, 1974, p. 28.

[36] Barry M. Kroll and John C. Shafer, "Error-Analysis and the Teaching of Composition," *CCC*, 29(October 1978), 244.

[37] In "Writer-Based Prose: A Cognitive Basis for Problems in Writing," *CE*, 41(September 1979), 19-37, Linda Flower argues that poor or inexperienced writers often produce "writer-based prose," which lacks acceptability specifically because these writers cannot envision an audience.

[38] See, for example, J. A. Daly, "The Empirical Development of an Instrument to Measure Writing Comprehension," *Research in the Teaching of English*, 9(1975), 242-48; also J. A. Daly and W. Shamo, "Academic Decisions as a Function of Writing Apprehension," *RTE*, 12(1978), 119-26.

[39] Roy C. Maize, "Two Methods of Teaching English Composition to Retarded College Freshmen," *Journal of Educational Psychology*, 45, (1954), 28.

[40] Doris Sutton and Daniel Arnold, "The Effects of Two Methods of Compensatory Freshman English," *RTE*, 8(Fall 1974), 248.

[41] Lewis Meyers, "Texts and Teaching: Basic Writing," *CE*, 39(April 1978), 929.

[42] Michael Paul and Jack Kligerman, "Invention, Composition, and the Urban College," *CE*, 33(March 1972), 652.

[43] Harvey Wiener, "The Single Narrative Paragraph and College Remediation," *CE*, 33(March 1972), reprinted in Ohmann, *Ideas for English 101*, p. 175.

[44] Meyers, p. 930.

[45] Andrea Lunsford, "Cognitive Development and the Basic Writer," *CE*, 41(September 1979), 41.

Chapter IV
PLANNING THE COURSE
Six Key Questions

Planning next semester's writing courses often sends writing teachers into uneasy—if not agonizing—reappraisals. Have the texts really been useful? Have students used them, or merely lugged them around, to be dumped at the bookstore for a fraction of their cost at semester's end? And was it really necessary to assign all that writing this semester? Wouldn't students have improved just as much (or little) with less writing, and less work for the instructor? Should so much time be spent talking about dangling modifiers when as many modifiers dangle in the last piece of writing as in the first? Incompleteness haunts writing courses. Nothing ever seems really finished at the end of the semester; for every student who shows remarkable improvement there is one who doesn't seem to have gained any skill in writing, despite papers dutifully done and returned. Students often despair of improving their writing when in paper after paper the instructor seems to find difficulties—sometimes the same ones, but often new ones as old ones are resolved. And teachers find equal cause for despair when despite their hours of labor and their faith in a foolproof text, many students do not appear to have improved their writing and vent their frustration in their evaluation sheets.

We saw in Chapter I that writing is an "open" capacity, always susceptible to change and difficult to evaluate at a given moment. It's not surprising, therefore, that teaching writing can be as frustrating as attempting to learn it. For just as learners continually discover new aspects of writing that require mastery, so teachers find that an appealing, innovative strategy may convey only part of what students must learn. New texts, incorporating even the most recent developments in composition theory and touted as the final solution to teachers' needs, often lose their appeal for students and teachers by semester's end because they seem, after all, not to provide all the answers—or even some of the necessary ones. Indeed, because writing *is* so open a capacity, the more a text focuses on one central strategy the less satisfactory it usually proves to be. An unfortunate consequence of such misdirection for teachers can be a pervasive cynicism. When nothing really seems to work well, why should we continue trying to discover more effective teaching strategies? Wearied by this prospect, most teachers planning for next semester are tempted to recycle their present course plan and allow custom to triumph.

Just because writing is an open capacity, however, and teaching it may produce indeterminate results, we must not be seduced into the comfortable fiction that what we do as teachers doesn't really matter. Just *because* teaching writing is frustrating and ambiguous, teachers must clarify for themselves what they expect from the methods they use, and just how they want to use them. The best defense against terminal cynicism is hard consideration of what may be expected of students and what strategies may best serve those expectations: in a word, planning. Such planning must begin with an understanding of some basic issues in structuring and administering a writing course.

The Issues

If the composition discipline today agrees on one thing, it is that writing teachers must be prepared to teach students *how to compose.* As we have seen in earlier chapters, the influences of psychology and linguistics have helped the composition discipline realize that it's not possible to "teach" the written product; teachers cannot make the writing itself better. Teachers *can* help students discover how to generate and revise writing, and how to edit it "up to code." However, we have seen that far too much energy has traditionally been spent on grammar drills and editing, when these elements of writing are secondary and tertiary effects rather than primary causes of good writing. We have seen that far too little attention has been paid to teaching students the nature of writing as a process, so that they can learn to exploit it. The models of composing described in Chapter I offer useful resources for teachers seeking insight into writing behavior. We need now to consider how, in Joseph Comprone's words, we can make writing "intrinsically related to a student's habits of perceiving, thinking, and expressing."[1] Teaching the whole language-shaping process must be the primary goal of writing teachers.

The difference between understanding language processes and just knowing language facts is the difference between "knowing how" and "knowing that." In the course of critiquing "Descartes' myth" of the dualism of mind and body, philosopher Gilbert Ryle argues that in actual human experience "the styles and procedures of people's activities *are* the way their minds work and are not merely imperfect reflections of the postulated secret processes which were supposed to be the workings of minds."[2] "Knowing that" and "knowing how" are two different kinds of knowledge, not antecedent and consequence. "Learning *that*" is "acquiring information," becoming "apprised of a truth"; "learning *how*" is "improving in ability," or "getting trained in a procedure" (59). These two capacities are both exercises of intelligence, but are not associated in a simple cause-and-effect fashion. "The intelligent reasoner . . . avoids fallacies and produces valid proofs and inferences," but "he probably observes the rules of logic without thinking about them" (48). To illustrate, Ryle resorts to analogies bearing relevance to writing:

> It would be quite possible for a boy to learn chess without ever hearing or reading the rules at all. By watching the moves made by others and by noticing which of his own moves were conceded and which were rejected, he could pick up the art of playing correctly while still quite unable to propound the regulations. . . . His knowledge *how* is exercised primarily in the moves that he avoids or vetoes. So long as he can observe the rules, we do not care if he cannot also formulate them. . . . Similarly a foreign scholar might not know how to speak grammatical English as well as an English child, for all that he had mastered was the theory of English grammar (41).

Ryle argues that "knowing *how*" is knowledge which manifests itself in a result, while "knowing *that*" is knowledge on an abstract level. "The execution of intelligent performances [knowing how] " does not necessarily "entail the additional execution of intellectual operations [knowing that,] " for "the intelligence in-

This distinction helps us see the purposelessness of much of the teaching of

volved in putting prescriptions into practice is not identical with that involved in intellectually grasping the prescription" (49). Both modes of knowing are processes of comprehension. While "knowing how" is measured by observable behavior and its products, "knowing that" is pure cognition.

language facts—"grammar"—in the schools. Linguist Martin Steinmann applies to writing pedagogy the transformationalists' distinction between *competence* (a native speaker's intuitive grasp of the rules of his language) and *performance* (the speaker's actual use of these rules in discourse). If, Steinmann suggests, a student learns to write more effectively by developing more skills, he may be said to hold knowledge in the sense that "he knows *how* to do something"; if "he possesses . . . a theory (of grammar and semantics) explaining exercise of a certain ability (speaking the language)," then "he has knowledge because he knows *that* something is the cause."[3] Learning to write is a matter of discovering how to do something; writing is an activity, not a set of ideas or a mass of information. That is why workbook drills on language facts serve no real purpose. Unlike math drills that help build computational skills, language-fact exercises do not contribute to a larger set of behaviors. Knowing compound-complex sentences and parts of speech does not enhance the ability to make sentences.

Grammar facts are abstractions, in "traditional grammar" categories of word function and type. Talking and writing are dynamic processes of language-making flowing from an innate competence that has no necessary relation to factual knowledge about language. It's for this reason that writing evaluation is usually shielded by warnings about intangibles and hidden variables. If writing skill were responsive to the writer's knowledge of language facts, then teaching and measuring writing would be far easier than they are. Yet English teachers have traditionally required as much "knowing that" as "knowing how" from students. Writing handbooks usually contain long enumerations of the rules of English syntax, standard usage and punctuation, and frequently, language history. Writing is often taught as though it were a matter of learning *that* certain facts of English syntax exist: that a clause has a noun and a verb, that adverbs are those words modifying verbs and modifiers, that parallel structures must be consistent. "Correct" writing is cited as the students' goal in learning that certain words, phrases, inflections and punctuation marks are "wrong," and that certain others are "right."

The ill-fated enthusiasm given transformational grammar by school-curriculum planners in the 1960s exemplifies this misguided emphasis. When transformational grammar first became known to educators, it was welcomed as a way of revolutionizing the teaching of writing. Many text-makers and teachers felt that for the first time a grammar theory had emerged that if taught to students could help them generate good sentences. But first the new theory had to be taught; and students were confronted with the spectacle of apparently simple sentences fragmented into baffling branching-tree diagrams:

The boy hit the ball.

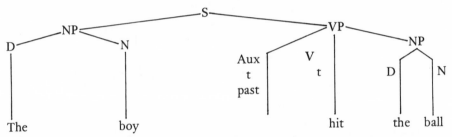

This information had to be learned as fact; little attention was paid to its usefulness in helping students write better. Many classrooms became battlefields in which both sides, teachers and students, surrendered in the face of their common enemy, leaving transformational grammar in possession of the field. Knowing *that* did not lead to knowing *how*. But the lure of "grammar" remains seductively strong for writing teachers fond of drilling students in language facts. What Ann Berthoff calls the "drill-for-skill" approach still pervades many upper elementary and junior high language arts texts. Later in this chapter we will see that grammar knowledge has only one specific justification in the writing classroom: it permits communication about style. Beyond this benefit, knowing grammar gives nothing more; it does not help students learn to invent, organize, or revise their writing more effectively.

Writing teachers must not only decide how much know-how and know-that they want to teach, they must also clarify for themselves the purposes for which writing instruction is valued in their institution. We can simplify this often ambiguous problem by dividing academic writing rather arbitrarily into two types: personal writing, exploring students' own experiences of the world (writing that occurs mostly in English courses), and the academic version of what Britton calls "transactional" writing, composed of all the papers, reports, and tests required for coursework. The personal uses of writing have been strongly advocated by participants in the Dartmouth Conference of the mid-1960s and those influenced by the Conference reports. The NCTE, for example, has urged that using language "can help students live more fully" by enabling them to "interpret, enjoy, and in part create" their worlds.[4] Participants in the Dartmouth Conference urged that drama, group interaction, and classroom writing should all be combined in writing classes in order to help students to "a new investment in the experience of writing, and a correspondingly original and personal vision." [5] But because such writing does not usually fit the purposes of academic work outside the English department, critics have opposed it as irrelevant and even dysfunctional at the college level. One critic suggests that its intensity and privateness cannot be matched in other writing tasks outside English courses, and consequently it creates false expectations for some students. When the "personal" is made to seem "more real than the objective," or the "reminiscence" more valid than the conjecture, students are ill-served, it is said.[6]

Britton and others have argued in response that topics drawn from personal experience confer value upon the act of writing for anxious and inexperienced writers. Inexperienced writers are often weak readers. If they are asked to write on a topic drawn from an anthologized essay or some other source outside personal experience (especially in a freshman-level course), the need to digest and respond to strange material compounds the student's difficulties. Inexperienced writers in particular must begin by learning *how* to compose; the forms and topics of personal writing lend themselves to this purpose. Writing anxiety is most acute in poor writers, as Mina Shaughnessy points out: the student needing remediation "lacks confidence in himself in academic situations and fears that writing will not only expose but magnify his inadequacies."[7] Particularly for these students, personal writing requiring narrative and descriptive patterns offers apprehensive writers the readiest starting point.

Unfortunately, faculty in other disciplines tend to regard personal writing as typical of "English"—the study of "flowery" writing on impractical, often literary subject matter. Such an attitude is understandable among teachers in the physical or social sciences, who traffic in "hard" knowledge empirically derived from "real" things in human life—the nature of matter, the composition of social groups, the observable behavior of human beings. Many of these instructors are convinced that writing in composition courses ought to deal in "real things." They wonder what use could come from a description of a night ride on an Alpine tramway or a narrative of a disagreement over a roommate's insistence on listening to the radio until 3 a.m. They wonder why students should be encouraged to write on such "frivolous" topics when there are so many "substantive" topics that will be required of them: historical or current events, descriptions and analyses of scientific experiments, or critiques of articles and books.

These "substantive things" make up what Britton calls "transactional writing"
—the bulk of academic (and "real-world") writing. Discourse aimed outside
the writer's personal experience comprises the major part of academic writing.
One textbook used by several generations of college students typifies the transactional orientation of many composition texts. In *Modern Rhetoric*, first published in 1949, Cleanth Brooks and Robert Penn Warren assert the purpose of
college writing: "Consider for a moment the college career before you," they
urge the student; "most of the instruction will be in language and you will be
required to respond in language."[8] They enumerate the essays and exams students will have to write, and urge that "once we start putting into words an
explanation—or an argument or an account of an event—we have to organize
the material in a way that will be readily understood by others" (3). The prose
anthology that accompanies the text is replete with descriptions, analyses, and
arguments focusing on academic topics, subject matter likely to be encountered
in political science, philosophy, psychology and the like.

Writing of this sort asks students not to inquire into their personal worlds,
but to put those worlds aside in favor of new ideas and information gleaned
from texts and lectures. Transactional writing requires the submission of the self
to the not-self, that body of thought and experience which society traditionally
posits as the content of formal education. Students' obligation to write pur-
posefully for academic assignments is reflected in the charge given students in
one recent text, which lists several writing goals for the "student-citizen,"
including writing papers for other classes, letters to the editor, and committee
reports.[9] According to a survey in one large American university, the three
writing tasks students most often face are essay questions on exams, research
papers, and short-answer tests.[10] In none of these forms of writing are students
permitted to explore their own purposes. Rather, in such writing students must
perform both types of knowing simultaneously: knowing that and knowing how.
To answer essay test questions or put together a research paper, students must
demonstrate knowing *how* to organize and present new ideas and information,
just as they are struggling to control such material cognitively—knowing *that* it
is so. The traditional library research paper is the best example of this, requiring
students to master the processes of collecting, analyzing, and documenting
information, as well as the process of composing it into a coherent report. The
typical composition course has the unenviable task of teaching both personal and
transactional writing to students of widely divergent abilities. As we will see,
a carefully planned syllabus must try to integrate these purposes and keep the
fault lines between them from serious fractures.

Some Planning Questions

We don't buy a garden spade if we plan to lay a brick wall, or get a mason's
trowel if we intend to plant shrubs. Nor do we buy texts before we decide what
kind of writing course we're going to teach. Contrary to the urgent petitions

of the book salespeople, many of them former English majors, composition texts cannot shape a course, despite their authoritative tone. Instructors must choose the kind of course to be taught; choosing a text first and trying to organize a course around it is like trying to eat soup in a straightjacket. Deciding the purpose and structure of the course, preparing materials, and devising appropriate teaching strategies are the first priorities in planning. The following questions will help teachers think about these points:

1. What are the purposes of the course?
2. What kinds of writing assignments should I set?
3. How much emphasis should I give to deliberately planned and revised writing? How much to spontaneous, impromptu writing?
4. How much should I try to teach about language itself? Should students know the terms and rules of grammar? What grammar?
5. Should I use an anthology or other outside source of writing in addition to students' own work in the course?
6. What kind of pacing should the assignments follow? How much writing should I require and how often?

These questions, which are by no means exhaustive, will help teachers discover the *what* of their course—its content and pattern. They are not aimed at the *how* of the course, its dynamics; the relative advantages of one-on-one, small-group and whole-class strategies, discussion methods, and evaluation strategies will be discussed in the next chapter. And even if the individual writing teacher must plan the course as part of a controlling general syllabus, there remain many choices that only the instructor can make. The discussion that follows is directed primarily towards those choices governed by the needs of the students and the teachers' own preferences.

1. What are the purposes of the course?

The most frequent demand made of writing teachers is that they produce students able to write adequately for other courses. It's never put so baldly in curriculum guidelines or college catalogs, which tend to grandiosities like "the importance of communication in human culture" or "the necessity for clarity in our thoughts and actions." But parents, administrators, other faculty, and employers all expect English teachers to give students skills fitted to their own respective preferences. Parents expect students to be able to write letters to grandparents; administrators expect them to score well on language tests; other faculty expect them to write coherent exams and reports; and employers expect them to enter the company ready to dash off letters, memos, and reports. Whether they are asked to write on the causes of the Civil War, the beauties of grandma's birthday gift, or the superiority of their employer's product, transactional writing will offer the most frequent challenge to students' immediate and future writing skills. And while they are still in school, the connecting of facts and ideas on essay tests, research papers, and reports will be their main writing chore in non-English courses. Comparing and contrasting, analyzing and synthesizing, relating the specific to the general—skills that make it possible to learn and communicate course content—will be essential to the academic uses of writing.

But as we have seen, personal writing does not exclude these cognitive skills, and it brings one crucial benefit as well: it requires students to write about their own experience within a universe of discourse larger than the family. That is, it offers student writers the chance to explore familiar experience under the expectation of a discriminating audience capable of genuinely educative feedback. This does not mean that students will necessarily discover their true aspirations and change their lives because they must write discriminatingly about their own experience. It does mean that they will take the act of writing about themselves more seriously because they perceive that others will—indeed are obliged to by the nature of the course context. And taking writing seriously is the first step in the student writer's discovery that writing is purposeful human activity, not just academic labor. Personal writing subjected to serious inquiry and feedback will take on value for writers themselves, as a reflection of its value for others. Causing writing about personal experience to take on reflexive significance for students can, in turn, give unique significance to that experience.

It's difficult to separate personal and transactional values in any given assignment, since some personal awareness may grow out of any writing task, in addition to an understanding of its transactional function. If writing assignments appear as just another sort of homework to satisfy a teacher, then that assignment has neither personal nor transactional meaning for the student. Thus, no writing task should be rejected because it does not appear to serve a practical purpose for students' future writing needs. For example, teachers may want to assign journals in addition to other writing tasks, but may hesitate because journals appear to serve only the personal writing goals in a curriculum that emphasizes practical writing purposes. But journals may well seem to students the most interesting, personally engaging kind of writing asked of them. Writing journals, may, in other words, bring home to students the power of discourse to clarify feelings and thoughts—power that gives writing a significance no merely practical purpose can confer. And their discovery of writing's power in a personal context may carry over into more routine transactional tasks. Any writing task that can help students discover writing as a way of giving meaning to experience automatically legitimizes itself. Even in the most practical kind of writing course, personal writing can be integrated with transactional work to give student writers the feel of significant discourse.

2. What kinds of writing assignments should I set?

Making up writing assignments is the most important part of planning a writing course. Writing assignments determine the way in which students will perceive the course, the amount and seriousness of their labor, and the attitude toward writing they will carry into their work. We have already seen in Chapter II that small-scale, a-rhetorical writing tasks—sentence-combining problems, paragraph exercises, error-correction exercises—can easily fill up class time and be assigned as homework. But students tend to perceive such labor, however useful for literacy skills, as makework, typical "English course" activity. For where outside the writing classroom do we combine sentence kernels, correct a list of twenty sentence errors, or rearrange paragraphs? Indeed, a major reason why students do not write effectively, or regard writing as serious work, is that they have seldom been asked to *do* genuine writing in school. They have filled in countless workbooks, written out spelling and definition lists, and diagrammed endless sentences. But they have not done much writing. Here is where writing teachers who want to make a difference in students' lives can do so: they can build a sequence of significant writing assignments, and help students see, perhaps for the first time, that writing is essential human activity.

The basis of a good writing course is a series of purposeful writing tasks. This series can be organized in several ways: for example, by means of the writer's logical processes, or in terms of a sequence of topics, or as a sequence of different rhetorical situations. The best assignment sequence will bring together subject matter, writing purpose, and audience in clearly defined writing situations. For inexperienced writers, the invention and organization of the subject matter are the first concerns, before the consideration of specific audience strategies. Such writers must first discover *what* they have to say about a topic, before they are able to envision *how* they can adjust their styles to different audiences. That's why inexperienced writers often produce what Linda Flower calls "writer-based prose," writing which primarily reflects the writers' attempts to master the material. Teachers must expect organizational and stylistic problems in the early efforts of such students; students must first learn how to use the composing process fully to focus and develop their topics before they can begin to adapt style and tone to specific audiences. The backbone of an effective writing course, therefore, must be a carefully planned sequence of tasks set in gradually broader and more complex contexts.

Composing is thinking, argues Ann Berthoff: "thinking is a matter of seeing relationships—relationships of parts to wholes, of items in a sequence, of causes and effects; composition is a matter of seeing and naming relationships, of putting the relationships together, ordering them."[11] These movements of connecting and ordering represent the mind in the act of creating levels of generality, expressed in language as the abstract and concrete, general and particular. Establishing these logical hierarchies is essential to virtually every writing task college students may face, from laboratory reports to poetry. No logical pattern can be effectively developed without control over levels of generality, no paragraph built (no matter what its pattern of development), and no assertion supported (factual or conjectural). Berthoff's "putting relationships together, ordering them" defines the movements of mind that range from the particular and the immediate to the universal and speculative—from "he's mad" to "people get mad." In Piagetian terms, all learners who have reached the stage of formal operations are capable of this generalizing and particularizing, and of recognizing the logical need for their interrelationship.

But grasping the interaction between universal and particular requires the experience of it *in language*. We generalize and particularize continuously in our thoughts, but we often recognize this process only when we discover it expressed in language, in something we say or write. When teachers find "muddy thinking" behind "bad writing," it may be that the writer has never fully grasped the processes of logical ordering that can best be perceived in language. The writing course should begin with this dimension of language.

Discovering the relationships between particular and general occurs most readily in the contexts of private experience. All students have memories of specific experiences that can readily be particularized in description and narration, even though such experiences may not have been rationalized or reflected upon. James Kinneavy argues that the "sensitivity to uniqueness" inherent in descriptive writing makes description "psychologically prior" to other uses of language.[12] Writing tasks for inexperienced writers should include description as a way of teaching the rendering of particularity in language. Description and narration are the easiest modes to control because they are normally structured in terms of time and space. As students gain control over the composing process and the language of particularity, they will more readily be able to generalize and reason about experience. As student writers begin to *reflect* on what has happened, to compare one experience with another, to classify an encounter in terms of other encounters like it, or to find reasons why it occurred, they are moving beyond telling about experience (which gives life to particulars) into the modes that connect particulars to form general patterns. In such writing students are obliged to recognize particularity and manipulate it into patterns that reveal general and abstract meanings. They will be able to do this effectively only to the extent, however, that they have come to recognize *the language of the particular* and *the language of the general* as the two interact to make meaning. Such recognition must be taught carefully and thoroughly if students are to master these languages for their own purposes.

A series of writing tasks based on the logical processes of discourse offers a good basis for a course outline. Berthoff proposes a "method of composing" which begins with "naming" and "renaming," as items are identified first individually and then together in classes and groups.[13] Students are then asked to "generalize and interpret" the classes which have been named, and among the classes themselves. These processes Berthoff terms "forming concepts"; they are taught by means of brief writing tasks, including making lists (at the outset), writing dialogues, and creating a series of dialectical statements. Only after these activities of composing have been presented does Berthoff introduce strategies for developing these movements of mind into units of discourse like paragraphs. The effect of this strategy is to emphasize that finding words and composing sentences and paragraphs *is* "making meaning." A different kind of sequence is described by Marilyn Katz, who outlines a series of essays moving from concrete personal experience to general, impersonal subject matter.[14] The first assignment asks students to describe a geographical place and discuss its meaning for them. Later assignments ask students to describe and analyze a relationship with someone else, an internal conflict, and an experience that left them with a strong opinion. The final task is the traditional research paper requiring discovery of knowledge beyond students' personal experience. Within each assignment, and from earlier to later assignments, the same principle holds: students are asked to particularize experience and then to universalize those particulars—to exploit relationships between the specific and the general, concrete and abstract. Each assigned essay except the term paper is rooted in students' personal experience, but requires making general, speculative statements about that experience. Katz pays less attention to the activity of composing than Berthoff; she describes writing situations which require the expression of meaning in longer units of discourse.

Another way of organizing writing tasks is by means of a sequence of topics. This method requires the instructor to build into each topic the logical and rhetorical strategies desired. One influential model of sequencing by topic is that of William Coles, who proposes a series of assignments on the idea of "teaching and learning."[15] Students are asked to write a series of papers, each developing an aspect of the central topic, and each emerging from previous papers and class discussions. The entire focus of the course is the students' writing generated in response to the sequence of topics. No outside reading is required and class discussions center on students' own writing and issues raised in it. Coles' method draws exclusively upon the students' own inventiveness, as it is challenged by a series of writing tasks carefully articulated to pose issues and problems. Another kind of topical writing sequence requires students to draw upon outside readings in addressing a central theme. A series of assignments, for example, exploring "The Anti-Hero in Literature" could draw from literary and nonliterary readings and require students to go beyond their own experience in defining the writing topics. Such a sequence has the weakness of being limited to expository purposes for the most part, as students respond to thematic issues by defining, comparing, classifying, and analyzing.

But a topical, reading-based sequence need *not* be limited to exposition; it can encompass a variety of purposes and forms. One proposal offers a reading-based series of assignments that asks students to understand the published writers "as writers" and to write in ways that represent "an essential component of a particular writer's performance, a component that the writer used often, and with variety, throughout the piece in question."[16] Students in this course wrote descriptive analyses on a geographical place (representing Cather's technique in *Death Comes for the Archbishop*) and stream-of-consciousness meditations within a moment of time (embodying Virginia Woolf's strategy). Such exercises are intended to enlarge students' awareness of context in writing, and facilitate "the transfer of technique from the reading to the writing" (27). Another, more traditional proposal suggests the use of literary contexts for the routine sequence from autobiography to the library research paper. The major writers in the British canon are surveyed and writings derived from the students' responses to literature. The first assignment is an autobiographical meditation on how the student has experienced literature in the past; other assignments ask students to write a character description after Chaucer and to compose an argument over the value-conflicts in *The Rape of the Lock.* Such tasks presume some literary sensitivity on the students' part and, obviously, the teacher's tolerance for inexperienced writers' exaggeration of effect. But both these strategies leave students free to explore, develop, and articulate their own experiences within the discipline of specific forms and styles.

These assignment strategies attempt to create meaningful contexts for student writing. Unfortunately, the assignment sequence implied in many big-selling texts relies primarily on modes or discourse forms as the basis for framing assignments. Textbook discussions of purpose and form are often followed by assignment suggestions that are formal and without rhetorical context. Implied in this conventional handling of writing tasks is that composing begins with a sense of form. The practical result is often a series labeled "a description paper," "a comparison and contrast paper," "an argument," and so on. The absence of content and context means that students must devise a topic without seeing any connection with what they may have written previously, or what they may write about later. The lack of rhetorical context encourages "writer-based prose," or at best a piece aimed at what students have discovered about the teacher's expectations. Above all, the task will strike students as just another exercise in doing what is expected of them, in which dutifulness—rather than inventiveness, uniqueness, or any form of risk-taking—is the supreme virtue. They know perfectly well that no one writes simply to compare and contrast things, or classify things, or argue with a shadowy audience about some abstract issue—except, of course, in a classroom.

Telling students to "define *politics*" or "compare and contrast roommates" or "argue for gun control" simply will not do. It's not only that such tasks do not cohere as a sequence; they also lack self-justifying significance for student writers. Such topics are important, to be sure, and their structural patterns are relevant to other kinds of writing. But packaged in a semester's time, as a series of jobs students must perform to get the reward of a good grade, the purely modal sequence confirms students' sense that academic writing is like lab experimentation in basic science courses. Students know that the teacher knows what to expect: there are "more right" and "less right" responses. Students (particularly the best ones) quickly learn to divine the teacher's wants and write to them. This is writing as academic gameplaying; from it students learn that writing is just another form of test-taking. Like taking tests, writing papers requires a canny judgment about the teacher's biases and a dutiful attempt to do what is asked. If the job is done with a modicum of care, the reward will come in the form of an A or a B. But, of course, this is not writing, any more than drawing up a lab report on the structure of a daisy is real botanizing. For neither activity has real consequences; they are merely training exercises. To be sure, botany students need to learn how to dissect and classify flowers in the lab, but only in order to be able to go into the field and botanize in a way that makes a difference to someone somewhere. And this, finally, is what genuine writing instruction must encourage: composing and writing that makes a difference, that exists within a context students perceive as fraught with consequences beyond merely good or bad grades.

Writing in the "real world" always bears consequences. A feasibility report may launch or kill a new venture. A performance evaluation may do the same for a career. A legal brief may impress a judge and help a client, or muff the job and lose the case. An article by a research engineer may present the research and its results persuasively and change the state of the art, or garble the facts and their interpretations so badly that the work has no impact. The list of consequences could go on, of course, but the point is made: "real world" writing always has an outcome, always makes some difference, even if only for the writers themselves. But writing that emerges from an assignment to "compare your values with your parents' " has no significance for the student writer unless it is engendered by the writer's genuine *need* to make such a comparison, to address some issue that lends importance to the effort.

What attributes, then, should an effective assignment sequence—the backbone of the writing course—possess? It should at all costs avoid a mere stringing together of modal tasks. Each assignment should have some rhetorical context: a clear topic, a distinct audience when students have gained some composing experience, and an underlying purpose that makes certain structures and styles appropriate. And a useful assignment should also make it possible for the student writer to use all elements of the composing process. This does not mean that students should always be promised the chance to revise their work after it is returned to them; it means that the assignment must be planned so that students will be able to work through the whole composing process within the time allowed, even if the work is an impromptu piece. Thus, the scope of the task should be adjusted to the setting within which students are asked to write.

But sometimes, even when assignments have all these things, students may still perceive them as mere exercises, the more so as elements of the assignment appear remote or unfamiliar. An essential aspect of writing assignments is their genuine significance for the writer: something that gives discourse the promise of a meaningful outcome. Take, for example, the common assignment requiring students to match their values or attitudes with those of an older generation. The topic has many versions ("Compare your ideas about something with those of your parents" is the most common). Most students will have engaged in some dialectic on this general theme for years with their parents. But simply writing a paper explaining their disagreements is not a natural writing purpose; it's a laboratory formulation only. Suppose instead that students were asked to write a letter to a younger brother or sister having similar conflicts with the parents; the letter should explain the writer's perceptions of the conflict and offer some suggestions to the reader about coping with conflict, based on the writer's longer perspective. Or suppose students were asked to imagine themselves as

65-year-olds writing the chapter of the autobiographies dealing with family relationships. They would be required to trace a family conflict, clarify their youthful role in it, and trace the impact of this conflict upon decisions made at the time. The audience in this case would be a distant and general readership quite unlike the sibling audience of the previous assignment, a readership for whom assumptions and motivations would need to be clarified. Both such assignments have a rhetorical context; one requires a descriptive analysis for a familiar audience, the other an analysis for a general audience seeking understanding rather than advice.

The topic of value conflict is part of the dialectic of maturation present in all our lives. Neither of the assignments just described would reconcile the generations, though either one might help the student writer change her feelings about herself or her parents. And this in itself would be a significant outcome, but it would not be the point of the assignment. Writing teachers are not in the business of changing lives; their responsibility is rather to help students learn to move freely within the universe of discourse where change and growth are articulated and recognized. By learning to form discourse, students will discover the power inherent in this basic activity of life. But they will not experience the genuine power of effective writing until they are given the chance to see its consequences as more than merely the gaining of a certain mark. The instructor can make this possible by establishing writing tasks that students must take seriously. Family relationships are only one part of students' lives; any topic, private or public, provided it has context and bears some implications for students, can call out their seriousness and invite them to discover the power of writing.

3. How much emphasis should I give to deliberately planned and revised writing? How much to spontaneous, impromptu writing?

Traditional rhetoric emphasizes deliberate, reasoned discourse; "precise and well-reasoned expression" is a common catch-phrase. The definition of writing as the expression of deliberate reasoning appears as a matter of course in writing texts, wherein students are urged to outline their writing, formulate a "thesis sentence," and carefully plan out their essays as a series of logical propositions to be amplified and made coherent. Even the models of composing described in Chapter I suggest prewriting activities that may include a systematic heuristic or discovery process which can frame random ideas into organized sequences (Burke's "pentad," for example). The assumption behind this emphasis upon careful composing is that better writing will emerge if students deliberately work out ideas in writing, revising intensively.

The traditional wisdom that effective writing can only come from planning and revision has been challenged in recent years. Some critics of conventional writing instruction have urged the value of rapid and spontaneous composing as a way of helping students gain fluency. One elaborate effort to justify spontaneity in composing has been made by Robert Zoellner, who argues that instead of seeing writing as "a two-step transaction of meaning-into-language," it should be seen as "an organic, developmental process in which you start writing at the very beginning—before you know your meaning at all—and encourage your words gradually to change and evolve."[17] Splitting what he calls the "think-write" process is the goal of his "talk-write" doctrine. He urges teachers to develop students' writing fluency by requiring them to put spoken words into writing without "thinking"—i.e., without deliberate prewriting and without being conscious of the encoding conventions of writing. Deliberate composing strategies (heuristic activities, outlining, and the like) hurt rather than help students in producing effective prose, in this view. Freewriting has emerged as the best-known technique for bypassing deliberate composing and emphasizing fluency in writing. Ken Macrorie urges students to "write for ten minutes as fast as you can, never stopping to ponder a thought. Put down whatever comes to your mind."[18] Macrorie wants students to write so rapidly and freely that they won't have a chance to use their stock of clichés Macrorie labels "Engfish." He argues that too often students labor diligently to write pretentious and overwrought prose in order to please the English teacher; freewriting is an intensive experience in generating writing in the student's own voice—writing that is "telling." He points out that freewritten prose is not "fully realized" writing (10), however, and must undergo revision and reworking. Peter Elbow argues the other side; brief freewritten pieces, he says, can be "less random, more coherent, more highly organized" than deliberately composed writing because the writer's intention is intensively focused to achieve an "integration of meanings."[19] However freewriting may be justified, its immediate effect is clear: it deliberately telescopes the normal phases of composing into brief, intensive spurts. It prevents young writers from reflecting on those phases as they pass through them in their writing. Macrorie and Elbow argue strongly—but from different standpoints—that this telescoping helps counteract bad habits and gives students confidence as writers. The largest danger in spontaneous writing, of course, is that in shortcircuiting the composing process, it conveys to students that this is how effective writing is *normally* generated—a notion that belies the conclusions of all recent research into the composing process.

Some attempts have been made to measure empirically the impact of spontaneous writing on student writers. One study reports that students who were allowed to write "what they wanted, when they wanted, in whatever way they chose," without being required to address a specific topic, produce a rough draft, or revise, wrote more fluent, error-free prose than those following prescribed modes and following steps of planning and revision.[20] The enticement of unstructured writing has led one writing teacher to laud the wholesome effect of nongrammatical, free-form writing upon student writers. Writing under what he terms "the powerful and autonomous dynamics of the unconscious," this teacher's students produce the "authentic yet untutored voices" that he finds essential to student writing.[21] Beyond the psychedelic jargon, there is here the existential notion of "authenticity" misapplied to freewriting. Deliberately planned and revised writing is not less "authentic" to the writer's intention than an impromptu writing. Indeed, if composing is a complex and recursive process, all of whose phases are important to completed intentions, then deliberate obedience to the writing process will produce more, not less, authentic writing. Spontaneous writing, produced within strict time limits, always requires the writer to circumvent full composing. Such composing should, as wise advocates like Macrorie suggest, be used only as a carefully arranged loosening-up exercise. It should not be exalted as a cure for composing disabilities it can make worse.

Indeed, the value of revision in student writing has been thoroughly documented in recent years. In questioning the need for students to "rewrite," one researcher argues that no differences could be found between the posttests of students taught to rewrite and those taught to submit only first-draft writing.[22] But her discussion of rewriting appears naive in light of the work of Donald Murray and Nancy Sommers, who have demonstrated that a major weakness of inexperienced writers is their failure to understand what genuine revision is. Murray divides the revising process into "internal revision," in which writers "discover and develop what they have to say, beginning with the reading of a first draft," and "external revision," which is "editing and proofreading."[23] He points out what we have already seen in Chapter I of this book—that writing texts tend to emphasize "the etiquette of writing" (91) rather than the essential work of discovering content, form, and voice. Sommers extends this argument by showing that student writers generally have a far narrower grasp of the revision process than "experienced adult writers," largely because the students have been taught that revising is putting commas in the right places and spelling correctly.[24] Experienced writers in Sommers' study saw revision as a way of "finding form and shape for their argument" (384), and making stylistic and tonal choices appropriate to their audience. Revision is re-seeing and re-shaping; it must be taught as an integral part of composing, not merely as the fixing of grammar and punctuation errors.

4. How much should I try to teach about language itself? Should students know the terminology and the rules of grammar? Which grammar?

The split between "knowing *that*" and "knowing *how*" is sharp and clear in these questions. We saw earlier that knowledge of the nature of language has no necessary connection with the ability to use it. Can "writing," still a poorly understood behavior, be nurtured without considering grammar at all? Those arguing that grammar is not needed for writing often argue by analogy. Does a child need to know the laws of physics in order to learn to swim? Does he have to grasp the principles of optics to learn to read? Is an understanding of the principles of internal combustion needed by a student driver?

Yet there is disagreement both about whether grammar is necessary to help students learn to write, and about what kind of grammar might be best. Structural and transformational grammars are the bases of current linguistics, yet traditional word-grammar still prevails in secondary and even college texts. As Frank O'Hare notes, a number of experiments have shown no useful relationship between grammar and the improvement of writing skills: "study after study tested the hypothesis that there was a positive relationship between the study of grammar and . . . composition. Result after result denied this hypothesis."[25] Yet argument over the role of grammar in the writing class continues unabated in journals and convention programs.

The plain fact is that even aside from the arguments-on-principle suggested earlier in this chapter, no convincing empirical evidence has shown any link between knowing grammar—traditional or transformational—and writing well. O'Hare himself, arguing that "grammar study is in disrepute at the present time largely because it has failed to help students write any better," offers a sentence-combining strategy that "does not necessitate the study of a grammar, traditional or transformational."[26] While O'Hare demonstrates his doubts about grammar in the writing class by devising a sentence-exercise plan not requiring it, some researchers have hailed transformational grammar as an essential part of the writing class. Defending transformational grammar as offering "meaningful explanations for what traditional grammars ignore," Elaine Chaika argues that the focus of "new grammar" is on "the creative process itself" and is useful in helping students learn to compose sentences. Writing teachers should select only texts with a transformational basis to its grammar material, she concludes.[27] Opponents of grammar teaching in the writing class argue that forcing students to learn grammar notations, particularly those of the transformational system, burdens students without improving their writing by substituting a knowing that for what writing really is, a knowing how.[28]

Moffett makes a strong argument against grammar in the writing classroom. "Poor punctuation, illogicality, ambiguous pronoun reference, run-on or rambling sentences, inaccurate vocabulary, lack of transition or coherence or subordination"—problems often lumped under the heading of "grammar"—are not grammar problems at all, says Moffett, but questions of usage and mechanics having nothing to do with the grammaticality of sentences.[29] "Can anyone seriously believe," he asks, "that theorizing about habits as deep and automatic as those of speech will alter practice?" (21). Poor writers, Moffett suggest, may generate ungrammatical sentences, but knowing what a subject or a finite verb *is* will not guarantee their being able to write one. Only making sentences—i.e., writing—will improve students' skills in making sentences. This insultingly simple tautology, Moffett argues, is not accepted in schools and colleges because of educational politics, not because teachers do not recognize its truth. And "the best way to improve grammar is to practice discourse in all its forms," he concludes (464).

But this conclusion leaves writing teachers in a quandary. On the one hand, teaching the abstract categories of syntax doesn't help students learn writing. But if students don't know the names of a few basic sentence elements, teachers will not be able to communicate with them about sentence structure. It comes to this: some common vocabulary for discussing sentence elements must be found. Such a vocabulary has two parts: terms for the elements of syntax, and terms for the operations that combine those elements. Traditional word-grammar provides the terms for sentence parts: clause, phrase, subject, predicate, modifier, pronoun, conjunction. Transformational grammar offers the best descriptions of the sentence operations students must work with—largely the embedding operations which are part of transformational rules. Sentence-combining work is the quickest way to familiarize inexperienced writers with the labels and operations of sentence making and to build a minimal working knowledge of syntax. As we saw in Chapter II, however, sentence combining itself is an exercise strategy designed to help students recognize and write more complex sentences. It's an enabling skill and not a replacement for discourse itself. Grammar terms should be taught in the same way—as enabling knowledge useful only to permit students to understand the complexities of real writing in real contexts.

5. Should there be collateral reading in the course? Should I use anthologies or other sources of writing outside students' own work?

To question the need for collateral readings is to threaten the profitability of great publishing houses and send tremors through the academic cottage industry of anthology-making. Yet an anthology of readings should be chosen only after the teacher has asked a fundamental question: do students need to read as well as write in a writing course? Berthoff argues strongly that they do: "reading and writing, I believe, should always be taught together. . . . composing is best nurtured by interpreting texts as well as [interpreting] experience."[30] On the other hand, Peter Elbow argues that any writing teacher hoping to get students to work hard should focus in class on their own work, the only writing "the members of the class can take seriously."[31] Professional writing may seem remote to inexperienced writers, who will despair of their own writing as it contrasts with polished work. They can read such writing with interest and still find little in it that they can absorb into their own composing.

So there may be excellent reasons for an instructor's decision not to include collateral readings in the writing course. But suppose the teacher wants students to confront topics and writing styles beyond their own experience? Kinneavy argues that student writers may examine samples of good writing, draw principles inductively from them, and apply those principles to their own writing.[32] Students may imitate these examples directly, or they may study them for techniques they can apply to their own writing. Or, the examples may provide an opinion or idea that will spur students' interest and aid them in the invention process. Collateral reading may serve two fundamental purposes: it offers students examples of rhetorical or stylistic strategies which they can imitate, and it may stimulate students' own exploration of the subject matter.

Teachers can help demystify professional writing for students by clarifying the composing processes experienced writers use, and by showing how thoroughly such writers generally exploit these processes. Published writing can be examined in terms of the stages of its composition (John Ciardi's essay on Frost's labor with "Stopping by Woods" is an example); teachers can show their own composing methods in pieces they may be working on. Another way to help students feel the power of good prose is to require them to imitate directly the styles of good writers. One teacher advocates requiring students to "think of writing in terms of form, and in terms of the particular linguistic devices that . . . contribute to form" in the work of established writers.[33] And, he continues, copying the styles of great writers does not have to be mechanical imitation, but can be a way for students to integrate into their own composing the strategies of professional writers, allowing students "to squeeze or to stretch them to their needs" (494). Such apparently "servile copying" has a place in teaching students the range and flexibility of the sentence, by asking students to imitate in their own words the sentence patterns and tone of writers as different as Mark Twain and Aldous Huxley. Anthologies are not the only source of topical material for students. Newspapers, magazines and journals, and films can all be used as sources for writing in all modes, from narrative descriptions of sensational murder cases to reviews of current films. Another kind of collateral material emphasizing cultural and social experience outside academe is fieldwork, wherein students are required to develop a project exploring some person, profession, or situation in the community outside the academic institution.[34] Even non-verbal materials can provide the subject matter of composition, such as paintings and photographs whose interpretations offer challenging writing tasks.

6. What kind of pacing should I use? How much writing should I require and how often?

There's little empirical research on the most effective patterns and frequencies in writing assignments, perhaps because of the overwhelming tradition of 500 words every week or two. This standard has some obvious advantages for the student and the instructor. It's short enough to allow students to develop, write, and revise within a three-to-five hour span, about as long as the average student is likely to spend on one paper. And it's long enough to permit the development of two or three major points in some detail. Training students to write within a 500-word scope is nothing more than developing their artfulness in exploiting a given form as fully as possible. Transactional writing in most disciplines (and in most business settings) occurs within limited formats that demand conciseness as a primary virtue. It's not the brevity (or length) of assigned writing that brands it as routine school writing. As we saw earlier in this chapter, that stigma results from the lack of context and significance in most assignments. Indeed, brevity is the governing condition of much "real world" writing—most of it shorter even than 500 words. Learning to establish and develop all that can be said within a certain limit is a valuable composing skill, and assignments of various lengths can help develop it.

Small amounts of writing oftener than once a week—a paragraph or two in a class period—can help students learn specific sentence or paragraph patterns. The advantage of small-scale assignments is the narrow focus it permits upon specific strategies, and the immediate feedback to the students available in the classroom setting. The disadvantage is the effect of small assignments upon the students' need to push beyond a paragraph or two if a topic calls up their inventive potential. Larger writing tasks afford scope for inventing and developing topics, for creating larger rhetorical units, and for composing more complex logical patterns. For the average freshman composition student, somewhere between 500 and 1000 words is the limit to ask on a weekly or biweekly basis. Some students could produce more without strain, but inexperienced writers cannot cope with a larger regular writing task without at some point abandoning planning or revision and simply putting down words as fast as possible. Most students will feel too badgered by other academic and social commitments to put in sufficient time for longer writing tasks on a weekly basis. Meanwhile, for the instructor teaching two (or more) writing courses, the obligation to evaluate fifty or more 500-word papers will require (at a quick ten minutes per paper) eight hours or more of reading per week, in addition to preparation for class meetings and student conferences. In Chapter V various evaluation strategies are analyzed; as these strategies show, teachers are not limited to the conventional editing-plus-terminal-comment routine.

For too many students, however, all assigned writing is an imposition regarded with an equal measure of fear and loathing. Recent interest in "student-centered" pedagogy lies behind other strategies: requiring "some writing each week" of no set length, or simply allowing students to write "what they want when they want."[35] While "some writing each week" gives students freedom to exploit whatever material or sources they want, but on a regular basis, writing "whenever they want" throws students back squarely upon their own self-directedness. This freedom of output no doubt accounts for what one study describes as students' great "personal satisfaction" in their work under this regimen.[36] Indeed, students' delight in work they alone have generated is a natural advantage of such an assignment pattern. But are the benefits of regular required assignments worth sacrificing for the increased pleasure students may find in setting their own pace?

Undoubtedly a few well-motivated students thrive under such freedom; they enjoy seeing how far their abilities can take them. The majority, however, cannot use the freedom because they do not have the discipline. They discover that some kind of pressure—peer pressure, grade pressure, instructor's nagging—is essential to motivate them into regular effort. And if these covert pressures do not stimulate poorly-motivated students, their gradually increasing guilt could alienate them from the course and ultimately from themselves. They will have confirmed themselves failures. The course that has no specific assignments or deadlines also creates difficulty in the feedback process. The student who puts off writing for weeks or months at a time and then turns in a mass of work as make-up will fail to get the regular attention that might have enhanced his critical awareness of his own work. Able students may flourish under a regime of freedom; but poor or even average students, lacking the discipline of structured assignments or deadlines, may fall short of their own capacity for growth because it has not been called up in them sharply enough. These students need the challenge of regular assignments.

There is a popular assignment pattern that stops short of absolute deadlines and a required number of writings, but offers more intrinsic structure than the "open" course. This is the "contract" course that matches certain totals and types of written work with specific grades, so that students know what and how much they must write in order to get a certain grade. The psychological basis of this course pattern is a deliberate, forthright correlation of work and reward. Students see clearly that "achievement" is a relative term, depending on realistic goal-setting, and their their own persistence as much as their writing ability will determine how far they go. Especially for students whose fear of writing is based on unhappy previous experience, a course that requires drive and ambition as much as skill is highly attractive. Any task that promises to yield to effort, rather than to be totally dependent upon an ability doubtful in the holding, will attract students with even modest motivation. One "contract" system sets forth several levels of achievement based on the number of papers completed, and evaluated on a graduated scale of polish and complexity, so that an "A" grade represents eight successful papers judged by increasingly rigorous standards, a "B" six papers judged by the same incremental standards, etc.[37] Other contract patterns may involve more (or fewer) papers, may require experimentation with a variety of modes or topics, or may allow for students to select several of what they judge to be their best writings for final evaluation. However administered, the contract pattern offers an attractive blend of discipline and freedom. Students may legitimately be asked to write in a variety of modes, use a wide range of rhetorical strategies, and still be offered their own choice of how much work they will do and what reward they are willing to settle for. Few other courses in school or university can provide self-fulfilling latitude within a structured situation.

In this chapter we have sketched some of the most important issues writing teachers confront as they plan their courses. As we said earlier, these questions are not the only ones teachers must ask themselves, but they are among the most important. If they are not answered reasonably, the course that emerges will lack definition, though that may not become clear until the course is well underway, when it will be too late. The basic course purposes, the writing assignments, outside readings, handling of grammar, and the amount and pacing of work must all be established at the outset, and students must be given the chance to understand them clearly. A syllabus that ends halfway through the semester or is filled with blank spaces invites students to disregard it. When this happens, the teacher will have lost an important control over the students and will have squandered an opportunity to guide and support their efforts. We have now to consider another important dimension of the writing course: its dynamics, the ways of structuring its interactions and shaping the learning process.

Notes

[1] Joseph Comprone, "Burke and Teaching Writing," *College Composition and Communication*, 29(December 1978), 336.

[2] Gilbert Ryle, *The Concept of Mind* (London: Hutchinson House, 1949), p. 58.

[3] Martin Steinmann, "Rhetorical Research," *New Rhetorics*. New York: Charles Scribner's Sons, 1967, p. 18.

[4] "Teaching Composition: A Position Statement," NCTE Commission on Composition, *College English* 36(October 1974), 219. See Appendix A.

[5] John Dixon, *Growth Through English Set in the Perspective of the Seventies* (London: Oxford University Press, 1975), p. 45.

[6] James B. Vopat, *"Uptaught* Rethought," *CE,* 40(September, 1978), 42.

[7] Shaughnessy, 85.

[8] Cleanth Brooks and Robert Penn Warren, *Modern Rhetoric* (New York: Harcourt, Brace and World, 1961), p. 2.

[9] Maxine Hairston, *A Contemporary Rhetoric,* 2nd ed. Boston: Houghton Mifflin Co., 1978, p. xvi.

[10] Anne R. Gere, "Writing and WRITING," *English Journal,* 77(November 1977), 60-4.

[11] Ann E. Berthoff, *Forming/Thinking/Writing* (Montclair, NJ: Boynton/Cook, 1978), p. 71.

[12] James L. Kinneavy, John Q. Cope and J. W. Campbell, *Writing: Basic Modes of Organization* (Dubuque: Kendall/Hunt, 1976), p. 24.

[13] Berthoff, *Forming/Thinking/Writing,* Part II.

[14] Marilyn Katz, "From Self-Analysis to Academic Analysis," *CE,* 40(1978), 288-92.

[15] William E. Coles, Jr., *Teaching Composing* (Rochelle Park, NJ: Hayden Book Company, 1974).

[16] Charles Moran, "Teaching Writing/Teaching Literature," *CCC,* 32(February 1981), 22.

[17] Robert Zoellner, "Talk-Write: A Behavioral Pedagogy for Composition," *CE,* 30(January 1969), 267-320. This monograph-length article had a spectacular launching, as the sole presentation of an entire issue of *College English.* It is couched in the jargon of behavioral psychology and appears to the unwary as the last word on writing as a mental process. As many critics have pointed out, however, its concepts are blurred and its attitude toward what it calls the "scribal act" (i. e. writing things down) is reductive and mechanical. Its basic conclusion that students ought to be taught to write the way they talk (or as Zoellner puts it, "the superimposition of a behavioral dimension upon our present think-write pedagogy, involving the transmodal manipulation of successive vocal-to-scribal approximations"), has been criticized by, among others, Janet Emig in "Writing as a Mode of Learning," *CCC,* 28(May 1977), 122-27.

[18] Ken Macrorie, *Telling Writing,* 3rd ed. (Rochelle Park, NJ: Hayden Book Company, 1980), p. 8.

[19] Peter Elbow, *Writing Without Teachers* (New York: Oxford University Press, 1973), p. 8.

[20] Robert Baden, "College Freshmen Can't Write?" *CCC*, 25(December 1974), 431.

[21] David Siff, "The Sense of Nonsense: An Approach to Freshman Composition," *CCC*, 27(October 1976), 276.

[22] Barbara Hansen, "Rewriting Is a Waste of Time," *CE*, 39(April 1978), 956-60.

[23] Donald Murray, "Internal Revision: A Process of Discovery," *Research on Composing*, ed. Charles R. Cooper and Lee Odell (Urbana, IL: NCTE, 1978), 85-103.

[24] Nancy Sommers, "Revision Strategies of Student Writers and Experienced Adult Writers," *CCC*, 31(December 1980), 378-87.

[25] Frank O'Hare, *Sentence Combining: Improving Student Writing Without Formal Grammar Instruction* (Urbana, IL: NCTE, 1973), p. 5.

[26] O'Hare, *Sentence Combining*, p. 30.

[27] Chaika, "Grammars and Teaching," *CE*, 39(March 1978), 771.

[28] Two articles typify opposition to grammar in the writing class: W. B. Elley, *et al.*, "The Role of Grammar in a Secondary School English Classroom," *RTE*, 10(Spring 1976), 5-21; and Melvin J. Luthy, "Why Transformational Grammar Fails in the Classroom," *CCC*, 28(December 1977), 352-55.

[29] James Moffett and Betty Jane Wagner, *Student-Centered Language Arts and Reading, K-13*, 2nd ed. (Boston: Houghton Mifflin, 1976), p. 19.

[30] Berthoff, *Forming/Thinking/Writing*, p. 10.

[31] Peter Elbow, "A Method of Teaching Writing," in *Ideas for English 101*, ed. Richard Ohmann and W. B. Coley (Urbana, IL: NCTE, 1976), p. 20.

[32] James Kinneavy, "Theories of Composition and Actual Writing," *Kansas English*, 59(December 1973), 3-17.

[33] William Gruber, " 'Servile Copying' and the Teaching of English Composition," *CE*, 39(December 1977), 493.

[34] R. C. Townsend, "The Possibilities of Fieldwork, " *English 101*, ed. Ohmann and Coley, pp. 74-92.

[35] See Timothy McCracken and W. Allen Ashby, "The Widow's Walk: An Alternative for English 101—Creative Communications," in *English 101*, and Robert Baden, "College Freshmen Can't Write?" cited above.

[36] Baden, 432.

[37] John Knapp, "Contract/Conference Evaluation of Freshman Composition," *CE*, 37(March 1976), 647-53.

Chapter V
TEACHING THE COURSE
Settings and Evaluation

In Dickens' *Dombey and Son,* during the search for a school for little Paul Dombey, Dr. Blimber's establishment is recommended: in it, remarks one character, "there is nothing but learning going on from morning to night." Adds Mr. Dombey, "And it's very expensive." In short, it's wonderfully fitted to Mr. Dombey's predilections about education and capitalism. It is efficient in the delivery of its product, learning, and prestigiously expensive. Dr. Blimber's establishment would suit an administrator of today perfectly; it embodies faculty and physical plant in continuous use, and makes a comfortable profit. The fact that Dr. Blimber's faculty is badly paid and worked day and night further enhances profitability, for learning is produced in the largest possible quantity at the lowest possible cost. English teachers well know such institutional logic, for they experience it in each writing class they're scheduled to teach.

A recent research article illustrates the contemporary relationship between education and capitalism. The authors describe an experiment which attempts to measure the relative improvement in writing skills of a group of students taught tutorially, on a one-to-one basis, and a group of students taught primarily in the classroom.[1] Their conclusion is that those taught primarily in large groups showed significantly greater improvement than those taught primarily through weekly conferences with the instructor. Although the article did not say so explicitly, it would appear from the conclusion ("we are all going back to the classroom") that the underlying issue is the familiar argument about the relative desirability of cost-effective classroom teaching and labor-intensive individualized teaching. Teachers of writing nurture a faith in the value of personal contact; for since writing is so personal, its demands and rewards so inner-directed, must its teaching not be personal? In English departments, administrators and teachers often battle over the size of the composition class and the number of sections assigned to each instructor. Does faculty want one section per semester (in addition to other assignments) with no more than twenty students? Impossible, says administration; faculty must teach at least two sections each semester with thirty students per class. But look at our load, cries faculty; we cannot adequately teach that many students. What can we do? blusters administration; we haven't the money to hire more teachers. If you don't want sixty writing students, we know some unemployed teachers and short-order cooks who'd step over your bodies to get them.

So the stakes are high in this game. If classroom methods improve writing more efficiently than individualized methods, then the perpetual clamor for smaller classes may be quieted. And those who keep insisting on the need for smaller and fewer writing sections may find their pleas silenced. The study itself does not urge teachers to abandon their convictions about personalized teaching. But all who have taught writing in a department divided between the desire for smaller classes and the push for larger enrolments know that convincing empirical evidence for abandoning personal contact in teaching writing would make institutional pressures even more intense. Indeed, *any* proof that writing courses make a measurable difference in students' writing skills is hard to come by. Some studies in recent years have suggested that students who take freshman composition don't perform any better either on writing tasks or in coursework generally than those who have not taken it.[2] If the measurable results— not only of different settings for writing instruction, but of writing instruction itself—are so ambiguous, what grounds of judgment are left writing teachers in selecting course settings and teaching strategies?

For the sake of reasonable discussion, we must take a leap of faith. Suppose we assume that these settings carry inherently different experiences with them, real enough for the student though not readily measurable by the usual empirical means. We shall assume that students do not necessarily feel the same way, behave identically, or learn the same things in the tutorial as they do in the classroom. Suppose also that small-group work adds yet another dimension to such differences. Are students likely to interact differently in a tutorial than in a classroom or small group? How do peer relationships affect students' attitudes toward writing, as opposed to their relationships with instructors? How are students likely to feel about peer evaluation as opposed to instructor evaluation? What aspects of the writing process can most effectively be presented tutorially? In small groups? In the classroom? Suppose, finally, we agree that a crucial difference among the tutorial, small group, and classroom settings is the nature (not the amount) of the feedback or reinforcement students receive in each. A fruitful comparison among all three settings may then be made, in terms of feedback given students in each type of setting.

Recent developments in learning theory have given new support to the argument that different settings involve different kinds of learning reinforcement. Since the emergence of the stimulus-response-reinforcement (SRR) model of learning behavior, increasing attention has been given to the third component of the model. Recent behaviorists, substituting "feedback" as a more comprehensive term for reinforcement, have argued that "the S-R-F system is primarily relevant to the immediate interactions between teacher and pupil."[3] But they also suggest that the feedback phase of the learning process may consist of any number of reinforcing behaviors, such as "reward, punishment . . . knowledge of results, encouragement, prompting, or information."[4] Feedback will come from the instructor, but it will also emerge from students' interaction with their peers, assignments and tests, and students' assessments of their own progress. A useful comparative analysis of three settings for writing instruction must take into account these varied sources of feedback in the learning process.

Tutorials

The term sounds faintly elitist, evoking the image of a tweedy, pipesmoking instructor conferring with a student about the weekly paper across a polished table. It implies a low student-teacher ratio, a leisurely, student-oriented faculty, and highly-motivated, intellectually independent students. Such a fantasy seems ill-suited to the pressures of today's universities, where most students do not burn with commitment to the life of the mind, and the professoriat finds itself driven to teach, publish, and often perish all at once. Yet the tutorial pattern has emerged in recent years as a popular alternative to the classroom arrangements typical of the modern university. The reason for its popularity and, obviously, the source of its effectiveness is the potentially strong relationship between instructor and student.

The student will be strikingly vulnerable to the teacher's immediate influence in this setting. Even before the first piece of writing is brought to the teacher, the student will begin to meditate on this authority to whom he must submit, without the customary group of peers around him in the classroom. No matter how humane the teacher may wish to appear, the student may be at first fearful of revealing weaknesses to the instructor, even perhaps resenting the instructor's authority. Yet despite the student's anxieties upon confronting a close, exacting relationship, the very intensity of the tutorial setting can develop into a strongly task-oriented partnership rapidly if conditions are right. Reciprocity is the crucial element in such a partnership. The expectations brought to it by teacher and student can shape a personal interaction with major advantages for the learning process, and with certain dangers as well.

Indeed, the flexibility and intensity of the tutorial have led some teachers of writing to urge it as a method of choice for all writing instruction. Yet learning theorists disagree on just how it creates learning, and just how its advantages should be weighed. Perhaps the sharpest disagreement concerns whether personal contact with the instructor or the learning activity itself is the key to the tutorial's effectiveness. The importance of a close, caring relationship in helping students learn has most forcefully been argued by psychotherapist Carl Rogers. The virtues in personal relationships that Rogers emphasizes—"prizing" and empathy—have frequently been cited by those who feel that the important thing in writing instruction is a caring relationship between instructor and student.[5] Rogerians assert that teachers must project themselves into their students' feelings, accept those feelings and nurture them into the positive self-regard that Rogers argues is essential to genuine learning. The teacher's ability to empathize, to leave her own standards at bay in the act of seeing the tasks she has set for the student as the student sees them, is in this point of view crucial to the writer's growth. However, some critics have questioned the value of the personal relationship itself in teaching writing. Not enough measurable connection between feelings and cognitive development can be shown, argues one critic, to justify the belief that there is "magic in individual attention."[6] Rather, "the significant variable in producing effective tutoring is the tutoring program— what tutors do" (137). Nevertheless, tutorial methods have been strongly advocated by teachers convinced that personal relationships are essential to real writing growth.

The tutorial principle has been variously applied to writing instruction. Roger Garrison insists that while "the *least* effective method is the regular class meeting," "the *most* effective teaching method is one-to-one: tutorial, or editor-to-writer."[7] Garrison's premise is that students best learn to write by writing with the instructor's "creative intervention in [their] work process" (69). It would take less time, maintains Garrison, to teach one hundred writing students tutorially than in the classroom, because direct contact between instructor and student provides necessary editorial advice more efficiently than the laborious written commentaries often ignored by students. Garrison urges that the classroom be turned into a workshop in which the instructor gives rapid, sharply focused attention to fifteen or twenty students per class hour, so that students' work can be evaluated in early and finished stages as the revision process goes on. Only continuous, intense contact between instructor and student, concludes Garrison, can bring out that student's best potential as a writer. Another teacher describes a method which places all contact time in regular conferences, during which the instructor evaluates the student's work as he reads it with him, to demystify the evaluation process and enhance "on-going communication" about the student's work.[8] The tutorial method takes no more total time than a classroom arrangement, and "three hours of conference time is, in quality, as well as in practical necessity, worth almost twice as much time as the other method" (653). The assumption here is that the directness of tutorial interaction shapes the student's writing growth more efficiently than the more distant, less controlled interactions of the classroom. The structure of the tutorial conference has also received attention from another writer who draws on practical psychology and speech communication to outline the conference as a planned sequence of steps from "engagement" to "termination."[9] Though she sees the conference only as an adjunct to classroom work, she follows Garrison in urging the value of particularized feedback in conferences.

Tutorial advocates emphasize the instructor's control over feedback the student receives. If students do not see why the paper's focus is too broad, they can be brought to recognize paragraph by paragraph where it wanders and where it can be trapped and held onto. If they cannot recognize sentence difficulties, they can work through sentences with the instructor, leaving the conference with specific instructions to practice needed sentence variations. Perhaps most importantly, with oral feedback the instructor can avoid the intimidating simultaneity of written comments on returned papers. When papers are returned, students may read whatever final evaluation is on them before, or in place of, a sequential scrutiny of marginal or interlinear comments. In the tutorial the instructor can begin with whatever fact seems necessary to the student's feelings, and then track through the paper in the order and at the speed appropriate to the student. All these advantages carry the virtues of immediacy and appropriateness in the feedback process.

The successful tutorial depends upon a routine of conferences, writing, and revision. If each student is to be met once a week, a regular meeting time should be set so that students may pace their writing and revision, internalizing as self-discipline the external pressure of regular conferences. Some teachers do not read students' work ahead of conference time, preferring to read quickly at the outset of each meeting.[10] In-conference reading requires intense concentration by the instructor, while the student waits anxiously for the verdict. This strategy primarily benefits the instructor by saving the time required for pre-conference reading. A large teaching load may justify it, particularly if it makes conferences possible where they might not otherwise be feasible. But a quick reading cannot fully comprehend a paper's essential organization or adequately diagnose stylistic difficulties, particularly obtuse ones. Requiring that writing be submitted in time for the instructor's prior reading will make it easier to appraise the work in terms of what the student has already written and what improvements need to be made. To engineer a situation requiring rapid, immediate reading of student work is to invite superficiality and misdiagnosis on the teacher's part.

The tutorial has two major disadvantages. The first is that the real audience for the student's writing is limited to the instructor, the only source of feedback for the student. This limitation runs directly counter to the urgings of recent writing theorists that students write for different audiences after gaining some writing experience. Moffett's "abstractive scale" of writer-audience relations suggest students' need to understand the rhetorical demands of audiences ranging from "interpersonal" to "impersonal," the latter a "large anonymous group" such as the readership of a published article or book.[11] The progression from expressive writing into "broadly differentiated kinds of writing" urged upon all writing students by Britton also supports the idea of confronting writers with a range of audiences, to nurture flexibility in the use of voice and tone.[12] But the tutorial affords students only the constant viewpoint of the instructor, who, while she may conscientiously shape her demands to the student's level, cannot change her identity. The tutorial provides neither the large, diverse audience of a classroom group nor the supportive responsiveness of a small peer group. A student taught only by tutorial conference will lose the benefits of learning to deal with a variety of audience expectations and feedback.

The second disadvantage lies in the potential loss of objectivity in an exclusively mentorial relationship. In a close tutorial setting, instructor and student alike may forget that a certain distance is needed for objective evaluation and feedback. The tutorial relationship, in other words, is not necessarily a friendship; criticism must be given and received without constraint. If the student sees the instructor primarily as a friend, then criticism may come to be perceived as betrayal; or the teacher may begin to overlook weaknesses or lack of progress as the student betrays the stresses all students face as the semester proceeds. A genuinely caring relationship requires the instructor to maintain a balance between support and needed criticism if the student is to derive full value from the tutorial.

The Classroom

If the instructor's control over the students is monolithic and intense in the tutorial, in the classroom it's often tenuous. In a class of twenty-five students the instructor will lecture some of the time; this, as we will see, can be fraught with danger for students and teacher. But even if a variety of activities occupies the writing class, interaction between instructor and students will be fragmented, discontinuous, and unpredictable. Classroom interaction seldom stays on a direct line of exchange, but varies as the instructor lectures and speaks specifically to certain students, and students reply to the instructor or to each other. The extent of a student's participation in lecture-discussions may vary widely from day to day, depending on the student's knowledge, interest, or other attitudinal factors. Thus, the instructor can never adequately plan for the level of student involvement, or be assured that students will either listen or respond well enough to understand the material under discussion. Recently an educational researcher measured the rate of information retention by students over the course of a sixty-minute lecture, and fashioned a graph representing the results:[13]

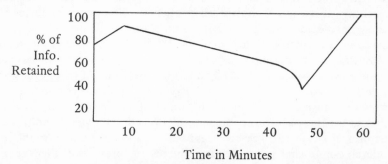

These findings suggest that students will retain information best in the first and last minutes of a lecture only, and that retention moves in roughly inverse proportion to the passage of time. This graphic representation only confirms what teachers know very well from their own experience: a class hour featuring only the instructor talking to students will bring few benefits to students struggling to learn an activity as complex as writing.

The classroom is, however, the most efficient setting for the dissemination of information. In a tutorial arrangement, students' actual time with the instuctor will be limited to the fifteen to thirty minutes per week. Thus, the classroom student will hear far more explanation and analysis than the tutorial student, though most will not be focused directly on the student's own work. Discussions of collateral reading, for which there will be no time in the tutorial setting, may be introduced into the classroom setting for the purposes of modeling and topic stimulation. Organizational patterns, sentence and paragraph forms, and grammar and usage may be illustrated at length from student and professional writing, with the aid of handouts, blackboard, or overhead projector. The classroom is an efficient forum for illustrating, and to a limited extent practicing, techniques of organization and style.

But the classroom offers the least effective setting for insuring that students absorb new strategies into their own writing behavior. The tutorial arrangement at least insures that each student will talk at length about his writing once a week. No classroom course of twenty-five students meeting three hours a week can target each student's writing for discussion with the thoroughness of the tutorial session. Student writing (reproduced prior to class) may be discussed by the whole class, but only a few pieces can be covered in an hour of class time. In the classroom students may benefit from the diversity of responses, but the instructor cannot control the impact of those responses upon the student. Nor will class discussion necessarily benefit poorer writers who need it most, because large groups tend to inhibit the less verbal student. For those basic writers who cannot progress at the same rate as their more skilled peers, points about grammar, logic, and mechanics may need repeating again and again before mastery occurs. This pedagogical repetition may well be crucial to the success, even the survival, of some students; yet a restless classroom group may easily deter the instructor from clarifying by repetition. Classroom groups, by virtue of their mass, resist the teacher's efforts to provide that specific feedback necessary to the writing growth of all students, skilled or unskilled.

The challenge for the teacher of a classroom-based writing course is to create systematic, appropriate feedback for each student, within the constraints of a classroom setting. Marking and returning student themes has traditionally been the method of choice for this purpose. But if classroom discussion often fails to make a point jell for a student, written comments on returned papers just as often lie useless on the page, unread or misunderstood. There's a curious paradox in the business of changing writing behavior: the written word itself, in the form of marginal emendations, lacks the force necessary to change a student's writing habits. It's not that teachers can't write wise and witty comments or that students always ignore them. Rather, writing fluency, like mathematical problem-solving, is a skill requiring the student's continuous incremental translation from the conceptual to the practical, from the abstract and general to the concrete and particularized. In composition as in geometry, abstract premises come to life only in their working-out, in the words, sentences, and paragraphs the student himself creates. From the lecture on history or literature the student may gather and process ideas and facts leisurely, integrating them gradually. To alter the way he composes written language, the student must immediately bridge the gap between the concept of writing and the behavior it entails, making a strong closure between received information and writing behavior. Written comments on returned papers cannot insure such closures in students' learning; if they do not grasp the concept of relativization or the requirements of sequential logic, they cannot write a convincing argument. The inevitable ambiguity and incompleteness of any written commentary will persistently block students' transformation of "knowing that " into "knowing how."

Clearly, writing teachers must comment on student work. But additional feedback from other sources can extend and diversify the instructor's point of view. W. E. Coles, Jr. has outlined a semester's writing program in which every "class meeting is devoted to a discussion of mimeographed samples of unidentified student writing and is confined solely to a discussion of that writing and the assignments to which it is addressed."[14] This relentless focus on student writing is intended to keep students aware that writing—not just any writing but *their* writing—is the only subject of the course. General classroom discussions of some student's work each week means that, over a quarter or semester's time, all students in the class would receive feedback not only privately on each returned paper, but several times publicly in company of their peers. Coles' model makes each class meeting a series of conferences about individual papers, taking advantage of the diversity of viewpoints within the classroom. Another model of student-centered strategy advocates the "first-sight, in-class reading of students' writing as the entire business of classroom meetings."[15] This model gives all class time to reading students' papers by means of transparencies and an overhead projector. Teacher-guided readings of student work by the whole class have distinct benefits: they confront student writers with a readership larger and more diverse than the instructor alone can offer, and at the same time expose students to the authority of the instructor.

Some students may find such public exposure of their work painful. For inexperienced writers particularly, sharing writing may be perceived as a violation of individuality, even when anonymity is preserved. When we share written work with a group of peers, says one researcher, we think immediately "of what they directly or indirectly say we are, and are reminded of what we are not—our failures, misplaced commitments, erroneous assumptions, self-delusions, and misguided intentions."[16] Students whose work is under discussion will only half listen to what is said about the writing itself. They will be acutely aware of their instructor's and peers' tone of voice, and of the possibility of implied judgments about themselves. Comments that might appear calm and disinterested to an uninvolved listener may sound negative or hostile to the sensitive student.

To minimize this threat, instructors must attune themselves to the tone of the discussion, judge its effect on students whose work is under discussion, and manipulate that discussion so that its impact on student writers is instructive without being judgmental. So done, classroom sharing can strongly benefit student writers. Their intense awareness of exposure may impress upon them, as private conferences cannot, the "realness" of writing, its power to elicit responses as a genuine act of communication. Such an awareness can deepen students' responsibility toward their writing, enabling them to see it as an instrument affecting others in ways that the writer can manipulate. In other words, public sharing of writing can sharpen students' respect for writing as a means of power.

Making the writing classroom a forum for discussions of each student's work can put students in a participatory role, while giving direct feedback to each in turn. But a classroom wholly given over to discussion of student writing omits other, equally useful activities. The benefits of reading and discussing work by published writers will be lost. Writing activity itself cannot take place. Perhaps most seriously, there will be no time for dyads or small groups, in which students interact with one another *without* the immediate presence of the instructor. Group work in writing classrooms has received much attention in recent years; we must now look carefully at its uses in the teaching of writing.

Small Groups

Small-group work can involve students more fully in learning activity than any other group setting. But several things can affect the success with which they give appropriate feedback to students. Writing ability may vary widely in groups from untracked classes, yet instructors' attempts to balance skilled and unskilled writers in the same group may prove counterproductive. Unskilled writers may resent being counseled by their peers, however skilled. Good writers may not be able to communicate what they know about writing, or be psychologically prepared to share their experience with others. Some students may find self-disclosure to a small group as threatening as disclosure to the whole class. Indeed, students can easily fear exposure to one another more than they flinch at direct contact with the teacher, who fills a familiar authoritarian role in their experience. Adolescent sensitivities may well have created a vulnerability that will resist group sharing. An ethos of trust may develop in a peer group, but only when that group fulfills certain basic conditions for success.

A small group must be the right size: "the smallest one that contains all the skills required for the accomplishment of the group task," says one researcher.[17] A pair of students (or "dyad") may be appropriate if one-to-one peer feedback is desired; a rough-draft or editing workshop for the class may use dyads, with students paired so that each has some skills that can help the other. Larger groups should be set up in odd-numbered sizes, from three to seven, to avoid deadlocks. A group of three offers a comfortably small size but with limited possibility of divergent judgments about work under discussion. Groups of five or seven offer more varied viewpoints for the group size, but are more vulnerable to fragmentation in sharing the work load and focusing on the task. Student groups should be deliberately structured by the teacher, to avoid the grouping of friends who may find personal discussions more interesting than the task at hand. In forming small groups, the teacher should strive to include a mix of these abilities in each group:

A. *Perceptiveness about writing.* Needless to say, not all students will have helpful things to say about their peers' writing, even after some instruction. One or more students in each group must have some skill with language, particularly at the sentence level, where students have the most difficulty making judgments.

B. *Self-confidence in group discussion.* At least one student in each group should have the self-confidence to announce opinions about writing. Such a student may not be as insightful about writing as others in the group; however, his main function is to stimulate discussion, even dispute.

C. *Mediating tactfulness.* One student should have an instinct toward moderation, be uncomfortable with negative comments and eager to sympathize with and defend others.

If these characteristics exist in some mixture in the group, there should be enough heterogeneity to create momentum in discussion, but sufficient cohesiveness to pursue tasks set by the instructor.

Group leadership may be set by the instructor or left to the group to establish. If the teacher's goal is to give all students experience with leadership responsibility, leaders may be assigned on a rotating basis for each session of the group. Or each group may choose its own leader or leaders for each task or session. Communication research suggests that, by whatever method it is chosen, student leadership challenged with genuine responsibility for group tasks will increase motivation of all group members. The leader of any small group, whatever the task, has some or all of the following responsibilities:

A. Clarifying the group's goals.
B. Asking exploratory questions.
C. Using responses to generate other responses.
D. Mediating disputes.
E. Summarizing viewpoints of group members.

One researcher has suggested that a major function of group leaders is to cope with the indifference, reserve, or hostility of group members by preventing "such a negative buildup, or bring it within control if it begins . . . . [The group leader] must be able to cope with the most dominant and negative members, but he must not be too dominant or negative himself."[18] The measure of the group leader's success is the extent to which the group members work together as listeners, reinforcers and critics for one another.

Kenneth Bruffee has described the "collaborative learning" that *can* emerge from the properly administered small-group experience: "Evidence provided by collaborative activity," he asserts, "suggests that people can gain both awareness and support as adequately in a small group of their peers, as from the ministrations of a teacher."[19] Bruffee suggests that in giving each others' writing sympathetic, nonjudgmental hearings, students can provide an "astute and demanding audience" that will detect "lack of clarity, organization, logic, and substance" in each others' work (55). Obviously, such feedback will not emerge immediately in group work at the beginning of the course. Students must first learn how to read analytically before being able to give useful feedback. For weeks in the course's beginning, the instructor must teach students how to analyze and evaluate writing; students must internalize the instructor's standards as part of their own competence.

Inexperienced writers will lack both the ability to recognize effective prose and the vocabulary to communicate their perceptions. The teacher must train the whole class in these things, before groups can function. The "showing" reactions which Peter Elbow, for example, prescribes for his peer-group feedback may be interesting as metaphors—"drizzling," "foggy" "gusty," "forested," "hilly," etc.—but they provide little explicit direction to the student about how to make foggy writing clear or hilly writing smooth.[20] Students must learn to recognize focus, proportionate organization, and abstraction and concreteness, and find explicit language for these elements, in order to give useful feedback about writing.

Small groups may be created either within the framework of regular class meetings or in independent work-groups meeting on their own schedules. Working with what he terms a "parceled classroom," Thom Hawkins pictures the instructor as a "floating resource" who sorts students into groups and establishes the tasks for their "group inquiry."[21] These consist of generating topics for student writing, discussing collateral readings, working rhetorical and grammatical exercises, and most importantly, evaluating group members' own writing. One day a week is devoted to the latter task, at the end of which the instructor collects students' writing and adds his own evaluations to those performed by the group. Nearly every class day of the semester will be given to one of these group tasks; the groups themselves retain the same membership through the semester. The basic advantage of such "group inquiry," says Hawkins, is that "it's more fun to work through problems together with other students your own age than to work in isolation under the direction of someone from a different generation" (64).

Peter Elbow's "teacherless writing class" goes further by rejecting prescriptive advice from teachers because "to improve your writing you don't need advice about what changes to make; you don't need theories of what is good and bad writing."[22] What the student does need, he argues, is a committed, stable, caring audience for his writing, so that he can "see and experience his own words *through* seven or more people. That's all" (77). Both models assume that peer support plays a crucial, even predominant role in students' writing growth, and that what's lacking in expertise can be made up for in the value of the freedom and responsibility offered.

In such groups, students may discover their own resources and gain perspective on the infinite ways to come at a piece of writing by listening to others discuss their labors. Invention, for example, can get a strong stimulus from small-group discussion. "I was trying to write about my roommate," one student may say, "but I just couldn't seem to say what I really thought about her." Why not, others ask. What's she like? What does she do? The speaker is thus encouraged to separate her feelings about her roommate from her observations of the roommate's behavior, and to discover concrete elements of appearance and behavior that can clarify the roommate's essential qualities. Another group member may say "I wanted to tell how great my fraternity is, but I just seemed to get stuck on the stuff we learned in pledge week." What did you do in pledge week? others ask. How did it make you feel? What's so great about your fraternity brothers? The instructor could ask such questions in class or conference, but when the writer hears other students asking them out of genuine curiosity, he senses the power of his own words to make others feel and see as he does. The small-group bull session becomes for him an important heuristic.

A cohesive small group—an entity not easy to create or sustain—will help all its members learn more about how to compose. It's just as important for students to witness each others' failures as it is for them to admire the successes. Reading her paper to a small group as Elbow has urged, or submitting it to a collaborative group of Bruffee's type, a student can enjoy praise if the work is liked, or, with relief, be able to explain and self-justify freely if it doesn't appeal. Neither the tutorial conference nor the classroom group can provide quite the same nurturing that the small-group atmosphere offers the frustrated, struggling student. The need for such nurturing is essential for the student to carry himself over what John Dewey called "dead places" in his progress as a learner. Without the small-group presence, the student will seek its supportive benefits elsewhere, in places like the dorm where specific task-orientation is absent. Peer groups offer students an opportunity that cannot be provided by other settings. But they require a great deal of effort by both teacher and students. For unless small groups, especially outside the classroom, have a self-renewing core, they will flicker out under the pressure of other commitments by their members. Ultimately the instructor must provide the stability of routine that will sustain the group's vitality and enable it to give each member needed feedback.

No test has yet been devised that can accurately measure the differing results of tutorial, small-group, and classroom methodologies. But the likely effects of these different settings may be enumerated. Enjoying consistent, particularized feedback on all aspects of their writing, students in the tutorial are most likely to have that trial-and-error freedom to develop specific elements of their work, and to accept the discipline of constant revision as an essential part of the writing process. On the other hand, in any writing course that deals with a variety of modes and styles, a lot of material—professional and student models, organizational varieties, sentence patterns, tonal effects—can most efficiently be presented first in broadcast form, until students can utilize it in their own writing. The dissemination of such material can best occur in the classroom, as can the forceful sense of "realness" and the diversity of response deriving from large-group exposure. Small groups and dyads offer a more particularized audience for students with the direct and supportive feedback available from a group of equals. We might say, then, that conference-taught students will recognize particularly well their own writing needs, and gain the disciplined ability to revise in accordance with a growing perceptiveness about the writing process. That awareness will lack scope, however, if it hasn't been enriched by a classroom discussion, and may suffer a tinge of narcissism if it hasn't been widened by the discovery of how differently and well other students may write. And in all group encounters students will grasp the communality of the act of writing, and benefit from the constuctive tensions of writing with and for others.

How will the differing experiences of classroom, tutorial, and small-group encounters show up on the standard pre- and posttests? Poorly, if at all, given the history of testing to date. If what students have learned is a *process* requiring time and patience—days and weeks for each satisfying accomplishment—no single-incident testing can measure that clearly. Indeed, research has indicated that students allowed time for research and revision on both pre- and posttests will show writing improvement more clearly than students reported in the common, single-incident testing method.[23] Certainly no final impromptu can reveal how well a student has internalized the process of self-criticism and revision, how deeply he may have come to enjoy his community of fellow writers, or how acutely he has gained the sense of writing's power to affect others. These are important goals for any writing course; yet because of the ambiguous, measure-resistant quality of such learning, empirical verification is elusive. In the last analysis, whatever influence the instructor has on his writing students may not appear on a multiple-choice or impromptu posttest, and may not yield positive correlations with any particular thing measurable in numbers.

Evaluation

Once a young teacher returned some papers to a class that included an aggressive male student who thought well of his own abilities. He rushed up to the instructor as the class ended and shouted, "What is this, giving me a D? I don't get grades like that!" The instructor, taken aback, asked him if he wanted to talk about it in his office. "No," muttered the cooling student, "there's no point in talking about it. It wouldn't do any good." The student's anger, boiling up and then subsiding, gave that instructor a sharp lesson in the pressures involved in grading. Students recognize that the only evaluation that "counts" is the grade which goes on their transcript. They may accept the teacher's verbal assessments of their work, but the grade is the crucial item. They may have enjoyed the class, they may believe they have learned in it, they may see how it has helped them grow, but if the grade is not what they expect, the whole experience is soured. The writing teacher faces an especially acute problem. The act of writing is bound up in the student's ego, its product tied to his self-identity more deeply than most of his other academic efforts. The insititutional demand that the instructor convert his judgment of a student's writing into a grade necessitates an often prickly, ambiguous judgment. Certain questions need to be asked about such judgments:

1. Should student writing be evaluated at all?

Certainly writing has to be evaluated, it might be said; how else will the student know what he's doing wrong, and thus improve? Yet this is not the idle question it seems, nor is the answer so obvious. As we have seen, the influence of Carl Rogers and others has convinced many writing teachers that only a supportive, caring atmosphere can create the psychological freedom within which students can grow as writers. Evaluation, it is argued, inhibits development of this freedom by implying criticism, which stifles the student's willingness to experiment with words and risk failure. For example, one teacher has proposed a "low-risk, affirmative" experience which avoids "inadvertent put-downs" and permits only positive feedback from peers, with "exclusive concentration on strengths," so that every paper the student submits to the class is an "experience of success."[24] The teacher is limited to devising positive situations in which "desired behavior" in writing is elicited and reinforced through supportive group interaction. Such a system emphasizes the importance of psychological factors in writing growth, and the beneficial power of peer nurturing.

Yet, as much as students may fear criticism and welcome feedback that dwells on their strong points, students also want to know how effective instructor and peers perceive their writing to be. If students are told, week after week, only that their work has certain strengths which may perhaps be improved, they'll grow restless. For most students recognize, if only from seeing other students' work, that some writing is more effective than theirs, and that some students can do more things with words than they. Most students also grasp the self-evident truth that unless they learn how to unclutter their syntax, make their paragraphs cohere, and organize their essays clearly, their grades on papers and essay tests will not improve. Perhaps the strongest argument against providing only positive feedback is that it may create a fool's paradise of students who love their own writing so much they will be devastated when somebody criticizes it later. To give feedback which is too positive, too vague, or too late is to lose the unique opportunity afforded every writing teacher to improve the single most important ability students require for success.

2. Who should evaluate student writing?

Until the last two decades, such a question would have seemed ridiculous to most writing teachers. Who else should it be but the teacher, who, after all, knows more about writing than any student? In particular, the tutorial setting offers both wide scope and specificity in the instructor's evaluative responses. Even in a classroom setting the instructor, by commenting orally and in writing on students' work, and by reinforcing classroom contact with conferences, can thoroughly impress his attitudes upon students. But it's precisely the instructor's unavoidable dominance in the teacher-student relationship, some argue, that can hinder the student from feeling free enough to risk failure in experimenting with various voices and styles.

Advocates of peer feedback and self-evaluation argue that the teacher's responses are usually too cursory, detached, and unsupportive to nurture the proper risk-taking attitudes in their students. "A teacher," says Elbow, "tells you what he thinks the weak and strong points were and suggests things you should try for. But you usually get little sense of what the words actually did to him—how he *perceived* and *experienced* them."[25] Only small, cohesive peer groups, say their advocates, can offer this kind of response to student writers—evaluation that is descriptive rather than judgmental, clarifying *what* the writing does to the audience, not how well it may carry out rhetorical or grammatical rules. One advantage for students evaluated by their peers is that their feedback can appear less threatening than the instructor's judgments. Also, analyzing others' work can help students become better critics of their own writing. One peer-evaluation strategist urges that students be trained to "assume more control" of the evaluative process, moving from more structured to less structured sessions as they learn how to make more discerning analyses of each others' work.[26] This progression assumes interaction between two learning processes. Students begin working in pairs and then in larger groups as they learn the interpersonal skills needful to cooperative work; they also begin evaluating each others' writing using "highly structured rating scales" (148), moving to less structured evaluations after they have gained experience. Such a graduated system of peer evaluation "helps student writers find their voices, develop a sense of audience, and experiment with revision strategies" (153).

Self-evaluation may also force students to take responsibility for their own writing growth, and internalize writing standards that may carry over into later writing efforts. In the beginning of the course they could, for example, be asked to write a narrative description of the writing process by which they shape their early writing tasks. Later, after being readers of their own and other's writing, they'll be better able to evaluate the effectiveness of their own writing objectively. Students should not be asked to evaluate their own work without some time spent in training for that task. Despite its potential for making students more responsible for their own progress, self-evaluation requires careful nurturing and support from instructors. It also demands that students be made to feel that their evaluations of themselves actually count—that the instructor will read their self-evaluations and count them in the final grade.

3. What standards should evaluation rest upon?

Clarifying the standards by which students' work will be evaluated is a difficult and often thankless task for teachers. Teacher and students may agree on the characteristics of "good writing," and students may convince themselves that they expect to be evaluated according to such characteristics. But some students may resist the instructor's standards from the outset of the course, if those standards threaten the student's self-image or the grade. Other students who struggle to meet the teacher's demands at the beginning may perceive the teacher as intransigent if they continually fail to meet the standards or if these standards appear to change as the semester proceeds. The latter situation may well emerge if the instructor feels it proper to expect more from students as the semester goes by, and reads succeeding papers with an ever-more-discriminating eye. This situation may arise particularly sharply when students submit one or more revisions of the same work. Problems hidden at first reading by the more obvious difficulties may be resolved in the first revision, only to be superseded by further, legitimate criticisms about remaining problems.

Clearly the best way to teach evaluative standards is to make them clear and to apply them systematically. If revisions or papers written later in the semester are to be evaluated more stringently than earlier ones, students must be made aware of this fact. It can be justified; it is important for students to understand that a text is never finished, and that one skillful element in a written piece does not guarantee the excellence of the whole. But instructors should not impose their standards *ex cathedra* upon students. The only standards students will learn effectively will be those understood and accepted as legitimate. Standards acquiesced to without comprehension will produce no real growth in writing skill and will inevitably lead to confusion and unhappiness as the course proceeds. General agreement on writing standards can best be achieved by teacher-shaped class discussion, focused on student writing illustrating varying levels of effectiveness. Such discussion will make students more aware of the openness and complexity of the very idea of "good writing" and will make them feel collectively responsible for the formulation of standards. Student writing rather than professional work should be used in discussing the actual standards to which students will be held, for students know they cannot write at the level of anthology prose, though they may well recognize the techniques embodied in that prose. On the other hand, they will feel challenged by effective writing produced by their peers.

Teachers must do more than make general standards clear to students. In feedback each student is given, the standards upon which a particular writing is being evaluated should be clear. This task-related feedback should relate specifically to the nature and requirements of the assignment. In giving such evaluation, instructors should emphasize one particular aspect of the work (organization, style, tone) and limit comments upon other things that may require attention later. To adhere strictly to the principle of task-relatedness, instructors may have to force themselves not to notice misspellings, mechanical errors, or stylistic problems in a paper whose organization and structure are the primary evaluative focus.

After the classes and conferences, the writing, the reading and rewriting comes the final, inevitable evaluation that must result in a grade for the course. Such decisions can sometimes tax the instructor's wisdom to its limit as he tries to decide whether a student's work has been strong enough for an A, or just a B+; a B, or just a C+; nor are decisions any easier if he must pick Honors, Pass, or Fail. All the semester's work comes to this last reduction of labor and hope to a single letter. Teachers may simply average all the grades awarded to the student's papers in the semester and leave it at that. But a more appropriate strategy is to grade on the basis of "progress," which generally means how well students have learned to write by course's end. There are variations of the "progress" basis: students may submit a certain number of what they think are their best writings; or they may be graded only on the major paper from each type of assignment; or they may be graded only on revisions rather than the original draft. Or the instructor may devise a grading system depending on several variables, including actual written work, willingness to revise, class or group participation, and attendance. If a contract has been formed between instructor and student, such as that described earlier in this chapter, the final grade will depend on the extent to which the contract has been fulfilled. The basic necessity in any of these grading patterns, of course, is that students should have understood clearly the basis upon which their work is to be evaluated.

But what of the complaint that Ms. X gives B's or C's to work that Mr. Y gives A's to? Is there any way to avoid the inherent subjectivity of grades on writing, measure-resistant as it is? Some teachers suggest a "portfolio system" of final evaluation that employs the instructor's colleagues in disinterested judgments of students' work.[27] After students select what they judge to be their best work at the end of the term, this "portfolio" is given a pass-fail evaluation, not by the instructor, but by a colleague. The outside reader's pass-or-fail judgment, based on department-wide standards, is final unless the original instructor strongly disagrees, in which case the matter may be appealed. Final evaluation by a disinterested party, it's argued, makes the students "more willing to accept the teacher in the role he or she actually fulfills, the friend and mentor who has a great stake in preparing the student to pass the portfolio" (952). Such a system requires cooperation among all writing teachers, a working together which can benefit all participants by developing a clearer consensus about standards.

Indeed, how can individual instructors be confident that their judgments represent the same standards their colleagues use? As they read volumes of student essays over the years, writing teachers inevitably form an intuitive sense about where a piece of writing falls on a scale of effectiveness. Usually the scale is structured along the A to F range required by the standard grading system; variations such as Honors-High Pass-Pass-Fail scale or the like allow the same sort of hierarchical scale. Nor is it difficult to articulate the differences in levels of such a scale. Most experienced readers can describe an "A" paper, a "B" paper, and so on down the scale, relying on degrees of effective organization, style, support, mechanics and usage, and tone, for example. It's in the application of the reader's intuitive scale to particular papers that the rub usually comes. What one teacher perceives as an "A" paper may appear to another as a "B-," *not* because they disagree on what an "A"paper is in the abstract, but because they perceive that particular paper differently. For an infinite variety of reasons, individual pieces of writing may cause sharp disputes among instructors who share the most serene theoretical agreement about standards of effective writing. New writing teachers especially may use inconsistent evaluative standards; they may be unprepared for the enormous variation in student abilities or for the complex mixture of strengths and weaknesses in a single piece of writing.

Evaluative standards can be harmonized among teachers, however. A crucially important activity can help: periodic, department-wide readings of student writing during which teachers' evaluations are openly discussed, compared, and adjusted if too far afield from the consensus. This "calibration" of grading standards (described in Chapter III) can help new and experienced teachers both. It can help new writing teachers articulate their standards and form a sense of where particular essays may fall on their personal evaluative scales. Experienced teachers may gain trust in their judgments by having them confirmed in public discussion and by articulating more clearly the reasons for them. If a teacher's judgments depart frequently from the judgments of colleagues, a change in his or her own evaluative scale may be needed. The joint reading must be followed by an open discussion for all participants. This process, by serving the writing teacher, ultimately serves the student: fairer and more consistent evaluations of student work will result from collaborative openness.

4. When should evaluation occur?

It's generally accepted that students should get feedback on their writing as quickly as possible after they have submitted it. Faith in the quick response is based partly on our collective memory of resentment at teachers who took weeks to read and return papers. Another justification for timely feedback lies in the stimulus-reinforcement behavioral model discussed earlier in this chapter. The SRR model suggests that the closer the reinforcement comes to the behavior itself, the sharper and more effective that reinforcement will be. In terms of composition pedagogy, this model asserts that the more quickly the evaluator responds to the writer, the more acutely subsequent writing behavior will be influenced. The longer the time elapsing between submission and return, according to the SRR model, the more likely it is that the original behavior to be reinforced will be lost amidst new and changing tasks. Responding to student writing is not the same as grading and returning tests. When returned to students, corrected tests may reveal misunderstanding and gaps in knowledge, but in many disciplines the student will not necessarily be handicapped by these lapses to the extent that new material cannot be learned meanwhile. In composition, on the other hand, uncorrected weaknesses will probably appear in the very next written performance and recur until altered by the student's changed behavior. The snowball effect of unchanged weaknesses in writing can grow very quickly when feedback is delayed beyond a reasonable point.

As strong as the case is for rapid feedback in writing, there's also some justification for a cooling-off period between the writing of the paper and its evaluative response. Students who, hot and expectant from writing papers, get immediate evaluations on them may resent the imposition of another's viewpoint on work they have not gained distance from. Timing in evaluation is really a matter of proportion; instantaneous feedback is liable to run afoul of students' intellectual and emotional involvement in their writing; delays of longer than a week allow them to forget the intentions they may have had and sentence them to repeat errors and to be ignorant of their strengths in their next assignment. One of the most dispiriting experiences for a student is to submit a paper within a deadline (perhaps at some cost to other courses) only to have weeks go by befor the instructor returns it. Not only does such delay short-circuit the feedback cycle, it also violates the implicit contract of good faith which gives the writing course its unique and invaluable humaneness on the college campus.

Notes

[1] Judith Butz and Terry Grabar, "Tutorial vs. Classroom in Freshman English," *College English,* 37 (March 1976), p. 654-56.

[2] See, for example, Ross M. Jewell, J. Cowley, and G. Rhum, *Final Report: The Effectiveness in College Level Instruction,* in Freshman Composition, Project 2188—Amended (Cedar Falls, IA: University of Northern Iowa, 1969), and Sara E. Sanders, "A Comparison of 'Aims' and 'Modes' Approaches to the Teaching of Junior College Freshmen" (Unpublished doctoral dissertation, University of Texas, 1973).

[3] Douglas G. Ellson, "Tutoring," in *The Psychology of Teaching Methods,* ed. N. L. Gage, National Society for the Study of Education (Chicago: NSSE, 1976), 150.

[4] Ellson, 150.

[5] Carl Rogers, *Freedom to Learn* (Columbus, OH: Merrill, 1969).

[6] Ellson, 133.

[7] Garrison, "One to One: Tutorial Instruction in Freshman Composition," *New Directions in Community Colleges,* 2 (September 1974), p. 69.

[8] John V. Knapp, "Contract/Conference Evaluations of Freshman Composition, *CE,* 37 (March 1976), p. 649.

[9] Rosemarie Arbur, "The Student-Teacher Conference," *College Composition and Communication,* 28 (December 1977), p. 338.

[10] See Knapp, above, and Barbara Fassler, "The Red Pen Revisited: Teaching Composition through Student Conferences," *CE,* 40 (October 1978), p. 186-90.

[11] James Moffett, *Teaching the Universe of Discourse* (Boston: Houghton Mifflin, 1968), 33.

[12] James Britton, *et al., The Development of Writing Abilities (11-18)* (London: Macmillan Education, 1975), Chaps. 4 and 8; p. 10.

[13] John MacLeish, "The Lecture Method," in *The Psychology of Teaching Methods,* 262.

[14] William E. Coles, Jr., "The Teaching of Writing as Writing," in *Ideas for English 101,* ed. Richard Ohmann and W. B. Coley (Urbana, IL: NCTE, 1975), 31.

[15] Leger Brosnahan, "Getting Freshman Composition All Together," *CE,* 37 (March 1976), p. 657.

[16] Robert Bales, "Communication in Small Groups," in *Communication, Language and Meaning,* ed. George A. Miller (New York: Basic Books, 1973), 217.

[17] Meredith and Joyce P. Gall, "The Discussion Method," in *The Psychology of Teaching Methods,* 176.

[18] Bales, 216.

[19] Kenneth Bruffee, "Collaborative Learning: Some Practical Models," in *English 101,* p. 54.

[20] Peter Elbow, *Writing Without Teachers* (New York: Oxford University Press, 1973), 90.

[21] Thom Hawkins, "Group Inquiry Techniques for Teaching Writing," *CE,* 38 (March 1976), 637-46.

[22] Elbow, 77.

[23] Sara Sanders and John Littlefield, "Perhaps Test Essays Can Reflect Significant Improvement in Freshman Composition," *RTE,* 9 (Fall 1975), pp. 145-53.

[24] Mary Denman, "The Measure of Success in Writing," *CCC,* 29(February 1978), 44.

[25] Elbow, 77.

[26] Mary Beaven, "Individualized Goal Setting, Self-Evaluation, and Peer Evaluation," in *Evaluating Writing,* ed. Charles R. Cooper and Lee Odell (Urbana, IL: NCTE, 1977), 150.

[27] James E. Ford and Gregory Larkin, "The Portfolio System: An End to Backsliding Writing Standards," *CE,* 39(April 1978), 950-55.

Appendix A
Text of "Teaching Composition: A Position Statement"

Teaching Composition: A Position Statement*

The following are general principles which members of the NCTE Commission on Composition believe should guide teachers in planning curricula and teaching writing. They are issued as an official position statement of the Commission. The Commission will welcome comments or questions.

1. *Life in Language.* In many senses, anyone's world is his language. Through language we understand, interpret, enjoy, control, and in part create our worlds. The teacher of English, in awakening students to the possibilities of language, can help students to expand and enlarge their worlds, to live more fully.

2. *Need for Writing.* Writing is an important medium for self-expression, for communication, and for the discovery of meaning—its need increased rather than decreased by the development of new media for mass communication. Practice and study of writing therefore remain significant parts of the school curriculum and central parts of the English course.

3. *Positive Instruction.* Since a major value of writing is self-expression and self-realization, instruction in writing should be positive. Students should be encouraged to use language clearly, vividly, and honestly; they should not be discouraged by negative correction and proscription. They should be freed from fear and restriction so that their sensitivity and their abilities can develop.

4. *Learning by Writing.* Learning to write requires writing; writing practice should be a major emphasis of the course. Workbook exercises, drill on usage, and analysis of existing prose are not adequate substitutes for writing.

5. *Required Writing.* No formula dictates the amount of writing that should be required in a course—a paper a day or a paper a week. Ideally students should be allowed to write when they want to, as much as they want to, and at their own speed. Practically, however, students need class discipline and class discussion as well as freedom, and they should be frequently encouraged and at times required to write.

*Published in *College English,* 36 (October 1974), 219-20.

6. *Classroom Writing.* Inexperienced writers especially should have an opportunity to compose in school, with help during the actual writing process in clarifying ideas, in choosing phrasing, and sometimes in dealing with mechanical problems. Writing outside the classroom, of course, should be encouraged and sometimes required.

7. *Range of Assignments.* Writing assignments should be individualized, adjusted to the age, interests, and abilities of the student. Particularly in the elementary grades, but also through high school and into college, the teacher should encourage writing from personal experience, sometimes developing classroom experiences to provide material for writing. The expository essay should not be the exclusive form of composition encouraged. Especially for students who have convinced themselves that composition must be boring, a chore to be avoided whenever possible, writing various kinds of narratives, vignettes, dialogues, fables, family folklore, parodies, and the like may create interest.

8. *Alternate Techniques.* Instruction in writing techniques and rhetorical strategies should be part of the writing course, adjusted to the age and need of the students and focused on positive advice, suggestions, information, and encouragement. Instruction can include discussion of various ways in which writing can achieve its ends—in units as brief as a word or two and as long as a book—observations of procedures followed in existing prose, and constructive criticism of student writing.

9. *Composing.* Since there is adequate subject matter for direct study of writing, courses or units of English courses dedicated to composition should not be converted to courses in literature or social problems, with compositions to be written on the side.

10. *Usage.* Usage is an aspect of rhetoric; learning to predict the social effects of different dialects or different linguistic constructions is part of learning how writing can achieve its purposes. Students should be provided with information that will allow them the largest possible body of alternatives from which to choose and will help them to choose wisely. They should know, for example, that *dragged* and *drug* are both used as past tense forms, but that some listeners will react to *drug* by considering it uneducated. Or students should learn that *we was* and *we were* are alternatives but that *we was* is not characteristic of a prestige dialect. Such information should be provided through positive instruction about how dialects develop and why variations occur—not through correction based on notions of right and wrong.

11. *Dialects.* No dialect should be presented as "right" or "pure" or "logical" or better than others. The student should be given an opportunity to learn a standard written English, but the teacher must resist the temptation to allow the cultivation of a standard written English to stifle self-expression or to overshadow emphasis on clear, forceful, interesting writing.

12. *Grammar.* The study of the structure and history of language, including English grammar, is a valuable asset to a liberal education and an important part of an English program. It should, however, be taught for its own sake, not as a substitute for composition and not with the pretense that it is taught only to improve writing.

13. *Support for Composing.* Various kinds of activities related to composition contribute to the student's ability to write—film-making, debates, collecting material for notebooks, library investigation, dramatics, field trips, television and film viewing. The attractions of such activities—because of their novelty or because they seem to gain more immediate student interest—should not be allowed to supersede instruction in writing

14. *Talking and Writing.* Students are influenced by mass media not only as consumers but also as producers. Children, for example, may find it easier to compose orally on tapes, without the labor of handwriting. The teacher can sometimes exploit this interest in oral composition as a step toward writing, but the importance of the written word remains, and practice in oral composition is not sufficient.

15. *Audience.* Although some writing may be intended to be private, writing implies an audience and students should be helped to use a voice appropriate to the interests, maturity, and ability of an audience. Furthermore, since young writers are especially concerned about response, their writing should be read by classmates as well as the teacher.

16. *Grading.* The mere assignment of grades is rarely an adequate way of encouraging and improving writing; whenever possible grades should be replaced by criticism or detailed evaluation. When grades are required, the teacher should avoid basing them primarily on negative considerations—for example, the number of misspelled words or sentence fragments.

17. *Class size.* Classes in writing should be limited to no more than twenty to facilitate frequent writing, reading of papers, and discussion of written work.

18. *Objectives.* Emphasis on instructional objectives or on accountability should not dictate the content of the course, particularly not to replace writing with attention to measurable skills—mechanics, for example. Teachers should retain responsibility for determining their objectives: demands for accountability should not interfere with independent thought among students.

Appendix B
Partial Text of "Students' Right to Their Own Language"*

IV. Why Do Some Dialects Have More Prestige Than Others?

In a specific setting, because of historical and other factors, certain dialects may be endowed with more prestige than others. Such dialects are sometimes called "standard" or "consensus" dialects. These designations of prestige are not inherent in the dialect itself, but are *externally imposed*, and the prestige of a dialect shifts as the power relationships of the speakers shift.

The English language at the beginning of its recorded history was already divided into distinct regional dialects. These enjoyed fairly equal prestige for centuries. However, the centralization of English political and commercial life at London gradually gave the dialect spoken there a preeminence over other dialects. This process was far advanced when printing was invented; consequently, the London dialect became the dialect of the printing press, and the dialect of the printing press became the so-called "standard" even though a number of oral readings of one text would reveal different pronunciations and rhythmic patterns across dialects. When the early American settlers arrived on this continent, they brought their British dialects with them. Those dialects were altered both by regional separation from England and concentration into sub-groups within this country as well as by contact with the various languages spoken by the Indians they found here and with the various languages spoken by the immigrants who followed.

At the same time, social and political attitudes formed in the old world followed to the new, so Americans sought to achieve linguistic marks of success as exemplified in what they regarded as proper, cultivated usage. Thus the dialect used by prestigious New England speakers early became the "standard" the schools attempted to teach. It remains, during our own time, the dialect that style books encourage us to represent in writing. The diversity of our cultural heritage, however, has created a corresponding language diversity and, in the 20th century, most linguists agree that there is no single, homogeneous American "standard." They also agree that, although the amount of prestige and power

*Published in *College Composition and Communication*, 25 (Fall 1974), Special Issue, 5-10 (partial text).

possessed by a group can be recognized through its dialect, no dialect is inherently good or bad.

The need for a written dialect to serve the larger, public community has resulted in a general commitment to what may be called "edited American English," that prose which is meant to carry information about our representative problems and interests. To carry such information through aural-oral media, "broadcast English" or "network standard" has been developed and given precedence. Yet these dialects are subject to change, too. Even now habit patterns from other types of dialects are being incorporated into them. Our pluralistic society requires many varieties of language to meet our multiplicity of needs.

V. How Can Concepts from Modern Linguistics Help Clarify the Question of Dialects?

Several concepts from modern linguistics clarify and define problems of dialect. Recent studies verify what our own casual observation should lead us to believe—namely, that intelligence is not a factor in the child's acquisition of a basic language system. In fact, only when I. Q. is at about fifty or below does it become significant in retarding the rate and completeness with which children master their native spoken dialect. Dialect switching, however, becomes progressively more difficult as the speaker grows older. As one passes from infancy to childhood to adolescence and to maturity, language patterns become more deeply ingrained and more a part of the individual's self-concept; hence they are more difficult to alter.

Despite ingrained patterns characteristic of older people, every speaker of a language has a tremendous range of versatility, constantly making subtle changes to meet various situations. That is, speakers of a language have mastered a variety of ranges and levels of usage; no one's idiolect, however well established, is monolithic and inflexible. This ability of the individual speaker to achieve constant and subtle modulations is so pervasive that it usually goes unnoticed by the speaker and the hearers alike.

The question, then, is not whether students can make language changes, for they do so all the time, but whether they can step over the hazily defined boundaries that separate dialects. Dialect switching is complicated by many factors, not the least of which is the individual's own cultural heritage. Since dialect is not separate from culture, but an intrinsic part of it, accepting a new dialect means accepting a new culture; rejecting one's native dialect is to some extent a rejection of one's culture.

Therefore, the question of whether or not students *will* change their dialect involves their acceptance of a new—and possibly strange or hostile—set of cultural values. Although many students *do* become bidialectal, and many *do* abandon their native dialects, those who don't switch may have any of a number of reasons, some of which may be beyond the school's right to interfere with.

In linguistic terms the normal teenager has *competence* in his native dialect, the ability to use all of its structural resources, but the actual *performance* of any speaker in any dialect always falls short of the totality implied by competence. No one can ever use all of the resources of a language, but one function of the English teacher is to activate the student's competence, that is, increase the range of his habitual performance.

Another insight from linguistic study is that differences among dialects in a given language are always confined to a limited range of *surface* features that have no effect on what linguists call *deep structure,* a term that might be roughly translated as "meaning." For instance, the following groups of sentences have minor surface differences, but obviously share meanings:

Herbert saw Hermione yesterday.
Herbert seen Hermione yesterday.

Mary's daddy is at home.
Mary's daddy is to home.
Mary daddy home.

Bill is going to the circus.
Bill, he's going to the circus.
Bill he going to the circus.

Preference for one form over another, then, is not based on meaning or even "exactness" of expression, but depends on social attitudes and cultural norms. The surface features are recognized as signs of social status.

VI. Does Dialect Affect the Ability to Read?

The linguistic concepts can bring a new understanding of the English teacher's function in dealing with reading and writing skills. Schools and colleges emphasize one form of language, the one we called Edited American English (EAE). It is the written language of the weekly newsmagazines, of almost all newspapers, and of most books. This variety of written English can be loosely termed a dialect, and it has pre-empted a great deal of attention in English classes.

If a speaker of any dialect of a language has competence (but not necessarily the ability to perform) in any other dialect of that language, then dialect itself cannot be posited as a reason for a student's failure to be able to read EAE. That is, dialect itself is not an impediment to reading, for the process of reading involves decoding to meaning (deep structure), not decoding to an utterance. Thus, the child who reads

Phillip's mother is in Chicago.

out loud as

Phillip mother in Chicago.

has read correctly, that is, has translated the surface of an EAE sentence into a meaning and has used his own dialect to give a surface form to that meaning.

Reading, in short, involves the acquisition of meanings, not the ability to reproduce meanings in any given surface forms.

Reading difficulties may be a result of inadequate vocabulary, problems in perception, ignorance of contextual cues that aid in the reading process, lack of familiarity with the stylistic ordering, interference from the emotional bias of the material, or combinations of these. In short, reading is so complicated a process that it provides temptations to people who want to offer easy explanations and solutions.

This larger view should make us cautious about the assumption that the students' dialect interferes with learning to read. Proceeding from such a premise, current "dialect" readers employ one of two methods. Some reading materials are written completely in the students' dialect with the understanding that later the students will be switched to materials written in the "standard" dialect. Other materials are written in companion sets of "Home" version and "School" version. Students first read through the "dialect" version, then through the *same* booklet written in "school" English. Both methods focus primarily on a limited set of surface linguistic features, as for example, the deletion of -*ed* in past tense verbs or the deletion of -*r* in final position.

To cope with our students' reading problem, then, we cannot confine ourselves to the constricting and ultimately ineffectual dialect readers designed for the "culturally deprived." We should structure and select materials geared to complex reading problems and oriented to the experience and sophistication of our students. An urban eight-year-old who has seen guns and knives in a street fight may not be much interested in reading how Jane's dog Spot dug in the neighbor's flower bed. Simply because "Johnny can't read" doesn't mean "Johnny is immature" or "Johnny can't think." He may be bored. Carefully chosen materials will certainly expose students to new horizons and should increase their awareness and heighten their perceptions of the social reality. Classroom reading materials can be employed to further our students' reading ability and, at the same time, can familiarize them with other varieties of English.

Admittedly, the kinds of materials we're advocating are, at present, difficult to find, but some publishers are beginning to move in this direction. In the meantime, we can use short, journalistic pieces, such as those found on the editorial pages of newspapers, we might rely on materials composed by our students, and we can certainly write our own materials. The important fact to remember is that speakers in any dialect encounter essentially the same difficulties in reading, and thus we should not be so much interested in changing our students' dialect as in improving their command of the reading process.

VII. Does Dialect Affect the Ability to Write?

The ability to write EAE is quite another matter, for learning to write a given dialect, like learning to speak a dialect, involves the activation of areas of competence. Further, learning to write in any dialect entails the mastery of such conventions as spelling and punctuation, surface features of the written language. Again, native speakers of any dialect of a language have virtually total competence in all dialects of that language, but they may not have learned (and may never learn) to punctuate or spell, and, indeed, may not even learn the mechanical skill of forming letters and sequences of letters with a writing instrument. And even if they do, they may have other problems in transferring ease and fluency in speech to skill in writing.

Even casual observation indicates that dialect as such plays little if any part in determining whether a child will ultimately acquire the ability to write EAE. In fact, if speakers of a great variety of American dialects do master EAE—from Senator Sam Ervin to Senator Edward Kennedy, from Ernest Hemingway to William Faulkner—there is no reason to assume that dialects such as urban black and Chicano impede the child's ability to learn to write EAE while countless others do not. Since the issue is not the capacity of the dialect itself, the teacher can concentrate on building up the students' confidence in their ability to write.

If we name the essential functions of writing as expressing oneself, communicating information and attitudes, and discovering meaning through both logic and metaphor, then we view variety of dialects as an advantage. In self-expression, not only one's dialect but one's idiolect is basic. In communication one may choose roles which imply certain dialects, but the decision is a social one, for the dialect itself does not limit the information which can be carried, and the attitudes may be most clearly conveyed in the dialect the writer finds most congenial. Dialects are equally serviceable in logic and metaphor.

Perhaps the most serious difficulty facing "nonstandard" dialect speakers in developing writing ability derives from their exaggerated concern for the least serious aspects of writing. If we can convince our students that spelling, punctuation, and usage are less important than content, we have removed a major obstacle in their developing the ability to write. Examples of student writing are useful for illustrating this point. In every composition class there are examples of writing which is clear and vigorous despite the use of nonstandard forms (at least as described by the handbook)—and there are certainly many examples of limp, vapid writing in "standard dialect." Comparing the writing allows the students to see for themselves that dialect seldom obscures clear, forceful writing. EAE is important for certain kinds of students, its features are easily identified and taught, and school patrons are often satisfied when it is mastered, but that should not tempt teachers to evade the still more important features of language.

When students want to play roles in dialects other than their own, they should be encouraged to experiment, but they can acquire the fundamental skills of writing in their own dialect. Their experiments are ways of becoming more versatile. We do not condone ill-organized, imprecise, undefined, inappropriate writing in any dialect; but we are especially distressed to find sloppy writing approved so long as it appears with finicky correctness in "school standard" while vigorous and thoughtful statements in less prestigious dialects are condemned.

VIII. Does Dialect Limit the Ability to Think?

All languages are the product of the same instrument, namely, the human brain. It follows, then, that all languages and all dialects are essentially the same in their deep structure, regardless of how varied the surface structures might be. (This is equal to saying that the human brain is the human brain.) And if these hypotheses are true, then all controverises over dialect will take on a new dimension. The question will no longer turn on language *per se*, but will concern the nature of a society which places great value on given surface features of language and proscribes others, for any language or any dialect will serve any purpose that its users want it to serve.

There is no evidence, in fact, that enables us to describe any language or any dialect as incomplete or deficient apart from the conditions of its use. The limits of a particular speaker should not be interpreted as a limit of the dialect.

Just as people suppose that speakers who omit the plural inflection as in "six cow" instead of "six cows" cannot manipulate the concept of plurality, so also some believe that absence of tense markers as in "yesterday they *look* at the flood damage" indicates that the speaker has no concept of time. Yet these same people have no difficulty in understanding the difference between "now I *cut* the meat / yesterday I *cut* the meat," also without a tense marker. The alternative forms are adequate to express meaning.

And experience tells us that when speakers of any dialect need a new word for a new thing, they will invent or learn the needed word. Just as most Americans added "sputnik" to their vocabularies a decade or more ago, so speakers of other dialects can add such words as "periostitis" or "interosculate" whenever their interests demand it.

IX. What Is the Background for Teaching One "Grammar"?

Since the eighteenth century, English grammar has come to mean for most people the rules telling one how to speak and write in the best society. When social groups were clearly stratified into "haves" and "have-nots," there was no need for defensiveness about variations in language—the landlord could understand the speech of the stable boy, and neither of them worried about language differences. But when social and economic changes increased social mobility, the members of the "rising middle class," recently liberated from and therefore immediately threatened by the lower class, demanded books of rules telling them how to act in ways that would not betray their background and would so-lidly establish them in their newly acquired social group. Rules regulating social behavior were compiled in books of etiquette; rules regulating linguistic behavior were compiled in dictionaries and grammar books. Traditional grammar books were unapologetically designed to instill linguistic habits which, though often inconsistent with actual language practice and sometimes in violation of common sense, were intended to separate those who had "made it" from those who had not, the powerful from the poor.

Practices developed in England in the eighteenth century were transported wholesale to the New World. Linguistic snobbery was tacitly encouraged by a slavish reliance on rules "more honored in the breach than the observance," and these attitudes had consequences far beyond the realm of language. People from different language and ethnic backgrounds were denied social privileges, legal rights, and economic opportunity, and their inability to manipulate the dialect used by the privileged group was used as an excuse for this denial. Many teachers, moved by the image of the "melting pot," conscientiously tried to eliminate every vestige of behavior not sanctioned in the grammar books, and the schools rejected as failures all those children who did not conform to the linguistic prejudices of the ruling middle class. With only slight modifications, many of our "rules," much of the "grammar" we still teach, reflects that history of social climbing and homogenizing.

List of Further Readings

Chapter I

General Histories of Rhetoric

Corbett, E. P. J. "A Survey of Rhetoric." In *Classical Rhetoric for the Modern Student.* New York: Oxford University Press, 1965.

Ehninger, Douglas. "On Systems of Rhetoric." *Philosophy and Rhetoric,* 1(Summer, 1968), 131-44.

Golden, James L., Goodwin F. Berquist and William E. Coleman. *The Rhetoric of Western Thought,* 2nd ed. Dubuque, IA: Kendall/Hunt Publishing Co. 1978.

Larson, Richard L. "Structure and Form in Non-Fiction Prose." In *Teaching Composition: 10 Bibliographical Essays,* ed. Gary Tate. Fort Worth, TX: Texas Christian University Press, 1976.

Scaglione, Aldo. *The Classical Theory of Composition from Its Origins to the Present: An Historical Survey.* Chapel Hill, NC: University of North Carolina Press, 1972.

Classical Rhetoric

Aristotle. *The Rhetoric of Aristotle,* trans. Lane Cooper. Englewood Cliffs, NJ: Prentice-Hall, 1960.

Corder, Jim. *The Uses of Rhetoric.* New York: J. B. Lippincott. 1971.

Hughes, Richard. "The Contemporaneity of Classical Rhetoric." *College Composition and Communication,* 16(October, 1965), 157-9.

Murphy, James A. *A Synoptic History of Classical Rhetoric.* New York: Random House, 1972.

Medieval Rhetoric

Atkins, J. W. H. *English Literary Criticism: The Medieval Phase.* New York: Macmillan, 1943.

Caplan, Harry. *Of Eloquence: Studies in Ancient and Medieval Rhetoric.* Ithaca: Cornell University Press, 1970.

McKeon, Richard. "Rhetoric in the Middle Ages." *Speculum,* 17(1942), 1-32. Reprinted in *Critics and Criticism: Ancient and Modern,* ed. R. S. Crane. Chicago: University of Chicago Press, 1952.

Murphy, James. *Rhetoric in the Middle Ages: A History of Rhetorical Theory from St. Augustine to the Renaissance.* Berkeley: University of California Press, 1974.

Renaissance and 17th Century Rhetoric

Corbett, E. P. J. "John Locke's Contributions to Rhetoric." *CCC,* 32(December 1981), 423-33.

Clark, Donald L. *John Milton at St. Paul's School: A Study of Ancient Rhetoric in English Renaissance Education.* New York: Columbia University Press, 1948.

Clark, Donald L. *Rhetoric and Poetry in the Renaissance.* New York: Columbia Unisity Press, 1963.

Croll, Morris W. *Style, Rhetoric and Rhythm.* Princeton: Princeton University Press, 1966.

Hardison, O. B. *The Enduring Monument.* Chapel Hill: University of North Carolina Press, 1962.

Ong, Walter J. *Rhetoric, Romance and Technology.* Ithaca: Cornell University Press, 1971.

Sonnino, Lee Ann. *A Handbook to Sixteenth Century Rhetoric.* London: Routledge and Kegan Paul, 1968.

18th and 19th Century Rhetoric

Berlin, James A. "Richard Whately and Current-Traditional Rhetoric." *College English,* 42(September, 1980), 10-17.

Blair, Hugh. *Lectures on Rhetoric and Belles Lettres* (1783), ed. Harold Harding, 2 vols. Carbondale: Southern Illinois University Press, 1965.

Connors, Robert J. "The Rise and Fall of the Modes of Discourse." *CCC,* 32(December, 1981), 444-55.

Ehninger, Douglas. "Dominant Trends in English Rhetorical Thought, 1750-1800." *Southern Speech Journal,* 18(September, 1952), 3-12.

Golden, James and E. P. J. Corbett, eds. *The Rhetoric of Blair, Campbell and Whately.* New York: Holt, Rinehart and Winston, 1968.

Howell, Wilbur S. *Eighteenth-Century British Logic and Rhetoric.* Princeton: Princeton University Press, 1971.

Larson, Richard. "Structure and Form in Non-Fiction Prose." In *Teaching Composition: 10 Bibliographical Essays,* ed. Gary Tate. Fort Worth: Texas Christian University Press, 1976.

Whately, Richard. *Elements of Rhetoric*(1828), ed. Douglas Ehninger. Carbondale: Southern Illinois University Press, 1963.

20th Century Rhetoric

Becker, Samuel L. "Rhetorical Studies for the Contemporary World." In *The Prospect of Rhetoric*, ed. Lloyd F. Bitzer and Edwin Black. Englewood Cliffs, NJ: Prentice-Hall, 1971.

Fogarty, Daniel J. *Roots for a New Rhetoric*. New York: Columbia University Press, 1959.

Halloran, S. M. "On the End of Rhetoric, Classical and Modern." *CE*, 36(February, 1975), 621-31.

Perelman, Chaim, and L. Olbrechts-Tyteca. *The New Rhetoric*. Notre Dame, IN: University of Notre Dame Press, 1969.

Richards, I. A. *The Philosophy of Rhetoric*. New York: Oxford University Press, 1936.

Snipes, Wilson C. "Notes on Choice in Rhetoric." *CCC*, 27(May, 1976), 148-54.

Steinmann, Martin, ed. *New Rhetorics*. New York: Charles Scribner's Sons, 1967.

Rhetoric and Teaching

Corder, Jim. "What I Learned at School." *CCC*, 26(December, 1975), 330-4.

Freedman, Aviva and Ian Pringle. *Reinventing the Rhetorical Tradition*. Urbana, IL: NCTE, 1980.

Gage, John T. "Conflicting Assumptions About Intention in Teaching Reading and Composition." *CE*, 40(November, 1978), 255-63.

Larson, Richard. "Teaching Rhetoric in the High School: Some Proposals." *English Journal*, 55(November, 1966), 1058-65.

Ong, Walter. "The Writer's Audience Is Always a Fiction." *PMLA*, 90(January, 1975), 9-21.

Stewart, Donald C. "Composition Textbooks and the Assault on Tradition." *CCC*, 29(May, 1978), 171-6. Reprinted in *The Writing Teacher's Sourcebook*, ed. Gary Tate. New York: Oxford University Press, 1981.

Walter, Otis M. "The Value of the Classics in Rhetoric." *CCC*, 32(December, 1981), 416-22.

Psychology and Language

Alexander, Hubert. *Language and Thinking*. New York: D. Van Nostrand, 1967.

Bartholomae, David. "The Study of Error." *CCC*, 31(October, 1980), 253-69.

Britton, James. *Language and Learning*. London: Penguin, 1970. Available from Boynton/Cook.

Bruner, Jerome. *The Process of Education*, Cambridge: Harvard University Press, 1960.

―――――. *On Knowing*. Cambridge: Harvard University Press, 1963.

Donahoe, John W. and Michael Wessels. *Learning, Language, and Memory*. New York: Harper & Row, 1979.

Flavell, John H. *The Developmental Psychology of Jean Piaget.* New York: D. Van Nostrand, 1963.

Ginsburg, Herbert and Sylvia Opper. *Piaget's Theory of Intellectual Development.* Englewood Cliffs, NJ: Prentice-Hall, 1969.

Golman Eisler, F. *Psycholinguistics.* London: Academic Press, 1968.

Hunt, Kellogg. *Grammatical Structures Written at Three Grade Levels.* Urbana, IL: NCTE: 1965.

——————."Early Blooming and Late Blooming Syntactic Structures." In *Evaluating Writing,* ed. Charles R. Cooper and Lee Odell. Urbana, IL: NCTE, 1977.

Jakobson, Roman. "Linguistics and Poetics." In *Style and Language,* ed. T. A. Sebeok. New York: John Wiley, 1960.

Paivio, Allan. *Imagery and Verbal Process.* New York: Holt, Rinehart and Winston, 1971.

Piaget, Jean. *The Language and Thought of the Child,* tr. Marjorie Warden. New York: Harcourt, Brace and World, 1926.

Putnam, Hilary. *Mind, Language and Reality.* New York: Cambridge University Press, 1975.

Solokov, A. N. *Inner Speech and Thought,* tr. George T. Onischenko. New York: The Plenum Press, 1972.

Vinacke, Edgar. *The Psychology of Thinking.* New York: McGraw-Hill, 1974.

Whitehurst, Grover J. and Barry Zimmerman, eds. *The Functions of Language and Cognition.* San Francisco: Academic Press, 1979.

The Composing Process

Berthoff, Ann E. *The Making of Meaning: Metaphors, Models, and Maxims for Writing Teachers.* Montclair, NJ: Boynton/Cook, 1981.

Cooper, Charles R. and Lee Odell. *Research on Composing: Points of Departure.* Urbana, IL: NCTE, 1978.

Emig, Janet. "The Biology of Writing: Another View of the Process." In *The Writing Processes of Students,* eds. W. T. Petty and P. J. Finn. Buffalo: SUNY, Department of Elementary and Remedial Education, 1975.

——————.*The Web of Meaning: Essays on Writing, Teaching, Learning, and Thinking.* Montclair, NJ: Boynton/Cook, 1983.

Graves, Donald. "An Examination of the Writing Processes of Seven-Year-Old Children." *Research in the Teaching of English,* 9(1975), 227-41.

Petty, W. T. and P. J. Finn, eds. *The Writing Processes of Students.* Buffalo: SUNY, Department of Elementary and Remedial Education, 1975.

Sudol, Ronald A., ed. *Revising: New Essays for Teachers of Writing.* Urbana, IL: NCTE, 1982.

Wason, Peter, ed. *Dynamics of Writing.* Special Issue of *Visible Language.* Urbana, IL: NCTE, 1980

Invention

Berthoff, Ann E. "From Problem-Solving to a Theory of Imagination," *CE, 33* (March, 1972), 636-49.

Burke, Kenneth. "Questions and Answers About the Pentad." *CCC,* 29(December, 1978), 330-5.

Flower, Linda and John Hayes. "Problem-Solving Strategies and the Writing Process." *CE,* 39(December, 1977), 449-61.

_____."The Cognition of Discovery: Defining a Rhetorical Problem." *CCC,* 31(February, 1980), 21-32.

Harrington, David, et al. "A Critical Survey of Resources for Teaching Rhetorical Invention." *CE,* 31(February, 1979), 641-61.

Kaufman, Wallace. *The Writer's Mind.* Englewood Cliffs, NJ: Prentice-Hall, 1970.

Kinney, James. "Tagmemic Rhetoric: A Reconsideration." *CCC,* 29(May, 1978), 141-45.

Kneupper, Charles. "Revising the Tagmemic Heuristic: Theoretical and Pedagogical Considerations." *CCC,* 31(May, 1980), 160-67.

Larson, Richard. "Discovery through Questioning: A Plan for Teaching Rhetorical Invention." *CE,* 30(November, 1968), 126-34.

Chapter II

Burke, Moffett, Britton

Agee, Hugh. "Kenneth Burke's Pentad Format: A Rhetorical Model for Persuasive Writing." *Teaching English in the Two-Year College,* 5(Winter, 1979), 101-4.

Burke, Kenneth. "Questions and Answers About the Pentad." *CCC,* 29(December, 1978), 330.5.

Comprone, Joseph. "Kenneth Burke and the Teaching of Writing." *CCC,* 29(December, 1978), 336-40.

Heath, Robert L. "Kenneth Burke on Form." *Quarterly Journal of Speech,* 65 (December, 1979), 392-404.

Holland, L. Virginia. *Counterpoint* [Burke and Aristotle]. New York: The Philosophical Library, 1959.

Keith, Philip. "Burke for the Composition Class." *CCC,* 28(December, 1977), 348-51.

Sooby, Andrew. "What Is English? The Relevance of James Moffett's *The Universe of Discourse.*" *English in Australia,* 53(September, 1980), 6-17.

Kefford, R. E. "James Britton's Participant and Spectator Roles—A Problem in Conceptualisation." *English in Australia,* 35(May, 1976), 17-21.

Murray, Geraldine. "A Different Form." *English in Education,* 12(Fall, 1978), 10-19.

Rosen, Lois. "An Interview with James Britton, Tony Burgess, and Harold Rosen." *EJ,* 67(November, 1978), 50-8.

Kinneavy, D'Angelo

Harris, Elizabeth. "Applications of Kinneavy's *Theory of Discourse* to Technical Writing." *CE*, 40(February, 1979), 632-52.
Knoblauch, C. H. "Intentionality in the Writing Process: A Case Study." *CCC*, 31 (May, 1980), 153-9.
O'Bannion, John D. "*A Theory of Discourse:* A Retrospective." *CCC*, 33(May, 1982), 196-201.

D'Angelo, Frank. "The Search for Intelligible Structure in the Teaching of Composition." *CCC*, 27(May, 1976), 142-7. Reprinted in *The Writing Teacher's Sourcebook*, ed. Gary Tate and E. P. J. Corbett. New York: Oxford University Press, 1981, pp. 80-88.

Other Treatments of Discourse Theory

DeBeaugrande, Robert. "Psychology and Composition." *CCC*, 30(February, 1979), 50-57.
Eckhardt, Caroline and David H. Stewart. "Towards a Functional Taxonomy of Composition." *CCC*, 30(December, 1979), 338-42. Reprinted in *The Writing Teacher's Sourcebook*, pp. 100-06.
Grady, Michael. "A Conceptual Rhetoric of Composition." *CCC*, 22(December, 1971), 348-54.
Larson, Richard L. "Language Studies and Composing Processes." In *Linguistics, Stylistics and the Teaching of Composition.* ed. Donald McQuade. Akron, OH: University of Akron, 1979, pp. 182-90.
Odell, Lee. "Teachers of Composition and Needed Research in Discourse Theory." *CCC*, 30(February, 1979), 39-45. Reprinted in *The Writing Teacher's Sourcebook*, pp. 53-61.
Ong, Walter J. *Interfaces of the Word.* Ithaca: Cornell University Press, 1977.

Sentences

Arena, Louis A. *Linguistics and Composition: A Method to Improve Expository Writing Skills.* Washington: Georgetown University Press, 1975.
Christensen, Francis and Bonniejean L. *A New Rhetoric.* New York: Harper & Row, 1976.
Cooper, Charles R. "An Outline for Writing Sentence-Combining Problems." *English Journal,* 62(January, 1973), 96-102. Reprinted in *The Writing Teacher's Sourcebook*, pp. 368-78.
Faigley, Lester. "Generative Rhetoric as a Way of Increasing Syntactic Fluency." *CCC*, 30(May, 1979), 176-81.
Gibson, Walker. *Tough, Sweet and Stuffy.* Bloomington: Indiana University Press, 1966.
Maimon, Elaine P. and Barbara F. Nodine. "Measuring Syntactic Growth: Errors and Expectations in Sentence-Combining Practice with College Freshmen." *RTE*, 12(October, 1978), 233-44.

Milic, Louis. "Theories of Style and Their Implications for the Teacher of English." *CCC,* 16(May, 1965), 66-9, 126.

Morenberg, Max, Donald Daiker, Andrew Kerek. "Sentence-Combining at the College Level: An Experimental Study." *RTE,* 12(October, 1978), 245-56.

——————— and Andrew Kerek. "Bibliography on Sentence-Combining: Theory and Practice, 1964-1979." *Rhetoric Society Quarterly,* 9(Spring, 1979) 97-111.

Ney, James W. "The Hazards of the Course: Sentence-Combining in Freshman English." *English Record,* 27(Summer/Autumn, 1976), 70-77.

Ohmann, Richard. "Use Definite, Specific, Concrete Language." *CE,* 41(December, 1979), 390-97. Reprinted in *The Writing Teacher's Sourcebook,* 379-89.

Weathers, Winston. "The Rhetoric of the Series." *CCC,* 17(December, 1966), 217-222.

Paragraphs

Braddock, Richard. "The Frequency and Placement of Topic Sentences in Expository Prose." *RTE,* 8(Winter, 1974), 287-304. Reprinted in *The Writing Teacher's Sourcebook,* pp. 310-23.

Burke, Virginia. "The Paragraph: Dancer in Chains." In *Rhetoric: Theories for Application,* ed. Robert Gorrell. Urbana, IL: NCTE, 1967, pp. 37-44.

D'Angelo, Frank. "A Generative Rhetoric of the Essay." *CCC,* 25(December, 1974), 388-96.

Halliday, M. A. K. and Ruquaiya Hassan. *Cohesion in English.* London: Longman, 1973.

Karrfalt, David. "The Generation of Paragraphs and Larger Units." *CCC,* 19(October, 1968), 211-17.

Meade, Richard A. and W. Geiger Ellis. "Paragraph Development in the Modern Age of Rhetoric." *EJ,* 59(February, 1970), 219-26.

Nold, Ellen and Brent Davis. "The Discourse Matrix." *CCC,* 31(May, 1980), 141-52.

Shearer, Ned. "Alexander Bain and the Genesis of Paragraph Theory." *QJS,* 58(December, 1972), 408-17.

Stern, Arthur. "When Is a Paragraph?" *CCC,* 27(October, 1976), 253-57. Reprinted in *The Writing Teacher's Sourcebook,* pp. 294-300.

Warner, Richard. "Teaching the Paragraph as a Structural Unit." *CCC,* 20(May, 1979), 152-5.

Chapter III

Literacy and Other Social Issues of Language

Cross, K. Patricia. *Beyond the Open Door: New Students to Higher Education.* San Francisco: Jossey-Bass, 1971.

Dreeben, Robert. *On What Is Learned in Schools.* Reading, MA: Addison-Wesley, 1968.

Gere, Anne R. and Eugene Smith. *Attitudes, Language and Change.* Urbana, IL:
NCTE, 1979.
Moffett, James. *Coming on Center: English Education in Evolution.* Montclair, NJ:
Boynton/Cook, 1981.
Mosteller, Frederick and Daniel P. Moynihan, eds. *On Equality of Educational
Opportunity.* New York: Random House, 1972.
Nordstom, Carl, Edward Friedenberg, Hilary A. Gold. *Society's Children: A Study
of Resentment in the Secondary Schools.* New York: Random House, 1967.

Dialect and Code

Bolinger, Dwight. *Aspects of Language.* New York: Harcourt Brace Jovanovich, 1968.
Davis, A. L., ed. *Culture, Class and Language Variety: A Resource Book for Teachers.*
Urbana, IL: NCTE, 1972.
Dillard, J. L. *Black English: Its History and Usage in the United States.* New York:
Random House, 1972.
Gray, Barbara. "Dialect Interference in Writing: A Tripartite Analysis." *Journal
of Basic Writing,* 1(Spring, 1975), 14-22.
Hoover, Mary R. "Community Attitudes Toward Black English." *Language in
Society,* 7(1978), 65-87.
Labov, William. *The Study of Nonstandard English.* Urbana, IL: NCTE, 1970.
Nattinger, James R. "Second Dialect and Second Language in the Composition
Class." *TESOL Quarterly,* 12(March, 1978), 77-84.
Nist, John. *Handicapped English: The Language of the Socially Disadvantaged.*
Springfield, IL: Charles C. Thomas, 1974.
Ohmann, Richard. "Reflections on Class and Language." *CE,* 44(January, 1982),
1-17.
Reed, Carroll. *Dialects of American English,* Urbana, IL: NCTE, 1977.
Shuy, Roger. *Discovering American Dialects.* Urbana, IL: NCTE, 1967.
Sternglass, Marilyn. "Dialect Features in the Composition of Black and White
College Students: The Same or Different?" *CCC,* 25(October, 1974), 259-63.
Williams, Frederick, ed. *Language and Poverty: Perspectives on a Theme.* Chicago:
Markham, 1970.

Also see any issue of *Language in Society.*

Measuring Language Skills

Clark, Michael. "Contests and Contexts: Writing and Testing in School." *CE,* 42
(November, 1980), 217-27.
Cohen, Arthur. "Assessing College Students' Ability to Write Composition." *RTE,*
7(Winter, 1973), 356-71.
Cooper, Charles R., ed. *The Nature and Measurement of Competency in English.*
Urbana, IL: NCTE, 1981.
Diederich, Paul B. *Measuring Growth in English.* Urbana, IL: NCTE, 1974.

Fagan, William T., Charles Cooper, Julie Jensen. "Measures: Writing." In *Measures for Research and Evaluation in English Language Arts*. Urbana, IL: NCTE, 1975, pp. 185-206.

Gere, Anne R. "Written Composition: Toward a Theory of Evaluation." *CE, 42* (September, 1980), 44-58.

Grommon, Alfred H., ed. *Reviews of Selected Published Tests in English*. Urbana, IL: NCTE, 1976.

Mellon, John C. *National Assessment and the Teaching of English*. Urbana, IL: NCTE, 1975.

Meyer, Russell J. "Take-Home Placement Tests: A Preliminary Report." *CE, 44* (September, 1982), 506-10.

Modu, Christopher and Eric Wimmer. "The Validity of the Advanced Placement English Language and Composition Exam." *CE, 43*(October, 1981), 609-20.

Myers, Miles. *A Procedure for Writing Assessment and Holistic Scoring*. Urbana, IL: NCTE, 1980.

NAACP Special Contribution Fund. *NAACP Report on Minority Testing*. New York: NAACP, 1976.

National Association of Secondary School Principals. *Competency Tests and Graduation Requirements*. Reston, VA: The Association, 1976.

Noreen, Robert G. "Placement Procedures for Freshman Composition: A Survey." *CCC, 28*(May, 1977), 141-4.

Odell, Lee and Charles R. Cooper. "Procedures for Evaluating Writing: Assumptions and Needed Research." *CE, 42*(September, 1980), 35-43.

Purves, Alan, et al. *Common Sense and Testing in English*. Urbana, IL: NCTE, 1975.

Basic Writing

Carkeet, David. "Understanding Syntactic Errors in Remedial Writing." *CE, 38* (March, 1977), 682-86, 695.

Gorrell, Donna, "Controlled Composition for Basic Writers." *CCC, 32*(October, 1981), 308-16.

Higgins, John A. "Remedial Students' Needs vs. Emphases in Text-Workbooks," *CCC, 24*(May, 1973), 188-92.

Kasden, Lawrence and Donald Hoeber, eds. *Basic Writing: Essays for Teachers, Researchers and Administrators*. Urbana, IL: NCTE, 1980.

Kroll, Barry. "Developmental Perspectives and the Teaching of Composition." *CE, 41*(March, 1980), 741-52.

———— and John Schafer. "Error-Analysis and the Teaching of Composition." *CCC, 29*(October, 1978), 242-48.

Lunsford, Andrea. "Cognitive Development and the Basic Writer." *CE, 41*(September, 1979), 38-46.

Myers, Lewis. "Texts and Teaching: Basic Writing." *CE, 39*(April, 1978), 918-33.

Perl, Sondra. "The Composing Processes of Unskilled College Writers." *RTE, 13* (December, 1979), 317-36.

Rouse, John. "The Politics of Composition." *CE,* 41(September, 1979), 1-12.

Shaughnessy, Mina. "Basic Writing." In *Teaching Composition: 10 Bibliographical Essays,* ed. Gary Tate. Fort Worth: Texas Christian University, 1976, pp. 137-167.

Sutton, Doris and Daniel Arnold. "The Effects of Two Methods of Compensatory Freshman English." *RTE,* 8(February, 1974), 241-9.

Also see any issue of *The Journal of Basic Writing.*

Chapter IV

Institutional Perspectives

Applebee, Arthur N. *Writing in the Secondary School: English and the Content Areas.* Urbana, IL: NCTE, 1981.

Barnes, Douglas, James Britton, Harold Rosen. *Language, the Learner and the School.* London: Penguin, 1969. Available from Boynton/Cook.

Hillocks, George, Jr., ed. *The English Curriculum under Fire: What Are the Real Basics?* Urbana, IL: NCTE, 1982.

Martin, Nancy, Pat D'Arcy, Bryan Newton, Robert Parker. *Writing and Learning Across the Curriculum, 11-16.* London: Ward Lock, 1976. Available from Boynton/Cook.

Moffett, James. *Coming on Center: English Education in Evolution.* Montclair, NJ: Boynton/Cook, 1981.

NCTE Secondary Section Committee. *Workload and the Teaching of Secondary School English.* Urbana, IL: NCTE, 1981.

Torbe, Mike and Peter Medway. *The Climate for Learning.* London: Ward Lock, 1982. Available from Boynton/Cook.

Planning the Course

Barr, Mary, Pat D'Arcy, Mary K. Healy. *What's Going On? Language/Learning Episodes in British and American Classrooms, Grades 4-13.* Montclair, NJ: Boynton/Cook, 1982.

Brady, Philip L., ed. *The "Why's" of Teaching Composition.* Urbana, IL: NCTE, 1978.

Bushman, John H. and Sandra Jones. *Teaching English and the Humanities through Thematic Units.* Urbana, IL: NCTE, 1979.

Crowley, Sharon, ed. *The Teaching of Composition.* Urbana, IL: NCTE, 1976.

Donovan, Timothy and Ben McClelland, eds. *Eight Approaches to Teaching Composition.* Urbana, IL: NCTE, 1980.

Emig, Janet. *The Web of Meaning: Essays on Writing, Teaching, Learning, and Thinking.* Montclair, NJ: Boynton/Cook, 1983.

Fleming, Margaret, ed. *Writing Projects.* Urbana, IL: NCTE, 1980.

Judy, Stephen N., ed. *Teaching English: Reflections on the State of the Art.* Boynton/Cook, 1979.

Mandel, Barrett J., ed. *Three Language-Arts Curriculum Models, Pre-Kindergarten through College.* Urbana, IL: NCTE, 1980.

Moffett, James. *Active Voice: A Writing Program Across the Curriculum.* Montclair, NJ: Boynton/Cook, 1982.

Murray, Donald. *Learning by Teaching: Selected Articles on Writing and Teaching.* Montclair, NJ: Boynton/Cook 1982.

Neel, Jasper, ed. *Options for the Teaching of English: Freshman Composition.* Urbana, IL: NCTE, 1978.

Ohmann, Richard and W. B. Coley. *Ideas for English 101: Teaching Writing in College.* Urbana, IL: NCTE, 1975.

Springer, Imogene, ed. *Recommended English Language Arts Curriculum Guides, K-12.* Urbana, IL: NCTE, 1981.

Classroom Activities

Corbin, Richard with Jonathan Corbin. *Research Papers: A Guided Experience for Senior High School Students.* Second Revised Edition. Urbana, IL: NCTE, 1978.

Gallo, Donald, ed. *The Heard Word.* Urbana, IL: NCTE, 1979.

Kirby, Dan and Tom Liner. *Inside Out: Developmental Strategies for Teaching Writing.* Montclair, NJ: Boynton/Cook, 1981.

Koch, Carl and James M. Brazil. *Strategies for Teaching the Composition Process.* Urbana, IL: NCTE, 1978.

Ponsot, Marie and Rosemary Deen. *Beat Not the Poor Desk. Writing: What to Teach, How to Teach It, and Why.* Montclair, NJ: Boynton/Cook, 1982.

NCTE Classroom Practices Series:

Classroom Practices in Teaching English, 1975-6: On Righting Writing. ed. Ouida M. Clapp.

Classroom Practices in Teaching English, 1977-8: Teaching the Basics—Really! ed. Ouida M. Clapp.

Classroom Practices in Teaching English, 1978-9: Activating the Passive Student. ed. Gene Stanford.

Classroom Practices in Teaching English, 1979-80: How to Handle the Paper Load. ed. Gene Stanford.

Classroom Practices in Teaching English, 1980-1: Dealing with Difference [Exceptional and Talented Students]. ed. Gene Stanford.

Structuring for Success in the English Classroom: Classroom Practices in Teaching English [1982]. ed. Candy Carter.

Writing Assignments

Bernhardt, Bill. *Just Writing: Exercises to Improve Your Writing.* Urbana, IL: NCTE, 1977.

Farrell, Edmund. "The Beginning Begets: Making Composition Assignments." *EJ,* 58(March, 1969), 428-31.

Jenkinson, Edward B. and Donald A. Seybold. *Writing as a Process of Discovery: Some Structured Theme Assignments for Grades Five through Twelve.* Bloomington: Indiana University Press, 1970.

Johannessen, Larry R., Elizabeth A. Kahn, and Carolyn Calhoun Walter. *Designing and Sequencing Prewriting Activities.* Urbana, IL: NCTE, 1982.

Kraus, W. Keith. *Murder, Mischief, and Mayhem: A Process for Creative Research Papers.* Urbana, IL: NCTE, 1978.

Long, Littleton, ed. *Writing Exercises from "Exercise Exchange."* Urbana, IL: NCTE, 1976.

Wilson, Grace, ed. *Composing Situations.* Urbana, IL: NCTE, 1966.

Grammar in the Writing Course

Elgin, Suzette Haden. *A Primer of Transformational Grammar: For Rank Beginners.* Urbana, IL: NCTE, 1975.

Elley, W. B., I. H. Barham, H. Lamb, and M. Wyllie, eds. *The Role of Grammar in a Secondary School Curriculum.* Urbana, IL: NCTE, 1979.

Fleming, Margaret, ed. *Language All Around Us.* Urbana, IL: NCTE, 1981.

Gliserman, Martin. "An Act of Theft: Teaching Grammar." *CE,* 39(March, 1978), 791-99.

Herndon, Jeanne H. *A Survey of Modern Grammars,* 2nd Ed. New York: Holt, Rinehart and Winston, 1976.

Loban, Walter. *Language Development: Kindergarten through Grade 12.* Urbana, IL: NCTE, 1976.

Milosh, Joseph E. Jr. *Teaching the History of the English Language in the Secondary Classroom.* Urbana, IL: NCTE, 1972.

Myers, L. M. "Development of the Language," in *Exploring Language,* 2nd Ed, ed. Gary Goshgarian. Boston: Little, Brown, 1980.

Pinnell, Gay Su, ed. *Discovering Language with Children.* Urbana, IL: NCTE, 1980.

Pooley, Robert C. *The Teaching of English Usage,* 2nd Ed. Urbana, IL: NCTE, 1974.

Weaver, Constance. *Grammar for Teachers: Perspectives and Definitions.* Urbana, IL: NCTE, 1979.

Chapter V

Conferences and Small Groups

Abercrombie, M. L. J. *Aims and Techniques of Group Teaching,* 3rd Ed. London: Society for Research Into Higher Education, 1974.

Bruffee, Kenneth. "The Brooklyn Plan: Attaining Intellectual Growth through Peer Group Tutoring." *Liberal Education,* 64(December, 1978), 447-69.

Fisher, Lester A. and Donald Murray. "Perhaps the Professor Should Cut Class." *CE,* 35(1973-4), 169-73.

Gall, Meredith D. and Joyce P. Gall. "The Discussion Method." In *The Psychology of Teaching Methods: The Seventy-fifth Yearbook of the National Society for the Study of Education.* Chicago: The University of Chicago Press, 1976.

Gerbrandt, Gary L. *An Idea Book: For Acting Out and Writing Language K-8.* Urbana, IL: NCTE, 1974.

Hawkins, Thom. *Group Inquiry Techniques for Teaching Writing.* Urbana, IL: NCTE, 1976.

Jacobs, Suzanne E. and Adela Karliner. "Helping Students to Think: The Effect of Speech Roles in Individual Conferences on Quality of Thought in Student Writing." *CE,* 38(January, 1977), 489-505.

Judy, Stephen, ed. *Lecture Alternatives in Teaching English.* Urbana, IL, NCTE, 1977.

Laque, Carol and Phyllis A. Sherwood. *A Laboratory Approach to Writing.* Urbana, IL: NCTE, 1977.

Reigstad, Thomas. "Conferencing Practices of Professional Writers." Paper, Conference on College Composition and Communication, March, 1980.

Seidner, Constance. "Teaching with Simulations and Games." In *The Psychology of Teaching Methods,* 217-251.

Steiner, Karen. "A Selected Bibliography of Individualized Approaches to College Composition." *CCC,* 28(October, 1977), 232-4.

Evaluating and Responding to Writing

Bolker, Joan L. "Reflections on Reading Student Writing." *CE,* 40(October, 1978), 181-185.

Brannon, Lil and C. H. Knoblauch. "On Students' Rights to Their Own Texts: A Model of Teacher Response." *CCC,* 33(May, 1982), 157-66.

Gee, T. C. "Students' Responses to Teacher Comments." *RTE,* 6(1972), 212-21.

Judine, Sister I. H. M., ed. *A Guide for Evaluating Student Composition.* Urbana, IL: NCTE, 1965.

Kehl, D. G. "The Art of Writing Evaluative Comments on Student Themes." *EJ,* 59(1970), 972-80.

Lotto, Edward and Bruce Smith. "Making Grading Work." *CE,* 41(December, 1979), 423-431.

Lynch, Catherine and Patricia Klemans. "Evaluating Our Evaluations." *CE,* 40 (October, 1978), 166-180.

Mandel, Barrett John. "Teaching Without Judgment." In *Ideas for English 101: Teaching Writing in College,* ed. Richard Ohmann and W. B. Coley. Urbana, IL: NCTE, 1975.

National Council of Teachers of English. *A Scale for Evaluation of High School Student Essays.* Urbana, IL: NCTE, 1960.

Palmer, Orville. *Seven Classic Ways of Grading Dishonestly.* Urbana, IL: NCTE, 1962.

Platt, Michael. "Correcting Papers in Public and Private." *CE,* 37(September, 1975), 22-27.

Sommers, Nancy. "Responding to Student Writing." *CCC,* 33(May, 1982), 148-156.

Index